THE
Shuberts Present

100 YEARS OF AMERICAN THEATER

By the Staff of the Shubert Archive:

MARYANN CHACH · REAGAN FLETCHER
MARK E. SWARTZ · SYLVIA WANG

Foreword by GERALD SCHOENFELD

Afterword by HUGH HARDY

HARRY N. ABRAMS, INC., Publishers,

in Association with

THE SHUBERT ORGANIZATION, INC.

EDITOR: Harriet Whelchel
DESIGNER: Judith Michael
PHOTO CONSULTANT (ABRAMS): John K. Crowley
VISUAL CONSULTANT (SHUBERT): Kevin Kwan

On the end pages: *The Shuberts' 44th Street (front pages)
and 45th Street (back pages) theaters*
Page 1: *Curtain call for the Ziegfeld Follies of 1943 at the Winter Garden Theatre.
A perennial favorite, the Follies in 1943 included Milton Berle, Arthur Treacher,
and Ilona Massey.*
Pages 2–3: *Detail, the Royale Theatre*
Page 5: *Liza Minnelli in* The Act, *1977*
Pages 34–35: *Detail, the Majestic Theatre*
Pages 105–6: *Detail, the Imperial Theatre*
Pages 206–7: *Detail, the Cort Theatre*
Pages 254–55: *Winter Garden Theatre, 1929*
Pages 296–97: *Crescent Theatre, Brooklyn, c.1922*

LIBRARY OF CONGRESS CATALOGING-IN-PUBLICATION DATA

The Shuberts present : 100 years of American theater.
p. cm.
ISBN 0–8109–0614–7 (hardcover)
1. Theaters—New York (State)—New York—History—20th century. 2.
Performing arts—New York (State)—New York—History—20th century. 3.
Shubert Organization—History. I. Title: Shuberts present, one hundred
years of American theater

PN2277.N5 S495 2001
792'.09747'10904—dc21

2001001265

Published in 2001 by Harry N. Abrams, Incorporated, New York
Printed and bound in Japan
10 9 8 7 6 5 4 3 2 1

Harry N. Abrams, Inc.
100 Fifth Avenue
New York, N.Y. 10011
www.abramsbooks.com

Contents

Foreword

I fell into a career in the theater serendipitously. Prior to my getting a job in June 1949 at Klein & Weir, the law firm that represented Lee and J. J. Shubert and their theatrical business, I had never even been to the theater. Nor did I know anything about it or, for that matter, have any inclination to become affiliated with it. The only Shubert I had ever heard of was Franz Schubert, the great composer. Lee and J. J. Shubert were totally unfamiliar names—I had no idea that they were the emperors of the American theater during the first half of the twentieth century, or that they had created a theatrical dynasty out of the business started by their brother Sam, who unfortunately died at the age of twenty-nine in a train crash in 1905. The Shubert family had endured the rigors of abject poverty, including the loss of a sister to malnutrition. Though uneducated and forced to work before they were ten years old, they embraced an art form totally alien to them, crushed a virulent monopoly called the Theatrical Syndicate, and produced 520 plays, musicals, and dramas. But I knew none of this.

I met Lee Shubert only once—in 1952 at a conference attended by a team of lawyers defending an antitrust case brought by the United States of America against the brothers, their partner Marcus Heiman, the United Booking Office, and the Shubert-owned Select Theatres Corporation. Since I had been working on the defense, William Klein, the senior partner in my law firm, invited me to the meeting. During the course of the proceedings, Lee Shubert made a suggestion, to which Klein responded by saying in the presence of the others, "I don't think we should do that, Lee." Lee replied, "We? We? Since when did I make you my partner?" Both men were then in their eighties.

This experience, however, gave me some idea of what I might expect from Lee's brother, J. J., whom I was destined to meet in 1955. I subsequently learned that these brothers were not ordinary men. For while they possessed courage, ruthlessness, and an innate intelligence, they had no regard for what others thought of them or their actions. Devoid of guilt and lacking the desire to be liked, admired, or respected, they conducted their business and personal lives as they saw fit.

Meanwhile, the two senior members of Klein & Weir both fell upon the sword of J. J. Shubert. A younger member, Adolph

Lund, my mentor and friend, died on January 1, 1957. It was on that day that Mr. J. J., as he was called, asked me if I would handle his affairs. He said that he did not want old people handling his affairs, since old people had old views. I immediately accepted his offer.

On March 17, 1957, a little over seven years after I started my career, Bernard B. Jacobs joined me as my partner. Miraculously, we withstood the wrath of J. J. until he weakened in late 1961 and died in 1963.

Despite the many hardships I endured during those years, I rationalized my continuing at Shubert with the knowledge that through their undying devotion these two brothers undoubtedly saved the institution of the commercial theater from the threats posed by the advent of motion pictures, the Depression, bankruptcy, and the coming of television. In retrospect, they were to theater what Ford was to the motor car and the Wright Brothers to aviation.

From 1957 to November 17, 1962, Bernie Jacobs and I worked closely with John Shubert, J. J.'s son. Because of the relationship we forged with him, as well as the support and affection given us by his wife Kerttu (Eckie), Bernie and I became President, Chairman, and board members of the Shubert Organization and Foundation in 1972.

Fifty years may be a long time, but these years have passed with the speed of light. The theater and the Shubert Organization ultimately became an enduring love affair for Bernie and me, and now for Philip J. Smith, the Organization's current President, for Robert Wankel, our Executive Vice-President and CFO, and for all of the thousands of people who work under the Shubert banner—from the staffs of our various departments to the stars of our shows.

Today the Shubert business is vastly different—and quite a bit smaller—than it was at its peak in 1927, when it owned and operated 104 theaters and booked productions into more than 1,000 theaters nationwide. Nevertheless, the Shubert name still shines like a beacon upon the American theater scene, and I expect that our record of success and accomplishment will carry us through the next one hundred years.

Gerald Schoenfeld

Although Lee and J. J. Shubert hoarded their business records and production materials, it certainly was not with the intention of establishing an archive of company documents. In fact, it would be more than seventy-five years after the brothers' arrival in New York City and long after all the Shuberts were dead that the Shubert Foundation first considered the idea.

In 1976, Lynn Seidler, then executive director of the Shubert Foundation, had the foresight to realize the historical value of the existing Shubert records and thought that an educator with an arts background might evaluate their potential significance to academic researchers. She contacted Brooks McNamara, a faculty member in New York University's Graduate Drama Department and a pioneer in the study of popular entertainments. They subsequently met with the chairman of the Shubert board, Gerald Schoenfeld, and its president, Bernard B. Jacobs.

McNamara sensed a fascinating project unfolding—one quite unlike anything else he had been involved with so far. An archive of Shubert-related papers could, he thought, be an exciting new resource for historians across the world. After a careful sample appraisal of the Shubert material, McNamara enthusiastically recommended the establishment of a formal archive that would concentrate on the work of Sam, Lee, and J. J. Shubert, the company they founded, and the history of Broadway and the Shubert Organization. The primary focus of the archive would be to meet the needs of scholars and students. Because the new archive would not be open to researchers for some time to come, he proposed creating a newsletter, which would be sent to theater academics and libraries to inform them about research opportunities in this new facility to be called the Shubert Archive.

Seidler, Schoenfeld, and Jacobs liked McNamara's proposal, and Seidler brought it to the attention of the Shubert board, whose response was positive. In short order, McNamara set to work and hired as archivist Brigitte Kueppers, from the Theatre Collection of the New York Public Library at Lincoln Center, and he secured a

OPPOSITE:
The Belle of New York, *poster for the American tour. This musical, originally produced by George Lederer, first opened in 1897 at New York's Casino Theatre, where it ran for only 54 performances. Subsequently,* Belle *enjoyed a great success in London where it played for 674 performances and made a big star out of a Shubert friend, Syracuse's own Edna May, who took the role of the Salvation Army lass. The Shuberts successfully toured the show throughout America during the 1899–1900, 1900–1901, and 1901–2 seasons. Later updated, the musical reappeared as* The Whirl of New York, *which Lee and J. J. produced in 1921 at the Winter Garden.*

group of interns from New York University's Ph.D. program. The Shubert Archive was born.

Initially, some rooms in the Shubert-owned Longacre Theatre on 48th Street were designated as the new archive's home, but within a few months it became apparent that this would not suffice. Soon after, the Archive relocated to the Lyceum Theatre, where it has remained.

Among the materials that were gathered, appraised, sorted, and inventoried were artistic records, such as costume sketches, scene designs, scripts, posters, photographs, miscellaneous production materials, and architectural plans; business papers, including correspondence, account books, route books, legal materials, and financial ledgers; and various Shubert-related artifacts like old ticket grills and racks, antique lighting equipment, art objects, paintings, and prints. So great was the volume of materials being processed that it took a full ten years before the new facility could officially open its doors to applicants requesting permission to use the Archive.

As for the newsletter, it was named *The Passing Show*, in honor of the famous and successful series of summer revues that the Shuberts produced in the 1910s and 1920s. Each issue contained articles about the wonderful materials the Archive was unearthing, as well as interviews with former Shubert employees. Still produced on a biannual basis, *The Passing Show* features in-depth articles on a wide variety of Shubert-related topics.

In recent years the Archive's collections have continued to grow, with extensive donations of theatrical materials from general managers and press agents who have worked on Shubert shows, from various other public and private collections, and from many individual collectors. In addition, its user base of graduate students, authors, educators, and theater practitioners has expanded. The Archive's Web site (http://www.shubertarchive.org), launched in 2000, reaches out to a worldwide audience.

From its somewhat chaotic early days, the Shubert Archive has evolved into one of the most unique and valuable specialized research collections in the world. The Shubert brothers, through their business acumen, their canny knowledge of their audiences, their keen eye for creative talent, their wide-ranging real-estate holdings, and their utter devotion to the medium of live theater, not only guided the course of the theater business in this century, but are also largely responsible for its survival as we enter the next. Any attempt to understand the theater industry in America during the last one hundred years must include an examination of the history of the Shubert brothers and the company they founded. The work being done at the Shubert Archive preserves their rich legacy and makes such an examination possible and meaningful.

OPPOSITE:
Lyceum Theatre, c. 1910s, depicted on one of a series of souvenir cigar cards that were tucked into packages of Between the Acts Little Cigars. The front of these cards, which are now much in demand on the collector's market, highlighted in color a given playhouse's exterior, while the verso gave a brief description and history of the building along with an ad for the cigars. The Lyceum, Broadway's oldest continually operating legitimate theater, has been home to the Shubert Archive since 1977.

On a bright spring day in 1900, Sam and Lee Shubert stood together, brimming with anticipation, on the northeast corner of 35th Street and Broadway. Across the street in front of them was the Herald Square Theatre, in the heart of what was then the city's bustling theater district. They had just leased it—their first venue in New York City. As proud and excited as the Shubert brothers undoubtedly were, they would have been even happier to know that this was only the beginning of a hugely successful run on

Located on the northwest corner of Broadway and 35th Street, the Herald Square Theatre stood due north from where Macy's is today. At the turn of the century, the theater district was moving north along Broadway from Union Square, its previous center, and was gradually approaching Times Square. Five years before the Shuberts took over the theater, The Heart of Maryland *(1895), a Civil War melodrama written and directed by David Belasco, opened with Mrs. Leslie Carter and Maurice Barrymore, father of Ethel, Lionel, and John.*

Broadway—one that has lasted more than a century and shows no sign of slowing down.

The story of the Shuberts and the indelible mark they left on the American theater is somehow both typical and yet amazingly singular. Typical, because it is the story of three young, impoverished immigrants who wanted something better out of life and struggled to acquire it. In many ways, the ups and downs of the Shuberts and their theatrical enterprise mirror those of New York City and the rest of the country throughout the century. To explore the history of the Shuberts is to discover the kaleidoscope of changes that unfolded in twentieth-century American theater—both artistically and economically. In the end, that is what makes Sam S., Lee, and Jacob J. (J. J.) Shubert so singular—the story of the Shuberts is the story of Broadway.

The boys began their theatrical careers by selling newspapers on the sidewalks in front of the theaters of Syracuse, New York, in the 1880s. Sam S. Shubert, possessing vast amounts of energy, keen intelligence, and a winning personality, always stood out from the

OPPOSITE:
This image of J. J. Shubert and Lee Shubert on a boat is one of only two photographs in the Archive showing the two men together. There does not seem to be any surviving single image in which all three brothers appear.

pack, and before long was recruited for a walk-on role in a touring production of David Belasco's *May Blossom*. Now bitten by the theater bug, the young boy found a role model in Belasco, the great Broadway producer/director/playwright. He set his sights on a career in the theater and first found work as a ticket taker and usher before graduating to box-office treasurer and manager, learning by on-the-job training. It was not long before his taciturn but shrewd older brother Lee and his hot-tempered younger brother J. J. caught Sam's enthusiasm for the entertainment business. Quickly the Shuberts began amassing a small theatrical empire in upstate New York—they leased playhouses in Syracuse, Rochester, Buffalo, Troy, and Utica. Their acumen and trustworthiness in business had cemented strong friendships with many merchants and entrepreneurs in Syracuse who provided seed money for the Shuberts' undertakings.

But leasing venues was only a springboard for Sam, whose true desire was to become a producer. He approached popular play-

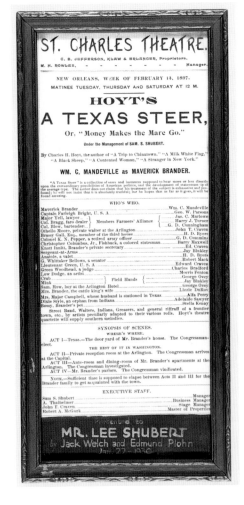

wright Charles Hoyt about procuring the touring rights to his show *A Texas Steer* (initial New York production, January 1894), a satire on political corruption. Although Sam, only in his early twenties, had no production experience, he persuaded Hoyt to give him a chance. He not only proved to be up to the challenge, but also was so successful with the tour that Hoyt awarded him the rights to his *A Stranger in New York* in 1898. As the twentieth century dawned, Sam and his brothers decided it was time to take on New York City—and the powerful Theatrical Syndicate.

Founded in 1896, the Syndicate was composed of major Broadway producers as well as theater owners in New York and around the country. It arose as an answer to the changes taking place in entertainment. The golden age of repertory—in which an in-house company of actors performed in a revolving series of plays at a given venue—was being replaced by the combination show, which featured a new hit play or a star performer not tied to a particular theater. The Theatrical Syndicate saw a need for a streamlined system for booking road tours and promised, for a fee, to make the whole process easier for both producers and

This is one of a series of snapshots of Sam Shubert (left) cutting up for the camera with unidentified individuals.

A former journalist, Charles Hoyt (1860–1900) turned to playwriting and focused his skills on satirizing contemporary problems; his most successful play was A Trip to Chinatown *(1891), which featured the song "The Bowery," for which Hoyt wrote the lyrics. While still a relatively small-time manager in Syracuse, Sam Shubert secured the touring rights to Hoyt's* A Texas Steer *in 1897 and earned his spurs as a general manager on the road with this production.* A Texas Steer *opened on Broadway in 1894. Sam's success on the road with this show enabled him to further develop his relationship with Hoyt. This framed program from 1897 was presented to Lee Shubert in 1930 and is the Shubert Archive's only program documenting a touring production from this period.*

theater owners. Several owners of the major theatrical circuits became backers of the Syndicate, which was run by Marc Klaw, Abraham Erlanger, Charles Frohman, and Alf Hayman, who were all theater owners and producers. Thus, if you were a producer or a theater owner, it behooved you to join the Syndicate.

When Sam and Lee set their sights on New York City in 1900, friends and business associates from Syracuse lent them the funds to obtain a lease on the Herald Square Theatre. (J. J. was left upstate to manage the five theaters the brothers already owned.) The brothers gradually acquired more theaters in the city—the Casino at 39th Street and Broadway, the Princess on West 39th Street, the Madison Square at 24th Street and Fifth Avenue, and the Lyric on 42nd Street, among others. Initially, the Shuberts cooperated with the Syndicate and booked Syndicate shows into their houses. But as the brothers expanded their operations and moved into production, the Syndicate

They Have Much Upon Their Shoulders.

tried to exert more control over them. The Shuberts began to chafe under their restrictive policies, until, finally, Sam and Lee devised a strategy to free themselves from the Syndicate's tyranny. Not surprisingly, they knew of other theater owners, producers, and performers who also resented the Syndicate's heavy-handed methods. The Shuberts' plan involved forming an alliance with these malcontents—a coalition of "Independents" composed of people like David Belasco, Harrison Gray Fiske (the publisher of the *New York Dramatic Mirror*), and his wife, the actress Mrs. Minnie Maddern Fiske. They would press the Syndicate for what they called an "open door" policy, which would afford producers and theater owners alike the opportunity to make bookings without going through the Syndicate if they so chose and without penalty or fear of retribution. By 1905 the opening salvo in the war between the Shuberts and the Syndicate had been fired.

The Shuberts had planned to present Sarah Bernhardt in a cross-country tour during the 1905–6 season, but were unable to book first-class venues in certain locales because those houses were under Syndicate control. So they

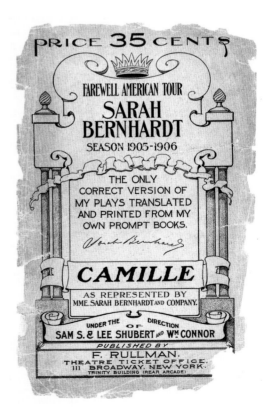

sought out available vaudeville theaters, second-class houses, and even resorted to erecting a large circus tent for Madame Bernhardt when no other suitable playhouse could be found. Despite these conditions, the Bernhardt tour was a tremendous hit.

The tour also underscored the Shuberts' need to acquire and/or build more theaters on the road in order to compete in earnest with the Syndicate. This, then, became their most pressing concern. In the spring of 1905, Sam was in London overseeing the construction of the Waldorf Theatre, the brothers' first foreign house, when Lee encountered some trouble with the transfer of a former Syndicate house, the Duquesne in Pittsburgh, to Shubert control. Thinking it best to attend to the matter himself, the take-charge Sam headed to Pittsburgh to switch places with Lee, whose financial savvy and detail-oriented personality made him well suited to supervise the completion of the Waldorf. Unfortunately, Sam never reached his destination. The train carrying him to the Steel City collided with a freight train full of dynamite. The resulting explosion and fire derailed both trains and, according to some reports, killed twenty-three people and injured about one hundred. Sam, not yet thirty, was one of the victims, and despite newspaper accounts that seemed to downplay his injuries, he succumbed to his burns within twenty-four hours.

"Sam S. Shubert Dies of His Burns," Syracuse (N.Y.) Telegram, *May 12, 1905. This is a page from Sam S. Shubert's obituary book, a scrapbook containing newspaper accounts from all over the country of the train wreck that took Sam's life.*

Sam's death was a tragic blow for Lee, J. J., and the rest of the Shubert family. Archival evidence suggests that Lee, still in London at the time of the accident, suffered a nervous breakdown as a result of his loss. There was much industry speculation that the Shuberts would not continue without Sam, but surviving correspondence and business records indicate that Lee and J. J. would proceed full speed ahead with the plans that Sam had set in motion. They began a practice of naming new theaters in honor of their late brother, and Sam S. Shubert Memorial Theatres soon dotted the American landscape.

Meanwhile, the war with the Syndicate raged on. Over the next two decades, the brothers vastly expanded their stock of theaters and enlisted outside investors—even going so far as to make a public offering on Wall Street, a business strategy never used by the Syndicate. By the mid-1920s, the Shuberts had outlasted the Syndicate. Charles Frohman had died on the *Lusitania* in 1915, Alf Hayman retired, and, in 1919, Marc Klaw split with Abraham Erlanger and sold his interests to the Shuberts. Erlanger now had no choice but to join with Lee and J. J. in the Shubert-controlled United Booking Office. As the 1920s began to roar, the Shuberts

were at the peak of their power. They now owned, operated, managed, or booked more than a thousand theaters nationwide. In 1924, the Shubert Theatre Corporation, which constituted a segment of all of Lee and J. J.'s business holdings, was incorporated. This public company sold shares on the stock exchange.

The kinds of productions that the Shuberts presented were, for the most part, geared toward mainstream audiences and consisted mainly of revues, operettas, melodramas, and light comedies. Lee, however, occasionally attempted to produce more serious work. Over the years, he had brief involvements with the New Theatre, as well as with artists like George Bernard Shaw, Maurice Maeterlinck, E. H. Sothern and Julia Marlowe, Alla Nazimova, Vincente Minnelli, Agnes de Mille, and George Balanchine. Although most of the brothers'

Lee Shubert, c. late 1940s, standing at the rear of the orchestra section of an unidentified theater

more than five hundred shows have not stood the test of time, they were nearly always extremely successful. Titles like *The Passing Show, The Greenwich Village Follies, Artists and Models, Sinbad, The Student Prince, Blossom Time, Bunty Pulls the Strings, Death Takes a Holiday, Dark of the Moon,* and *Ten Little Indians* were loved by audiences and have become classics of American popular culture. What is more, the Shuberts had a sharp eye for great talent, and many of the leading performers of the day appeared in Shubert productions. Among these were Abbott and Costello, Fred Allen, Fred and Adele Astaire, Josephine Baker, Tallulah Bankhead, the Barrymores (John, Lionel, and Ethel), Ray Bolger, Fanny Brice, Eddie Cantor, Ruth Gordon, Katharine Hepburn, Bob Hope, Al Jolson, Bert Lahr, Gypsy Rose Lee, Beatrice Lillie, Jeanette MacDonald,

Marilyn Miller, Carmen Miranda, Eleanor Powell, Mae West, and Ed Wynn.

The power and prosperity of the 1920s came to an abrupt halt with the market crash of 1929, and few were spared, including the Shuberts. The company filed for bankruptcy and lost a number of their theaters. On October 20, 1931, the Shubert Theatre Corporation went into receivership; Lee Shubert and the Irving Trust Company were appointed receivers. The receivership allowed the brothers to annul disadvantageous leases and to peel off a number of unprofitable holdings. Whatever remained after that was set to be sold at a court-appointed public auction. The brothers created a new corporation, Select Theatres Corporation, and, at the court-ordered sale on April 7, 1933, bought back a number of their properties (including almost all their New York venues) using their own personal funds, which they had managed to preserve to some extent through investment diversity. Former creditors and bond holders in the original corporation received shares in the new company.

THE MESSRS SHUBERT *present*
THE GREAT LONDON SUCCESS
THE BLUE LAGOON
A SPECTACULAR ROMANCE OF THE SOUTH SEAS
ADAPTED FROM H. DE-VERE STACPOOLE'S FAMOUS NOVEL
STAGED BY BASIL DEAN
INCIDENTAL MUSIC BY CLIVE CAREY

Poster, c. 1921. The Blue Lagoon played to packed houses for more than three years. It had been a great success in London as well.

Meanwhile, other parts of the Shubert business, composed of corporations personally owned by Lee and J. J., continued. Here too, however, financial difficulties set in, and, in order to sustain their enterprises, the brothers were forced to apply for loans through the government-owned Reconstruction Finance Corporation. And so, throughout the Depression, they kept the theaters operating, full or empty, until, by the middle of the 1930s, audience numbers once again started to rise. The Shuberts profited with some very successful revues, including *Life Begins at 8:40, The Show Is On, The Ziegfeld Follies of 1936,* and the smash hit *Hellzapoppin'*, the first of four Shubert productions created by the zany comedians Ole Olsen and Chic Johnson.

The 1940s were not the best of times, either, as far as the legitimate theater was concerned. At the beginning of the decade, anxiety over the war kept audiences away; at decade's end, the advent of television was the culprit. During its infancy, the television industry was centered in New York, and the networks—CBS, Dumont, NBC's Red Network and Blue Network (later ABC)—were desper-

ately looking for studio space. The logical solution to their problem was the legitimate theaters that sat dark for long stretches of time.

Ironically, although television competed with the theater for viewers, the growth of the television industry in New York motivated a major change in the Shuberts' holdings and in the landscape of American entertainment. While the Shuberts owned outright the majority of their theaters in the city, in many cases they only leased the land on which the buildings sat. In 1949, the Astor Estate, which did own the land under all of the Shubert theaters on 44th and 45th Streets, approached Lee with a proposition to sell ten theaters—the Shubert, Booth, Majestic, Broadhurst, Plymouth, Golden, Royale, St. James, Imperial, and Music Box—to the television studios. There was even some talk of demolishing the theaters to make way for a "Television City." Because the Shuberts' lease on the land under their buildings ran for a period of 99 years, the television people would have to pay dearly to buy out the Shuberts. At this point, Lee was reportedly in his early eighties, an age at which most people in his situation would probably have opted to take the money and retire. But the Shuberts' lease contained an option to buy the land, and the brothers decided to exercise that option. While the reticent brothers did not make their intentions known, it is a safe bet that Lee and J. J. viewed the theaters as their legacy (as is further evidenced by their forming, in 1945, the Sam S. Shubert Foundation, which would become the main benefactor of Lee and J. J.'s estates, including all of their real-estate holdings). With this decision, the Shuberts preserved the legitimate stage and kept the Broadway district intact.

When Lee Shubert died in 1953, his brother continued to run the company, but the Shuberts produced little during the decade. They were predominantly theatrical landlords of some of the most prized venues in the city. In 1950 the Shuberts and their United Booking Office had been sued by the United States and charged with violating the Sherman Anti-Trust Act. In 1956 the United States and the defendants entered into a consent decree. J. J. Shubert was ordered to divest some of his holdings (including the St. James and National theaters in New York and many venues on

Gerald Schoenfeld, Bernard B. Jacobs, and Irving Schoenfeld, Gerald's older brother, c. 1940s

OPPOSITE, ABOVE:
Shubert chairman Gerald Schoenfeld kisses president Bernard B. Jacobs on receiving an award from Hospital Audiences, Inc. in 1981.

OPPOSITE, BELOW:
Gerald Schoenfeld, on the right, with current president, Philip J. Smith, 2000

AL KAUFMAN · LEE SHUBERT

Mae West with Al Kaufman and Lee Shubert, c. 1930s

the road) and was restrained from booking any theaters other than those already owned by Shubert.

The Shubert brothers' glory days were over. In 1962, John Shubert, who had been running the company with his father since 1955, suffered a fatal heart attack, and the elderly and senile J. J. (in his mid- to late eighties) was not informed of his son's death. He died the following year. The company passed into the hands of the Shuberts' great-nephew, Lawrence Shubert Lawrence, Jr., who, by all accounts, was an inadequate manager. In 1972 he was ousted by the board of the Shubert Foundation. Board members and long-time Shubert attorneys Gerald Schoenfeld and Bernard B. Jacobs assumed control of the company.

In 1973, the various Shubert subsidiaries were reorganized under the new corporate name The Shubert Organization, Inc. Schoenfeld became the chairman and Jacobs the president. The two men ran the company together for some twenty-four years, and were often referred to as "the Shuberts." Under their leadership, the Shubert Organization emerged from near bankruptcy and once again began to thrive. The company introduced new ways of bringing audiences into their theaters by promoting shows on television and by introducing the use of credit cards and remote outlets for purchasing tickets for the legitimate stage. Today, theater audiences can purchase their tickets from the Shubert-owned-and-operated Telecharge, either over the telephone or via the Internet. Shubert has also played a vital role, commencing in 1970, in the renaissance of Times Square and the legitimate theater district. In 1996, following Jacobs's death, vice president Philip J. Smith became president.

As for the Shubert Foundation, it continues to fulfill its mandate of providing financial support to performing-arts groups across the United States. In the year 2000, the board announced more than $11 million in grants to 322 organizations. Another of its long-term projects is the Shubert Archive, which was established in 1976 in order to catalogue and preserve the rich legacy of the brothers and their company.

Most important, Shubert is once again an active producer of shows. Over the last twenty-seven years, the Shubert Organization has, with its partners, brought to the stage many outstanding and award-winning productions. A representative sample includes *Ain't Misbehavin'* (1978), *Amadeus* (1981), *Amy's View* (1999), *As Is* (1985), *The Blue Room* (1998), *Children of a Lesser God* (1980), *City of Angels* (1989), *Dancin'* (1978), *Dreamgirls* (1981), *A Few Good Men* (1989), *The Gin Game* (1977), *Glengarry Glen Ross* (1984), *The Grapes of Wrath* (1990), *The Heidi Chronicles* (1989), *Jerome Robbins' Broadway* (1989), *Lettice & Lovage* (1990), *The Life & Adventures of Nicholas Nickleby* (1981), *Master Harold . . . and the Boys* (1982), *A Moon for the Misbegotten* (1984), *'night Mother* (1983), *Passion* (1994), *The Real Thing* (1984), *Sunday in the Park with George* (1984), and *Tru* (1989); also revivals of *Joe Egg* (1985), *The Most Happy Fella* (1992), and *An Inspector Calls (1994)*. Their Off-Broadway productions include *Little Shop of Horrors* (1982), *Picasso at the Lapin Agile* (1995), *Nixon's Nixon* (1996), and *Stupid Kids* (1998). And on June 19, 1997, after performance number 6,138, the Shubert-produced *Cats* became the longest-running Broadway musical in history.

As the Shubert Organization embarks on its second century, a new 499-seat Off-Broadway theater is under construction, and the archive for the company's vast historical record is continuously supplemented by new additions. In a time of giant-screen motion pictures, high-definition television, elaborately realistic video games, and virtual-reality entertainments, the Shubert Organization remains committed to the live theatrical experience and looks eagerly ahead to the next one hundred years.

J. J. Shubert (left) with Busby Berkeley on the Warner Brothers lot, c. early 1930s. Berkeley had worked with the Shuberts on shows such as A Night in Venice *(1929) and* Pleasure Bound *(1929).*

The Shubert Family

The Shuberts immigrated from a sliver of land in eastern Europe that at different times was part of Prussia, Poland, or Russia. The name of their birthplace was Neustadt near what is now known as Königsburg.

David Shubert, father, seen sitting in front of the family home in Syracuse, New York. Shubert was an itinerant pack peddler and the first to arrive in America, probably in the 1880s. He settled in Syracuse because he had relatives there. Eventually, he was able to bring over his wife, Catherine, and his six children, Levi (Lee), Sam, Jacob (J. J.), Fannie, Sarah, and Dora.

Catherine Shubert, mother. Because the family was poor, Catherine took in boarders at the family's home in Syracuse. When Sam and Lee moved to New York, they relocated their mother and two youngest sisters, Sarah and Dora, to the city where they supported them.

Lee Shubert with (from left) his mother, Catherine, and sisters Dora and Sarah, c. 1910

J. J. Shubert on vacation in Egypt in the late 1930s

Sam S. Shubert on a transatlantic ship. The Shubert brothers made frequent scouting trips to Europe in their quest for new plays and musicals. In 1905, Sam and Lee opened their first theater in London, The Waldorf.

Lee Shubert at his desk, c. 1910s

OVERLEAF:
The wedding reception of Sarah Shubert to theatrical agent Edward Davidow was held at Delmonico's, September 20, 1911. Among the guests who can be identified are Mrs. Catherine Shubert and Lee Shubert (immediately to the right of the bride) and J. J. Shubert (fifth on the right). Also present are the oldest sister, Fannie Shubert Isaacs Weissager, and her son, Lawrence (Isaacs) Shubert Lawrence (on the far left, just under a mirror). Seated in front of Fannie are the youngest sister, Dora, and her husband, Milton Wolf. Next to Milton are Mrs. Catherine Dealy Shubert (J. J.'s first wife) and William Klein, the Shuberts' attorney. Missing from the picture is the bride's father.

SOUVENIR
OF THE MARRIAGE OF
MISS. SARAH SHUBERT
TO
MR. EDWARD DAVIDOW.
DELMONICO'S   SEPTEMBER 20, 1911.

PHOTO BY
DRUCKER & CO
204 W. 42ND ST.
NEW YORK

14D.

Lee Shubert (center) with his two nephews Milton (left) and John (right), who were viewed as the successors to the Shubert dynasty. Milton was the son of the oldest Shubert sister, Fannie, and her husband, Isaac Isaacs, a peddler from Syracuse. Both Milton and his brother, Lawrence Shubert Lawrence, Sr., went into their uncles' theater business. Lawrence's son, Lawrence, Jr., headed the Shubert enterprises into the early 1970s.

Lawrence Shubert Lawrence, Jr., is flanked by Dorothy Stickney (left, then appearing in *The Riot Act*) and Patricia Medina (in *Calculated Risk*) in Shubert Alley in 1963, the year the Shuberts celebrated the fiftieth anniversary of the Alley.

John Shubert's birthday party, when John (far right) was approximately five years old. He would grow up to assist his father, J. J., in running the Shubert business from 1955 to 1962.

Lee Shubert, the eldest and most taciturn of the Shubert brothers, was the one who handled the finances. He had no children; in fact, no one knew he was married until his wife, Marcella Swanson (at right, c. 1920s), filed for divorce in 1948, reportedly because she was tired of her "invisible" status. A year later, the couple remarried. Marcella had been one-half of the Swanson Sisters (the other being Beatrice), showgirls and minor actresses who appeared in a number of Shubert revues and plays.

Sam, the middle brother and by most contemporary reports the most charming and extroverted of the three male siblings, never married. The Shubert Archive, however, has two boxes of wonderful correspondence from female acquaintances— some are letters from friends and/or business associates, many are flirtatious (see Evelyn Nesbit's below, for example), and one entire box is devoted to letters from actress Mabel Carrier, an ingenue who seemed smitten with Sam. In her letters, Mabel alternates between chastising Sam for not writing to her and regaling him with stories about the activities of the touring company with which she traveled. Addie Marze, another performer, addressed her letters to "My darling old Dreamy Eyes." "L," who had probably been a chorus girl in *Piff! Paff!! Pouf!!!* wrote her notes to "My dear little Sambo." All of these actresses may indeed have been crazy about Sam, but they were doubtless well aware that he was a producer who could advance their careers.

To - Sam Shubert -
"Just me"
Evelyn Nesbit

J. J., John and Catherine Shubert
(the first Mrs. J. J. Shubert), c. 1913

Like his father, John Shubert also married a Shubert showgirl—Kerttu Helene Ecklund ("Eckie"). Eckie Shubert appeared with with Eugene and Willie Howard in *The Show Is On* in 1936. After her stage career ended, Eckie sat on the Shubert Foundation Board of Directors from the 1960s until her death in 1985. She was the last of the Shubert family involved in the business.

J. J., the youngest and most volatile brother, married twice: the first time, in 1907, to Catherine Dealy (above left), with whom he had a son, John. The beautiful, Gibson-Girl-ish Catherine concocted a story about meeting J. J. at a Shubert theater when she was on an outing with a class from a Catholic girls' school in the Bronx. In reality, it is likely that Catherine, like her sister Mae, was a chorus girl, not a schoolgirl. Catherine and J. J. were divorced in 1917, and their relationship after the divorce was as tempestuous as it had been when they were married. Muriel Knowles (with J. J. below, late 1940s), also a showgirl, became J. J.'s second wife. When she died in 1970, her ashes were purportedly scattered in Shubert Alley.

Behind the Scenes of "The New York Review"

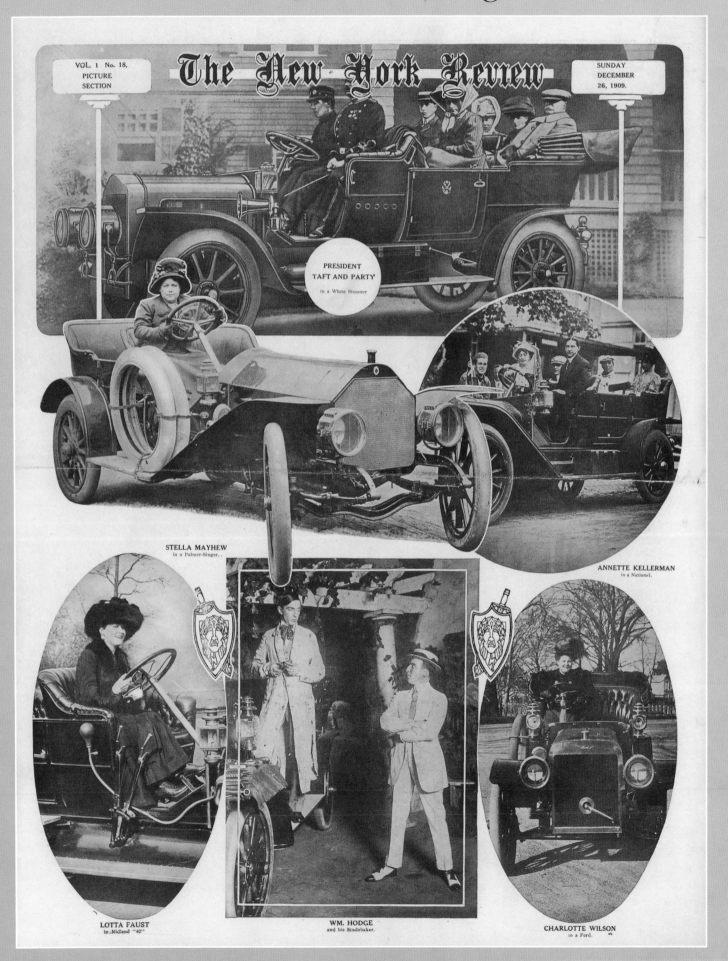

The New York Review

VOL. 1 No. 18, PICTURE SECTION

SUNDAY DECEMBER 26, 1909.

PRESIDENT TAFT AND PARTY in a White Steamer

STELLA MAYHEW in a Palmer-Singer.

ANNETTE KELLERMAN in a National.

LOTTA FAUST in Midland "40"

WM. HODGE and his Studebaker.

CHARLOTTE WILSON in a Ford.

Cartoon: "Source of a Stench Pervading the Entire United States." "The Real Open Sewers and their Inhabitants." Cascading from the "Debased Journalism" duct are the staff and reporters of *The Morning Telegraph*, the Syndicate paper, and streaming out of the "Debauched Theatricals" are Klaw, Erlanger, and Ziegfeld. *The New York Review* plainly made known the Shuberts' feelings about the Syndicate in a manner that would be unacceptable in a mainstream publication today.

PREVIOUS PAGE:
Rotogravure section from December 26, 1909, featuring celebrities and their cars. At that time, automobiles were considered luxuries.

The New York Review had its genesis in the great rivalry that the theater impresarios Marc Klaw and Abraham Lincoln Erlanger had with the Shuberts at the beginning of the twentieth century. Klaw and Erlanger headed the Theatrical Syndicate, the trust of producers and theater owners that controlled most of the hit plays and musicals on the New York stage. This control of product gave Klaw and Erlanger leverage in negotiating favorable bookings with independent theater owners across the country. Through the Syndicate, Klaw and Erlanger owned, operated, or influenced most of the major theaters in the country.

In 1900, when Sam and Lee Shubert arrived in New York City from Syracuse, they were forced to do business with the Syndicate and found themselves, like many others, treated in a high-handed fashion—often, for example, having their bookings abruptly canceled. It was not long before these upstarts from upstate took on the Syndicate by advocating an "open door" policy, a free market that would give theater owners and managers the freedom to do business with whomever they liked. This put the Shuberts at war with Klaw and Erlanger.

The opening volley was fired by the daily theatrical and sporting newspaper *The Morning Telegraph*, a close ally of the Syndicate. The paper boosted the shows of Klaw and Erlanger, while vilifying those of the Shuberts. When, according to Lee Shubert, "nasty little digs at Sam or J. J. or me began to appear in the *Telegraph*," Lee felt sure that a columnist named Rennold Wolf was responsible for the unsigned comments.

Unable to obtain fair treatment in the *Telegraph*, the Shuberts withdrew all their advertising. This meant, however, that the brothers now needed a theatrical paper in which to publicize their shows, express their views, and defend themselves against their enemies. As a result, *The New York Review* was born on Sunday, August 29, 1909. A large-format weekly newspaper, the *Review* had three or four sections—a pictorial or rotogravure section, one or two news sections, and a magazine. Sam Weller, the editor, and Charles Daniel, the business and advertising manager, operated the paper, with the persistent help of their not-so-silent partners, Lee and J. J. Shubert, who controlled the *Review*, although neither of their names appeared on the masthead.

At first, it was hoped that once the *Review* was on a firm financial footing, the newspaper might eventually become a daily or at least a semiweekly. But that never happened—the paper remained a weekly for its entire twenty-two-year run.

If the initial impetus behind the *Review* was to combat the Syndicate and all it stood for, then it certainly achieved its chief goal in its early issues. Nearly every news section featured a barbed anti-Syndicate cartoon by an artist named Howell. Many of these are extremely inventive as well as full of invective. In one example, ringmaster Abe Erlanger is forcing Bill Lewis, the editor of the *Telegraph*, and Rennold Wolf to jump through hoops.

Howell also drew more flattering caricatures of Shubert performers. Of course, shows produced by the Shuberts and their allies, as well as performers in those shows, were featured in the paper's articles and photographs. Among the spotlighted personalities were Alla Nazimova, Margaret Anglin, Victor Herbert, Nance O'Neil, William Morris, Harry Lauder, Maxine Elliott, Walter Hampden, and Maude Allen. Meanwhile, articles about the latest Syndicate outrage or any scandal touching its partners made the front page of the news section.

Although the *Review*'s editorial policy was far from unbiased, the paper nevertheless covered a wide spectrum of entertainment in New York and other major American cities. Every show scheduled to open in a given week was, at the very least, mentioned on the final page of the *Review*. Many were also described and summarized there. Even shows of Syndicate-associated producers, such as Charles Frohman, Cohan and Harris, and Henry B. Harris, were presented in an impartial way in this section of the paper. In other parts of the *Review*, however, Shubert-affiliated productions garnered the most attention and praise, while Syndicate shows often received less than full attention or were condemned.

Not all competitors' productions suffered neglect or vilification in the *Review*. Independent producers like Lew Fields, Oscar Hammerstein, and William Morris were treated as allies. The treatment of Syndicate producers varied according to their degree of closeness to Shubert nemesis Abe Erlanger. The paper was somewhat kindly disposed to the Frohman brothers, for example. The Frohmans, especially Charles, were powerful and respected managers with a large stable of popular stars, and although they were clearly allied with Klaw and Erlanger, Lee and J. J. considered them to be more fair-minded than other Syndicate members.

Undoubtedly, the three most-attacked producers in the *Review* were David Belasco, Florenz Ziegfeld, and Abe Erlanger. Belasco, who had once been a Shubert ally, was deeply resented for his defection to the Syndicate. Ziegfeld's shows were time and again referred to as "pornographic," and sarcastic comments about his purported gambling debts abounded. The attacks on the Syndicate chief, Abe ("Little Aby") Erlanger, were the most virulent and often sank to a personal level.

The *Review* included other newsworthy entertainment topics such as vaudeville, Sunday blue laws against theatrical performances, and the growth of motion pictures. Real-estate development in and around the Broadway theater district was also regularly covered.

The *Review* ceased publication sometime in 1931, its demise probably concurrent with the Shuberts' bankruptcy during the Depression. A complete run of the newspaper has not survived—only scattered issues are known to exist.

Caricature (1908) by Howell of Alla Nazimova, a Russian dramatic actress who was Lee Shubert's protégé and who introduced Ibsen in this country. Lee paid for her English instruction and named a theater on 39th Street "The Nazimova" after her. When she left his management, the theater's name was changed to the 39th Street Theatre.

THE 44TH
STREET
THEATERS

Belasco Theatre

When David Belasco opened his new theater on 44th Street on October 16, 1907, he named it the Stuyvesant because he had already named another playhouse after himself on 42nd Street (originally the Republic, then the Belasco, now the Victory). In 1910 he relinquished the 42nd Street space and immediately renamed the Stuyvesant the Belasco.

The Shubert brothers enjoyed an on-again/off-again relationship with David Belasco. Even before moving to Manhattan, Sam had considered him a role model. There are, in fact, two large portraits of Sam on the walls of the Shubert Archive that expertly mimic a painting of the great producer. According to Belasco's biographer, William Winter, the admiration was reciprocated. Upon Sam's untimely death in 1905, Belasco was quoted as saying that, had Sam not died so young, he would have "occupied a great place in the history of American theater. He had keen business instincts, a lovable nature, and was the soul of honor." Four years later, Belasco rejoined the Syndicate. Reportedly, Lee and J. J. never forgave him.

Belasco was recognized as a playwright, actor, director, producer, manager, and set designer. Never lacking in flamboyance, the self-dubbed "Bishop of Broadway" was wont to don clerical garb. His duplex apartment above the second Belasco Theatre had the decor of a Gothic church and included a grotto, a two-story room with a stained-glass dome, and a phone booth that resembled a confessional.

Although his lifestyle reflected a certain over-the-top theatricality, Belasco advocated realism in the theater. If a script called for a meal to be prepared, for example, he would insist that the set be equipped to do just that. He was a proponent of what was called the "Little Theater" movement, which held that the dramatic experience depended partly on the proximity of the audience to the actors. With this in mind, Belasco conceived the auditorium of his new theater as a "living room."

Door to Gentlemen's room with bottle-glass window and transom, and coat-check door with original lighting fixture. Bottle glass appears as a prominent decorative element of the theater's lobby as well.

OPPOSITE:

Stained-glass capital of column near the Belasco's proscenium, seen from house right

OPPOSITE, ABOVE:
An early Belasco production,
The Music Master, *starring one
of Belasco's favorite performers,
David Warfield*

OPPOSITE, BELOW:
*Publicity shot of the members of
the influential Group Theatre,
c. 1930s, which made the Belasco
their home for productions of* Awake
and Sing, Golden Boy, Rocket to the
Moon, *and* The Gentle People. *The
innovative ensemble included Elia
Kazan, Clifford Odets, Luther and
Stella Adler, Sanford Meisner, Sylvia
Sidney, Lee J. Cobb, Karl Malden,
Harold Clurman, and Franchot
Tone. Seated in the center of this portrait is one of the Group's most tragic
members, Frances Farmer.*

George Keister was commissioned to design the new venue
and Everett Shinn to produce murals and other interior decor.
Theaters became the architect's specialty, and he later designed
at least twelve others, including the Apollo in Harlem. The
Belasco is Keister's earliest surviving theater. For it, he used the

Sidney Kingsley's 1935 production of Dead End. *The set was an East Side Manhattan street that dead-ended into the East River. The orchestra pit was filled with water into which the neighborhood boys could actually dive and swim. The play was the genesis of a series of Hollywood-produced feature films starring the Dead End Kids.*

neo-Georgian style, often associated with residences, which complemented Belasco's desire for theatrical intimacy. The interior was done in dark woods and stained glass. The auditorium, fan shaped and wider than it is deep, allowed the audience to be close to the stage. The orchestra contained 450 seats, the first balcony 320, and the second balcony 240. The theater also boasted a state-of-the-art lighting board capable of producing magical lighting effects. Artist Everett Shinn executed eighteen murals in subdued tones that contributed to Belasco's desire for a cozy public room.

The theater opened with *A Grand Army Man,* which was chosen primarily as a vehicle for Belasco's protégé David Warfield. Among the cast was Antoinette Perry, for whom the Tony Awards are named. Over the next two decades, Belasco produced and directed nearly fifty shows, many of which he also wrote. Among the notable productions were *The Warrens of Virginia* (1907) featuring Cecil B. DeMille and Mary Pickford, *Polly with a Past* (1917), *Lulu Belle* (1926), *It's a Wise Child* (1929) starring Humphrey Bogart, and Belasco's last production, *Tonight or Never* (1930), which introduced Helen Gahagan to her future husband, Melvin Douglas.

Upon Belasco's death on May 14, 1931, the theater was leased to Katharine Cornell Productions, Inc., and later to Hazel Rice, wife of playwright Elmer Rice. Neither tenant seemed troubled by the persistent rumors that the space was haunted by David Belasco's ghost.

In 1935, the groundbreaking Group Theatre made the Belasco home for its production of *Awake and Sing!* by Clifford Odets, with Stella Adler, Morris Carnovsky, John Garfield, Luther Adler, and Sanford Meisner. Later in the year, the Group added *Waiting for Lefty* (also by Odets) to its repertoire. Sanford Meisner directed a cast that featured Elia Kazan and Odets. Other Group Theatre productions at the Belasco included *Golden Boy* (1937) starring Luther Adler, Frances Farmer, Lee J. Cobb, John Garfield, Elia Kazan, and Howard da Silva; *Rocket to the Moon* (1938); and *The Gentle People* (1939) with Karl Malden and Sylvia Sidney.

Later in 1935, the Belasco enjoyed one of its biggest hits with Norman Bel Geddes's production of Sidney Kingsley's *Dead End*, a play that Belasco himself would have been proud of. The realistic set re-created a dead-end street on Manhattan's East River.

It was at this time that the Shuberts became connected to the Belasco. Their earliest lease on the house dates to 1939. On October 29, 1948, they bought the theater and the the land on which it sits, and they have owned the venue ever since. Notable productions of the 1940s include John Barrymore's final Broadway appearance, in *My Dear Children* (1940); *Johnny*

Jayne Mansfield starred in the 1955 production of Will Success Spoil Rock Hunter? *along with Orson Bean (left) and Walter Matthau (not pictured).*

The realism of Oh! Calcutta! *may have proved too much even for the ghost of David Belasco. Once the nude revue transferred from Off Broadway to the theater on February 25, 1971, there were no more reported sightings of the oft-seen ghost of the great producer.*

Janet McTeer in the immensely popular 1997 revival of Ibsen's A Doll's House. *McTeer's highly acclaimed portrayal of Nora earned her a Tony Award for Best Actress in a Play.*

Belinda (1940); *Kiss Them for Me* (1945) with Judy Holliday; and *The Madwoman of Chaillot* (1948).

With the advent and popularity of radio, many empty houses were leased to radio networks. From mid-1949 to November 1953, the Shuberts leased the Belasco to NBC for use as a radio playhouse.

The Belasco returned to theatrical legitimacy with a powerhouse production of *The Solid Gold Cadillac* (1953) starring Josephine Hull. It ran for 568 performances. Other highlights of the 1950s included *The Flowering Peach* (1954) and *Will Success Spoil Rock Hunter?* (1955).

The 1960s were ushered in with Tad Mosel's poignant *All the Way Home* (1960), based on the James Agee novel and starring Arthur Hill, Lillian Gish, and Colleen Dewhurst. John Osborne's *Inadmissible Evidence* (1965), starring Nicol Williamson, and *The Killing of Sister George* (1966) were the other highlights of a rather lackluster decade for the Belasco.

When *The Rocky Horror Show* opened in 1975, all of the seats in the auditorium were removed and replaced with cabaret tables and chairs to create a nightclub atmosphere. Unfor-

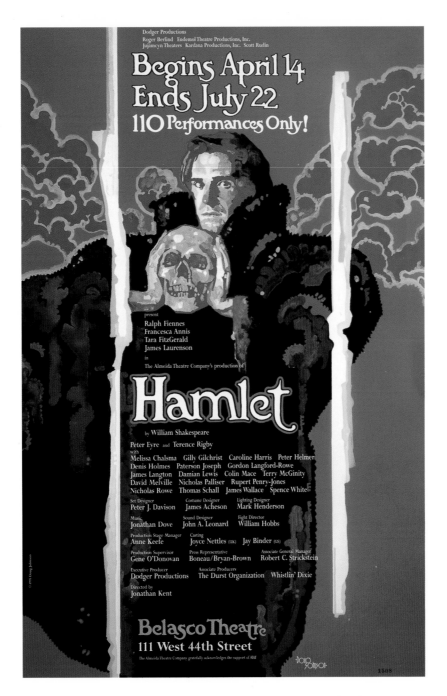

Dodger Productions
Roger Berlind   Endemol Theatre Productions, Inc.
Jujamcyn Theaters   Kardana Productions, Inc.   Scott Rudin

**Begins April 14
Ends July 22
110 Performances Only!**

present

Ralph Fiennes
Francesca Annis
Tara FitzGerald
James Laurenson

in

The Almeida Theatre Company's production of

Hamlet

by William Shakespeare

Peter Eyre and Terence Rigby

with

Melissa Chalsma   Gilly Gilchrist   Caroline Harris   Peter Helmer
Denis Holmes   Paterson Joseph   Gordon Langford-Rowe
James Langton   Damian Lewis   Colin Mace   Terry McGinity
David Melville   Nicholas Palliser   Rupert Penry-Jones
Nicholas Rowe   Thomas Schall   James Wallace   Spence White

| Set Designer | Costume Designer | Lighting Designer |
| Peter J. Davison | James Acheson | Mark Henderson |

| Music | Sound Designer | Fight Director |
| Jonathan Dove | John A. Leonard | William Hobbs |

| Production Stage Manager | Casting | |
| Anne Keefe | Joyce Nettles (UK)   Jay Binder (US) | |

| Production Supervisor | Press Representative | Associate General Manager |
| Gene O'Donovan | Boneau/Bryan-Brown | Robert C. Strickstein |

| Executive Producer | Associate Producers | |
| Dodger Productions | The Durst Organization   Whistlin' Dixie | |

Directed by
Jonathan Kent

**Belasco Theatre
111 West 44th Street**

The Almeida Theatre Company gratefully acknowledges the support of AT&T

tunately, because the production was set in the "Acme Demolition Company," original plasterwork from the lower boxes was sledgehammered off as well.

For the 1991–92 season, the Belasco became the home of Tony Randall's National Actors Theatre, whose inaugural productions were *The Crucible, A Little Hotel on the Side,* and *The Master Builder.* The following year Randall moved his home base to the Lyceum Theatre. The latter half of the 1990s at the Belasco included two highly acclaimed British imports: *Hamlet* (1995) starring Ralph Fiennes, and *A Doll's House* (1997) with Janet McTeer.

Window card for the 1995 revival of Hamlet *starring Ralph Fiennes, whose characterization of the brooding Danish prince won him a Tony Award for Best Actor in a Play*

The Belasco Theatre is located at 111 West 44th Street.

An exterior shot of the Broadhurst in 1917, the year it opened. The show on the marquee, Lord and Lady Algy, *was the third occupant of the new playhouse. It starred William Faversham and Maxine Elliott.*

OPPOSITE:
Exterior of the Broadhurst Theatre, 2000

For nearly a century, the Broadhurst has been home to a wonderful array of productions. Its location, commodious appointments, and size continue to make the theater one of the most desirable venues on Broadway. One of the Shubert Organization's most consistently booked houses, with a seating capacity of 1,155, the Broadhurst is ideal for both musicals and plays. The theater's opening in 1917 gave the Shubert brothers a further toehold in their eventual domination of 44th and 45th Streets. The Broadhurst and the Plymouth (on 45th Street) were both constructed in 1917 and opened within two weeks of each other. Both were also the brainchild of architect Herbert J. Krapp. Krapp had apprenticed with the prestigious firm of Herts and Tallant, but the two new houses would be his first independent commission.

The theater was built in association with and named for manager George H. Broadhurst, who was also an accomplished playwright—no less than six of his plays debuted at the structure named for him. Despite this, the Broadhurst did not open with one of his shows. That honor went to George Bernard Shaw's *Misalliance* with Maclyn Arbuckle on September 27, 1917— the play's United States premiere. Eva Le Gallienne's long

Detail on the lip of a hanging crystal light fixture in an auditorium box

OVERLEAF, LEFT:
Orchestra seat and boxes, far house left

OVERLEAF, RIGHT,
CLOCKWISE FROM TOP LEFT:
View of auditorium from upper box

Light fixture in box with a view through parted curtains to the auditorium's ceiling

Detail of molding near the ceiling

George Broadhurst, for whom the theater was named, immigrated to the United States from England in 1886. He wrote a number of popular plays and managed theaters across the country before opening the Broadhurst with the Shuberts in 1917.

association with the Broadhurst began later that year with a revival of *Lord and Lady Algy*. George Broadhurst's first play in his namesake theater was *He Didn't Want to Do It* (1918). Later that year, Nora Bayes opened in the theater's first musical hit, *Ladies First*.

The 1920s roared in with a Jeanne Eagels vehicle, *The Wonderful Thing* (1920). Other highlights of the decade included Broadhurst's adaptation of *Tarzan of the Apes* (1921); the lively revue *Topics of 1923;* George Kaufman and Marc Connelly's huge hit comedy *Beggar on Horseback* (1924) with Spring Byington; *The Green Hat* (1925) starring Leslie Howard and Katharine Cornell, which scandalized audiences with its theme of venereal disease; George Abbott's enormous hit *Broadway* (1926); and the musical *Hold Everything* (1928), which unleashed Bert Lahr on an unsuspecting audience.

As the country and Broadway soldiered on through the Great Depression, the Broadhurst continued to host a string of impressive shows. One of the venue's landmark productions opened in 1933—the Group Theatre's *Men in White*. Written by Sidney Kingsley and directed by Lee Strasberg, the play featured a stellar cast that included Luther

OPPOSITE, ABOVE:

The 1933 Pulitzer Prize–winning play, Men in White, *was a huge hit by the prestigious Group Theatre. The highlight of the production was this tense scene realistically depicting what appeared to be an actual medical operation.*

OPPOSITE, BELOW:

A flyer from the highly acclaimed 1935 production of Victoria Regina *with Helen Hayes as the British monarch. Many consider this to have been the highlight of her career. In it she was asked to age from a young girl to the beloved, older queen. Vincent Price played her adored Prince Albert.*

BELOW:

White Studio production shot of Ethel Barrymore (right) and Eva Le Gallienne in the 1934 production of L'Aiglon. *This was one of three plays presented by Le Gallienne's esteemed Civic Repertory Company. Among the cast of* L'Aiglon *were Barrymore's children, Ethel and Samuel Colt.*

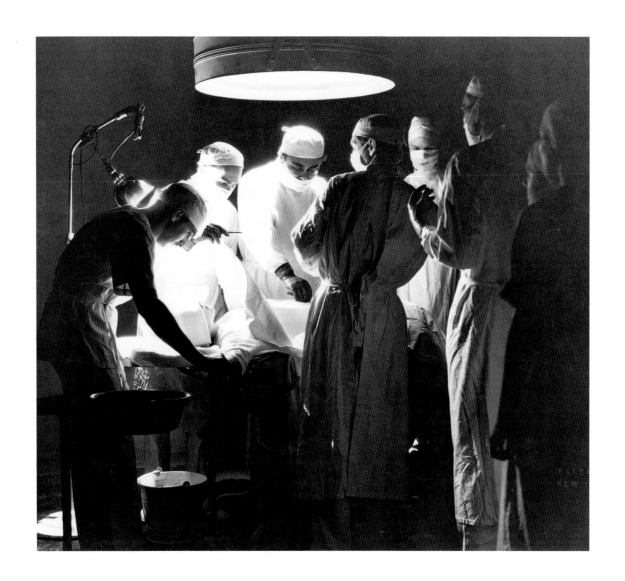

Agatha Christie's immensely popular
Ten Little Indians *haunted the*
Broadhurst in 1944. Cast members
were bumped off one at a time
throughout the evening. The play
became a perennial favorite for
college and community theater
groups for decades.

Adler, Sanford Meisner, Morris Carnovsky, Elia Kazan, and Clifford Odets. This medical drama heralded the arrival of the innovative company that would revolutionize American acting technique.

Next, Leslie Howard and Humphrey Bogart savored success with Robert E. Sherwood's *The Petrified Forest* (1935). The production was so successful, in fact, that Howard insisted that his costar reprise his role in the Hollywood version, which launched Bogart's film career. Later in 1935, the Broadhurst enjoyed another of its biggest hits with Helen Hayes in *Victoria Regina*. The decade culminated with two noteworthy musicals: Mike Todd's production *The Hot Mikado* (1939), a swing version of Gilbert and Sullivan's operetta, starring the legendary Bill "Bojangles" Robinson; and Olsen and Johnson's hit revue *Streets of Paris* (1939). The comic pair's follow-up to their smash *Hellzapoppin'* (see pages 19 and 290) marked Carmen Miranda's American debut. While vacationing in South America, Lee Shubert had discovered the Brazilian bombshell performing in a nightclub and immediately arranged to bring her to New York.

Against the backdrop of a raging world war, the Broadhurst offered 1940s audiences a haven for lighthearted entertainment. *Keep Off the Grass* (1940), a revue with a stellar cast made up of Jimmy Durante, Ray Bolger, José Limon, and Emmett Kelly, kicked off the decade. Two more revues followed: *Boys and Girls Together* (1940) starring Ed Wynn, and *High Kicks* (1941) with

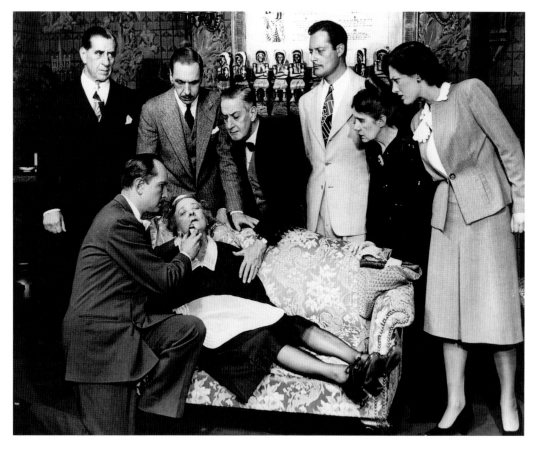

Auntie Mame *(1956), with Rosalind Russell as the irrepressible title character. She was succeeded in the role by Greer Garson, Bea Lillie, and Sylvia Sidney, and the production ran for a total of 639 performances. Russell later reprised her role in the motion-picture version of the show.*

George Jessel and Sophie Tucker. Agatha Christie's hit, *Ten Little Indians*, starring Estelle Winwood, scared up an audience in 1944, and Anita Loos's *Happy Birthday* with Helen Hayes settled in for a long run in 1946.

The 1950s saw a parade of well-received and long-running productions, such as a revival of Rodgers and Hart's *Pal Joey* (1952), *Anniversary Waltz* (1954), *The Desk Set* (1955), and *The World of Suzie Wong* (1958) starring France Nuyen and William Shatner. In 1956 the matchless Rosalind Russell introduced us to the equally unique *Auntie Mame*. The Pulitzer Prize–winning *Fiorello!* (1959), winner of a slew of Tony Awards, closed out the decade.

Elaine Stritch helped launch the 1960s with Noël Coward's *Sail Away* (1961), while *110 in the Shade*, a musical version of *The Rainmaker*, heated up the stage in 1963. The Broadhurst welcomed two British imports in 1964 and 1965: *Oh, What a Lovely War* and the Tommy Steele musical *Half a Sixpence*. One of the theater's biggest hits, Kander and Ebb's *Cabaret*, opened in 1966. Based on Christopher Isherwood's *The Berlin Stories*, the cutting-edge musical was directed by Harold Prince and starred Jill Haworth, Bert Convy, Lotte Lenya, Jack Gilford, and relative newcomer Joel Grey. In 1969, Woody Allen starred in his *Play It Again, Sam*, along with Diane Keaton and Tony Roberts.

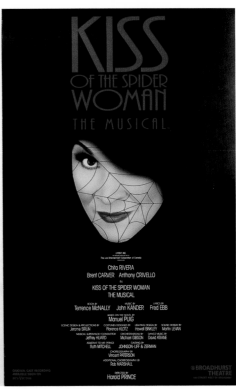

A triptych of window cards from three enormously popular Broadhurst productions: Amadeus (1980), Dancin' (1978), and Kiss of the Spider Woman (1993). Amadeus and Dancin' were both Shubert productions. Dancin', a dance concert by Bob Fosse, was the precursor to Fosse.

Fosse, winner of the 1999 Tony Award for Best Musical. The show is a retrospective valentine to the legendary Broadway choreographer and includes show-stopping numbers from his entire career. This image from the opening number captures some of his most recognizable trademarks: the bowler hat, black leotards, white gloves, and the angular isolation of the body.

Scene from the 1966 production of Cabaret *starring Joel Grey (top center). The musical about decadent, pre–World War II Berlin was based on Christopher Isherwood's writings of the time. The material had already been produced as the play* The Berlin Stories *(1952). The Broadhurst was the first of three homes for* Cabaret. *It moved to the Imperial in 1967 and then to the Broadway in 1968.*

Highlights of the 1970s include Sada Thompson's electrifying performance in George Furth's *Twigs* (1971), Neil Simon's *The Sunshine Boys* (1972), a rare appearance by Katharine Hepburn in *A Matter of Gravity* (1976), and Bob Fosse's popular dance revue *Dancin'* (1978). The 1980s began with a bang with Peter Shaffer's *Amadeus* (1980) starring Ian McKellan, Tim Curry, and Jane Seymour. The long-running drama about Salieri's toxic obsession with Mozart won that year's Tony Award as Best Play. It was followed by a successful urban musical, *The Tap Dance Kid* (1983), and two more Neil Simon smashes, *Broadway Bound* (1986) and *Rumors* (1988).

Kiss of the Spider Woman (1993), a musical based on the film, won several Tonys, including one for its beloved star, Broadway veteran Chita Rivera. And in 1999, Bob Fosse returned once again—at least in spirit—to the Broadhurst, in the Tony Award–winning *Fosse*, a song-and-dance retrospective of the career of this unique dancer, choreographer, and director.

The Broadhurst Theatre is located at 235 West 44th Street.

The Shuberts' War Efforts

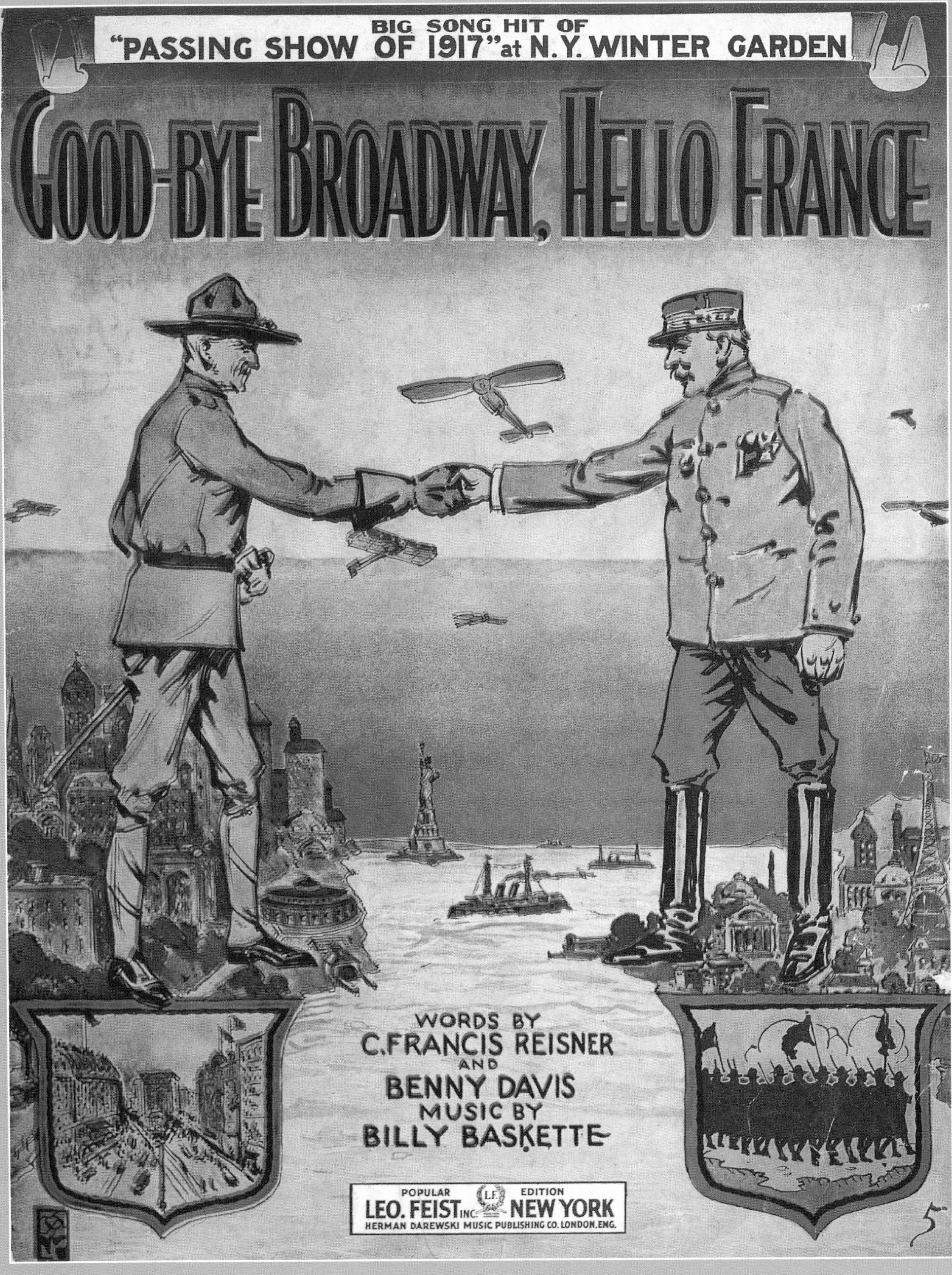

LEFT:
Homer Conant's costume sketch for a Postage Stamp Girl, from *The Passing Show* of 1917, a reminder to our boys to write home

BELOW:
Sketch by Homer Conant for World War I Service Girls, who all held auxiliary jobs to the military branches of the armed services. These included Red Cross nurses, YMCA girls, and Salvation Army girls.

PREVIOUS PAGE:
Sheet-music cover for "Good-Bye Broadway, Hello France," from *The Passing Show* of 1917. The song tells of how the Yanks are off to Europe to win the war quickly and pay off our debts to France, which "sent us Lafayette." By the time the United States entered the European war, revue songs and sketches were very pro-Britain and France.

Both world wars sparked a patriotic impulse in the Shuberts and their peers in the community. Lee and J. J. interpolated sketches and musical numbers in their revues that touched on the war in Europe and—eventually—strongly supported the Allies' cause. Initially, Shubert revues took their cues from President Wilson and Congress; in the 1915 edition of their annual, *The Passing Show*, for example, chorus girls sang "It's America First." By the next season, *The Passing Show* encouraged its audience to "Be prepared if we fight,—America." By 1917, there was no waffling. In the song "Johnny Get Your Gun," the hero is urged "to learn to shoot for your Uncle Sammy." Other numbers, like "Ring Out Liberty Bell," promised a haven here for people from oppressed lands, and in "Stamp Your Letter With a Kiss," a girl entreats her boyfriend to write to her and address the envelope, "My darling sweetheart, U.S.A."

The Shuberts cooperated with other theater people to make pitches in their venues in support of the war effort and the sale of liberty bonds. During World War I, the week beginning June 4, 1917, was designated "Liberty Loan Week." Stars like John Barrymore and De Wolf Hopper spoke from the stage between acts to encourage members of the audience to buy war bonds. After war was declared, the Shuberts were the first to announce that sailors and soldiers would get half-price tickets at their theaters. They donated the use of their venues to different societies engaged in charitable activities on behalf of the war effort. Lee and J. J. also instructed that "The Star-Spangled Banner" be played before every show and that the audience be encouraged to rise at the playing of the national anthem.

Much of what was done in support of the war effort grew from a spontaneous patriotism, but most was a response to war hysteria and anti-German fervor. Theater owners were ordered by the New York Order of Vigilantes to remove their ads from the German-language press. German periodicals were deemed to be anti-U.S., and selling, buying or advertising in the German press was considered to be aiding the enemy.

The United States involvement in World War II was more clear-cut. After the bombing of Pearl Harbor, most of the country supported the war effort, and the various branches of the entertainment industry cooperated to provide entertainment for the troops. In addition to organizing tours of professional performers to military bases, the United Service Organizations (USO) organized a Material and Writers Committee that compiled volumes of revue sketches, skits, and songs, which the soldiers could use to mount their own shows. John Shubert, chairman and chief editor of this committee, obtained the cooperation of producers, writers, composers, lyricists, and others to launch the project. Meanwhile, Lee Shubert became chairman of the Legitimate Theatre Campaign for the Army and Navy Emergency Relief, which raised money for the families of soldiers who were disabled, missing in action, or dead. From May 14 through May 20, 1942, actors made nightly appeals from stages all across the country on behalf of the campaign. Another project the Shuberts supported was the Stage Door Canteen, a club for servicemen in the basement of their 44th Street Theatre. The Stage Door Canteen, founded by the American Theatre Wing and the USO, provided food and entertainment to our boys in uniform.

L-I-B-E-R-T-Y

L stands for Lucy—she is learning how to fly

I stands for Ida—at farming she will try

B stands for Bertha—she is learning how to plow

E stands for Edna—who's a Red Cross nurse right now

R stands for Rosie—for the soldiers she will sew

T stands for Tessie—watch her motorcycle go
and
Y for Yvonne—who is selling bonds you see,

And L-I-B-E-R-T-Y spells Liberty

Lyric, *Doing Our Bit* (1917), words by Harold Atteridge, music by Sigmund Romberg and Herman Timberg

Audience of 2,500 soldiers and sailors at the Casino Theatre in New York on August 11, 1918, for a production of Jerome Kern's *Oh, Lady! Lady!*

Inset, clockwise from below left:
Lee Shubert talking with soldiers and sailors at the Stage Door Canteen

Flyer, *The Bistrew's Co.* In the aftermath of World War I, the Shuberts launched another foray into vaudeville and were inundated by acts promoting themselves for time on the Shubert Vaudeville circuit. In October 1920, the Bistrew's Co. from Belgium approached the Shuberts with their comedy act featuring one-legged acrobats in military uniforms performing jumps with military precision. This is an act that might have been created out of the accidents of war.

In *New Priorities of 1943*, unidentified actors play Winston Churchill and Franklin D. Roosevelt in the "Atlantic Charter" sketch.

The Majestic was built in 1926–27 by the Chanin brothers as part of a three-theater complex on the east side of Eighth Avenue between 44th and 45th Streets. Their decision to commence this ambitious building project ensured that one city block would become the heart of the theater district. The venues on these two streets formed the densest concentration of professional playhouses in the city, and they remain the core of the theater district today.

From the start, the Chanins envisioned a development that incorporated three differently sized venues into the centerpiece of their theater chain—a large musical house, the Majestic; a medium or "standard" house, the Royale; and an intimate house, the Golden (built as the Theatre Masque). Irwin Chanin's strategy in joining these theaters with a hotel was economy of scale; financially, the three the-

Carousel (1945), starring Jan Clayton as Julie and John Raitt as Billy. Based on Molnar's Liliom, *this Rodgers and Hammerstein musical was their follow-up to the hugely successful* Oklahoma!

aters worked as a unit with the hotel in purchasing supplies and furnishings and in sharing expenses. The Theatre Masque, the smallest house, would be the laboratory theater of the Chanin group—if a show introduced there became a hit, it could move to a larger house. Likewise, if a production opened at the

Majestic or Royale to lackluster business, it could transfer to the smaller house. Transferring productions from one venue to another was fairly routine at the time, because most sets consisted of easily transportable two-dimensional backdrops and scenery. This meant that producers and theater owners were more willing to gamble on small shows by unknown writers with unknown stars, because, in theory, profits from the two larger houses would help offset losses in the smaller one.

In November 1927, the Shuberts became partners with the Chanins when Theater Zone Realty, Inc., a Chanin subsidiary, sold ownership of the three houses to both the Shuberts and the Chanins, who then created a holding company, Royma (for Royale and Majestic), to hold the shares of the theaters. By 1930, however, the Depression had taken its toll on the Chanins and they exchanged their interest in the trio of theaters for a share of the Shuberts' New Theatre on Central Park West (currently the site of the Century Apartment Building). This made Lee and J. J. the sole shareholders of Royma. Then, on June 3, 1936, the Shuberts formed a subsidiary named Magoro (for Majestic, Golden, and Royale) and transferred ownership of the three theaters to the new company. Subsequently, Royma was dissolved.

From the start, the Majestic was considered one of the preeminent musical houses on Broadway—a status due, in part, to its architecture. The Chanins commissioned Herbert Krapp (see page 202) to design the theater complex in what he called a "modern Spanish" style, complete with terra-cotta base and brick-wall Spanish ornamentation, and arched windows. When it opened, the Majestic had the largest seating capacity on Broadway, and with 1,655 seats, it was the perfect venue for lavish musicals. Decades before the current vogue for stadium seating in movie theaters, Krapp had conceived of a similar concept for the orchestra of the Majestic. Because of its steep rake, the rear of the orchestra must be reached by a pair of staircases, but its sight lines are ideal. Another forward-thinking aspect of the design was the creation of a single large balcony rather than two smaller ones—today's producers are hesitant to book two-balcony houses because second-balcony seating is less desirable to modern audiences.

The Majestic opened with a revue, *Rufus LeMaire's Affairs*, on March 28, 1927, which was followed soon thereafter by its first Sigmund Romberg operetta, *The Love Call*. The next year the Majestic's stage was graced by John Gielgud in *The Patriot* and prizefighter Jack Dempsey in *The Big Fight*. In 1929, a newcomer named Archie Leach, soon to achieve stardom as Cary Grant, appeared with Jeannette MacDonald in *A Wonderful Night*, an operetta based on Strauss's *Die Fledermaus*.

The 1930s began with a new edition of the popular annual revue *Artists and Models* (see page 286). A little-known and short-lived George and Ira Gershwin show, *Pardon My English* (1933), was immediately followed by *Strike Me Pink* (1933), a more successful musical with Jimmy Durante as one of its stars. John Shubert, J. J.'s son, claimed a writing credit for 1934's *Music Hath Charms*. This Romberg operetta may have had charms, but it did not have legs—it closed after only 29 performances. Ethel Merman, Jimmy Durante, and Mildred Natwick led the cast of *Stars in Your Eyes* (1939), but despite good reviews and a chorus that included Jerome Robbins, the show was not a major success.

In 1945 *Carousel* became the first of four consecutive Rodgers and Hammerstein hit musicals to play the Majestic. Jan Clayton as Julie and John Raitt as Billy Bigelow dazzled wartime audiences. *Allegro*, with choreography by Agnes de Mille, debuted in 1947, followed two years later by

LEFT:
An eager audience anticipating the hit musical South Pacific *enters the Majestic.*

BELOW:
A surprised Mary Martin (far right) reacts to the appearance of (from left) Richard Rodgers, Oscar Hammerstein II, Joshua Logan, and Leland Heyward at her final curtain call as Nellie Forbush in South Pacific *on June 1, 1951. The Pulitzer Prize– and Tony Award–winning production opened at the Majestic on April 7, 1949. Martin left after two years, but it went on to chalk up 1,925 performances.*

Robert Preston as Harold Hill informs the denizens of River City that they've got "Trouble!" in the 1957 hit The Music Man. Preston's costar, Barbara Cook, helped the slice of middle-Americana achieve a run of 1,375 performances.

South Pacific (1949). Based on James Michener's book *Tales of the South Pacific*, the show was an immediate sensation. It ran for 1,925 performances and not only won the Pulitzer Prize, but also garnered Tony Awards for Rodgers and Hammerstein, director Josh Logan, and four of its stars: Mary Martin, Ezio Pinza, Juanita Hall, and Myron McCormick. The theater's last Rodgers and Hammerstein tenant, *Me and Juliet* (1953), a backstage musical, was not as successful as its predecessor, but nevertheless ran for almost a year.

Other noteworthy productions of the 1950s included: Herbert and Dorothy Fields and Arthur Schwartz's musical, *By the Beautiful Sea* (1954), starring Shirley Booth; Howard Lindsay and Russel Crouse's *Happy Hunting* (1956) with Ethel Merman and Fernando Lamas; and last, but not least, Meredith Willson's *The Music Man* (1957), which won eight Tony Awards and made Robert Preston and his 76 trombones famous.

No sooner had the residents of River City vacated the Majestic when King Arthur and his court moved in with *Camelot* (1960), the successful Alan Jay Lerner and Frederick Loewe musical starring Julie Andrews, Richard Burton, and Robert Goulet. Stephen Sondheim's *Anyone Can Whistle* (1964) is notable not only for its composer but also for the fact that even with its luminous stars—Harry Guardino, Lee Remick, and Angela Lansbury—it managed a run of only nine performances. The Majestic's next musical, *Golden Boy* (1964), was much more successful. Based on Clifford Odets's play, it starred Sammy Davis, Jr., in one of his signature roles.

OVERLEAF:
Camelot *(1960), Richard Burton as King Arthur and Julie Andrews as his beloved Guinevere. The show that Ed Sullivan saved! This highly anticipated musical directed by Moss Hart and written by Lerner and Loewe opened to mixed reviews and lagging ticket sales. The morning after Ed Sullivan presented selections from the show on his popular television program, the box office was mobbed. The new residents of the White House became fans, and it has forever been linked to the "one brief shining moment" of the Kennedy presidency.*

Inset:
Pallbearers shoulder the coffin of John Shubert following the funeral service on the stage of the Majestic. John was the only heir of the original three Shubert brothers. After graduating from the University of Pennsylvania, he was accepted to Harvard Law School. He left Harvard to work for his Uncle Lee and his father. He married Kerttu Helene Ecklund, a Shubert showgirl from Finland, in 1937. In 1962, at the age of fifty-three, he died suddenly of a heart attack on a Florida-bound train. There was some degree of shock when it was revealed that the soft-spoken, mild-mannered John had left directions for a very theatrical funeral on the stage of the Majestic.

Mabel King as Evillene, the Wicked Witch of the West, performs "No Bad News" in Geoffrey Holder's Tony Award–winning production of The Wiz (1975). Based on L. Frank Baum's The Wonderful Wizard of Oz (1900), the show used R&B music and black vernacular to retell the story of Dorothy's quest down the yellow brick road. The musical ran for over 1,600 performances and spawned a none-too-successful motion picture starring Diana Ross and Michael Jackson.

Sugar (1972) was the theater's first new musical hit of the 1970s. Based on Billy Wilder's film *Some Like It Hot*, the show featured a score by Jule Styne and a cast that included Robert Morse, Tony Roberts, Elaine Joyce, and Cyril Ritchard. Much was expected of Jerry Herman's *Mack and Mabel* (1974) starring Robert Preston and Bernadette Peters as Mack Sennett and Mabel Normand, but despite one of Herman's lushest scores, the show was not a success. The Majestic's next tenant, *The Wiz* (1975), more than made up for it, however. This African-American version of *The Wizard of Oz* swept the Tony Awards with seven wins. After it transferred to the Broadway Theatre, Liza Minnelli moved in with *The Act* (1977), directed by Martin Scorsese.

In 1981, David Merrick and Gower Champion's *42nd Street* transferred from the Winter Garden to the Majestic, where it stayed until 1987. That same year, the Landmarks Preservation

OPPOSITE:
Liza Minnelli in her Tony Award– winning performance in The Act at the Majestic in 1977. The weak script was only an excuse for Liza to strut her stuff in Vegas-inspired musical numbers.

The Phantom (Michael Crawford) introduces Christine (Sarah Brightman) to his otherworldly lair in The Phantom of the Opera, *which moved into the Majestic in 1988.*

Commission granted the Majestic Theatre landmark status. Extensive renovations to the stage and the area beneath it were then undertaken in preparation for the playhouse's next production, Andrew Lloyd Webber's *The Phantom of the Opera* (1988). The show's elaborate special effects necessitated these alterations, but the extra work was worth it. The elegant opening-night audience included Sarah Ferguson, Duchess of York, and the show took home seven Tony Awards that year. At the dawn of a new millennium, *Phantom* continues to drop chandeliers on awestruck audiences and the musical's appeal shows no signs of waning.

OPPOSITE:
The Majestic Theatre exterior, 2000

The Majestic Theatre is located at 245 West 44th Street.

R odgers and Hart, Lunt and Fontanne, Barrymore, Gielgud, Hepburn, Gleason, Streisand, Travolta: these are just a few of the famous names linked through time by an even bigger name—Shubert. The flagship theater of the Shubert brothers' empire has a rich and fabled history and, along with Shubert Alley, stands at the center of Broadway's lore and landmarks.

From the moment it opened, the Shubert Theatre was hailed as a welcome addition to the theater district, but although instantly successful, it was nevertheless born out of a Shubert failure. Lee Shubert was among those who in 1909 had founded the New Theatre, an "art" playhouse located on Central Park

OPPOSITE:

Shubert Theatre, 44th Street facade, c. 1913. The elaborate marquee that lent a strong presence to the sidewalk has since been replaced with a much simpler design.

RIGHT:

The Shubert's interior, taken from house left, shortly after the theater's opening in 1913

West that was devoted to serious repertory drama. Unfortunately, the project was a critical and commercial flop. In early 1911, the New Theatre group leased a plot of land stretching between 44th and 45th Streets behind the Hotel Astor, with the intention of erecting another theater there. The existing buildings on the site were razed in the spring of 1911, but the plan was ultimately abandoned.

One year later, Lee Shubert and Winthrop Ames, a former New Theatre partner, acquired a long-term lease on the site and built two adjoining playhouses there. Utilizing an unusual scheme, the new edifices shared an architecturally unified exterior described as being in the style of the "Venetian Renaissance, with certain modern adaptations," though the two interiors were totally distinct from one another. Lee and J. J. Shubert operated the larger of the two auditoriums (about 1,400 seats), which they named the Sam S. Shubert Memorial Theatre to commemorate their brother, who had died in May 1905. Ames managed the smaller Booth Theatre.

When the Shubert Theatre opened on September 29, 1913, it revealed a design that was truly remarkable. The sgraffito that decorated the exterior was architect Henry B. Herts's unusual solution to a statute in the city's building code dictating that no part of the edifice project beyond the building line. As the magazine *American Architect* described it, "the sgraffito panels have Renaissance ornament in light gray tone, executed on a background of purple gray. The trimmings, including the cornice, are of light terra cotta; the walls are buff colored, and the bricks are laid in alternate courses of headers and stretchers." *Architecture and Building* noted that the sgraffito was accomplished "by carving through several layers of varied colored cements, producing the figured decoration of the panels which decorates both fronts."

Another distinctive feature of the exterior was the private roadway connecting 44th and 45th Streets, which ran between the two new theaters and the rear of the Astor Hotel. This thoroughfare, which would come to be called Shubert Alley (see page 99), allowed each theater to occupy a corner lot.

The Shubert's interior is no less distinctive. A two-balcony house, its elegant decoration is marked by elaborate plasterwork and a series of painted panels that adorn the boxes, the area above the proscenium arch, and the ceiling. These panels, painted by artist J. Mortimer Lichtenauer, depict classical figures in a variety of poses, and include a series of figures flanking theatrical masks.

Because the new theater was both the centerpiece of the Shuberts' theatrical operations as well as a memorial to Sam,

OPPOSITE:
The Shubert Theatre, 2000. Except for the streamlined modern marquees and the banners advertising the musical Chicago, *little of the theater's exterior has changed over the years.*

CENTER:
*Shubert Theatre, interior
with renovation work crew
and Shubert Organization
executives in full force,
1996. In 1996 the Shubert
Organization embarked on
its largest theater restoration
project to date when it
decided to overhaul
completely its flagship
playhouse. Headed by
architects Barbara
Campagna and Francesca
Russo, the project aimed
not only to restore the venue
to its former brilliance,
but also to make added
improvements like
ergonomically correct
front-of-house seating and
thoroughly state-of-the-art
technical equipment
backstage. Toiling, at times,
around-the-clock, workers
completed the undertaking
in three short months. The
backstage renovation, in
fact, marked the first time
in the United States
that a completely new
counterweight and gridiron
system was installed in a
currently operating theater.*

Othello (1943), with Paul Robeson (left) in the title role, José Ferrer as Iago, and Uta Hagen as Desdemona. Critics and audiences alike enthusiastically welcomed this version of Shakespeare's tragedy. Robeson's performance was a benchmark for the actor, and the production design by Robert Edmund Jones was a prime example of the New Stagecraft.

Lee chose to build an office/apartment suite above the auditorium. This apartment, now the location of the Shubert Organization's executive offices, included a tiny circular office where Lee conducted business, as well as a large dining hall containing a working fountain and a minstrel's gallery.

Lee and J. J. chose the prestigious British actor Johnston Forbes-Robertson to open the theater with his repertory company. The plays presented from September 29 through December 29, 1913, included *Mice and Men*, *The Light That Failed*, *Caesar and Cleopatra*, *Hamlet*, *The Merchant of Venice*,

The Philadelphia Story (1939), souvenir program centerfold featuring Katharine Hepburn. Playwright Philip Barry had not enjoyed a Broadway hit since 1932, the Theatre Guild was on the brink of financial disaster, and the once popular movie star Katharine Hepburn had been labeled "box office poison" by Hollywood pundits after a series of poorly received films. Yet she and the witty and urbane play charmed audiences. Hepburn, who had wisely secured the film rights to the play, returned triumphantly to Hollywood and reestablished herself as a major screen presence.

Ivanov *(1966) with John Gielgud as Nikolai Alekseyevitch Ivanov and Vivien Leigh as Anna Petrovna. A British import that received mixed critical notices, this production nevertheless achieved hit status because of its distinguished cast. This was Leigh's last professional appearance on stage or screen—she died the following year at age fifty-four.*

Othello, The Sacrament of Judas, and *The Passing of the Third Floor Back.* After this premiere engagement, the Shubert played host to straight plays and musicals in equal measure—it was the brothers' most distinguished all-purpose venue. Some of the more significant plays to appear were *The Copperhead* (1918) starring Lionel Barrymore; *The Blue Flame* (1920) starring Theda Bara; *Dodsworth* (1934), based on Sinclair Lewis's novel and starring Walter Huston and Fay Bainter; *Love On the Dole* (1936) with Wendy Hiller; *The Philadelphia Story* (1939) starring Katharine Hepburn and Shirley Booth; *Othello* (1943) starring Paul Robeson, José Ferrer, and Uta Hagen; Mae West's *Catherine Was Great* (1944); *Anne of the Thousand Days* (1948) with Rex Harrison; Chekhov's *Ivanov* (1966) starring John Gielgud and Vivien Leigh; and *The Constant Wife* (1975) starring Ingrid Bergman.

As for musicals, a truly impressive roster has called the Shubert home. One of the brothers' most successful operettas, *Maytime* (1917) starring Peggy Wood, was the first of five Romberg shows to premiere here. The others were *The Magic Melody* (1919), *Marjorie* (1924), *My Princess* (1927), and *My Romance* (1948). Additional popular hits of the day were Rudolf Friml's *Sometime* (1918) with Mae West and Ed Wynn; four editions of the *Greenwich Village Follies* (1921, 1922, 1924, and 1926); *Artists and Models* (1923); *Vogues of 1924* starring Fred Allen; *Gay Paree* (1925) with Jack Haley; and another classic Shubert-produced operetta, *Countess Maritza* (1926). In *Padlocks of 1927*, star Texas Guinan first addressed Broadway fans with her trademark line, "Hello, suckers," and in 1931 Harold Atteridge and Sammy Fain's *Everybody's Welcome* introduced audiences to Herman Hupfeld's song "As Time Goes By."

Five Rodgers and Hart musicals occupied the Shubert during the last half of the 1930s and into the 1940s. Among these, *Babes in Arms* (1937), with Alfred Drake, gave us "My Funny Valentine" and "The Lady Is a Tramp," and *Pal Joey* (1941),

OPPOSITE:
Alfred Lunt and Lynn Fontanne, autographed portrait (date unknown). Married in 1928, Lunt and Fontanne were also professionally inseparable until their retirement from live theater in 1956. Considered by most to be the greatest husband-and-wife acting team ever to grace the legitimate stage, the couple made four appearances at the Shubert, the first being the Pulitzer Prize–winning Idiot's Delight *(1936), followed by* Amphitryon 38 *(1937),* The Seagull *(1938), and* I Know My Love *(1949).*

Artists and Models *(1923). Chorus girls hold up samples of the lightning sketch artist's handiwork. Artists such as this, popular staples on the vaudeville circuit, drew rapid portraits of characters in the manner of noted artists of the day.*

featuring Gene Kelly, put "Bewitched, Bothered, and Bewildered" on the musical map. Others that played the house during the 1940s were Yip Harburg and Burton Lane's *Hold Onto Your Hats* (1940) starring Martha Raye and Al Jolson in his last Broadway show; *Laugh Time* (1943), a vaudeville show featuring Ethel Waters; and the last operetta that the Shuberts would ever produce, *My Romance* (1948) starring Anne Jeffreys.

Cole Porter shows held sway at the Shubert for the first half of the 1950s. *Kiss Me Kate,* starring Alfred Drake and Patricia Morrison, transferred here in 1950 from the Shuberts' Century Theatre, while *Can-Can* (1952) enjoyed a long run with star Gwen Verdon. In between the two Porter shows, the playhouse hosted Lerner and Loewe's *Paint Your Wagon* (1951). In 1955 Richard Rodgers returned to the Shubert, this time with his new partner, Oscar Hammerstein II, and a new show, *Pipe Dream* (1955). Judy Holliday hit it big with Betty Comden, Adolph Green, and Jule Styne's *Bells Are Ringing* (1956), and Eugene O'Neill's *Ah, Wilderness!* was musicalized in Bob Merrill's *Take Me Along* (1959) starring Robert Morse, Jackie Gleason, and Valerie Harper.

The definitive 1960s and 1970s musicals that played the Shubert include *I Can Get It for You Wholesale* (1962), which

LEFT:

Artists and Models *(1923) advertising flyer.* Artists and Models *was one of the more successful of the Shubert-produced revues. It had its origin in the annual show of the Society of Illustrators, which played the Century Roof Theatre in May 1923. Shubert scenic designer Watson Barratt, who had supervised "The Illustrators Show," enlisted J. J.'s financial backing. The Shuberts received the right to use all sketches, scenery, and ideas for future productions, in exchange for paying the Society of Illustrators a small percentage of gross receipts. J.J. was also given the right to use in advertising the names of all the artists who participated in the original revue, whether or not their work was retained for the Broadway version of the show. In the end, it probably mattered little, however, since one of the show's biggest draws was the parade of "undraped beauty" that comprised many of the production's scenes. In all, the Shuberts presented six editions of the show between 1923 and 1943.*

ABOVE:

Babes in Arms *(1937), Lucas Pritchard Studio contact sheet featuring Alfred Drake, Ray Heatherton, Mitzi Green, and others. Several Rodgers and Hart musicals took up residence at the Shubert during the 1930s and 1940s. This one was the most youthfully exuberant of the bunch. With its "hey kids, let's put on a show" premise and songs like "My Funny Valentine," "Where or When," "The Lady Is a Tramp," "I Wish I Were in Love Again," and "Johnny One Note,"* Babes in Arms *was a huge success.*

introduced Barbra Streisand to Broadway; two Anthony Newley hits, *Stop the World, I Want to Get Off* (1962) and *The Roar of the Greasepaint, the Smell of the Crowd* (1965); Neil Simon and Burt Bacharach's *Promises, Promises* (1968); Stephen Sondheim's *A Little Night Music* (1973), which gave the world "Send in the Clowns"; and *Over Here!* (1974), pairing Patti and Maxine Andrews with then-unknown John Travolta. Then, on October 19, 1975, *A Chorus Line*, the Off-Broadway hit from the Public Theater, opened uptown at the Shubert. This "singular sensation" would remain for a record-breaking fifteen years before closing on April 28, 1990.

BELOW:

By Jupiter *(1942), autographed cast photograph. Starring Ray Bolger in one of his most acclaimed Broadway roles,* By Jupiter *was Rodgers and Hart's last collaboration on an original show. This lighthearted romp took audiences to the ancient Portus, a land where women are in power by virtue of a magic girdle, worn by their leader Hippolyta (Benay Venuta). A band of Greeks led by Theseus and Hercules invade, capture the girdle, and empower the country's men, including the previously "henpecked" King Sapiens (Bolger).*

A Little Night Music (1972), Glynis Johns as Desirée Armfeldt. Stephen Sondheim and Hugh Wheeler's version of Ingmar Bergman's film Smiles of a Summer Night was directed by Harold Prince and featured beautifully lush settings by scenic designer extraordinaire Boris Aronson.

OPPOSITE, ABOVE:

Can-Can (1953), Gwen Verdon as Claudine and cast kicking up their legs at a Montmartre café. This Cole Porter musical included the songs "Allez-Vous En," "C'est Magnifique," "I Love Paris," and "It's All Right With Me." With direction by Abe Burrows and musical staging by Michael Kidd, the show established Gwen Verdon as a rising star.

OPPOSITE, BELOW:

I Can Get It for You Wholesale (1962), Barbra Streisand singing "Miss Marmelstein." Playing a beleaguered secretary, Streisand, not yet twenty years old and appearing on a Broadway stage for the first time, literally stopped the show nightly and began her climb to superstardom with this comic song lamenting her character's plight. Produced by David Merrick, this Harold Rome musical set in New York's garment industry during the 1930s also starred Elliot Gould, whom Streisand would marry in 1963.

Crazy for You (1992), Harry Groener as Bobby Child and Jodi Benson as Polly Baker executing an "Astaire and Rogers" move. A compendium of well-known songs by George and Ira Gershwin, including five numbers from Girl Crazy (1930), this old-fashioned song-and-dance spectacular featured dazzlingly creative choreography by Susan Stroman.

A Chorus Line *(1975)*,
*window card showing
the cast in their finale
costumes performing
"One." Over the course of
its multi-year run, the
show's window card saw
many incarnations. This
one, produced in 1979,
touts the fact that the
production won both the
New York Drama Critics
Circle Award and the Tony
Award for Best Musical.*

Buddy (1990), a British musical based on the life and music of
Buddy Holly, was the Shubert's first post–*Chorus Line* tenant.
It was followed by the Tony-winning Gershwin musical *Crazy
for You* (1992). When that show closed in January 1996, the
Shubert Organization undertook a massive restoration and
upgrade of their flagship theater.

On April 3, 1996, a renovated and resplendent Sam S. Shubert
Theatre made its debut at a press conference hosted by composer Stephen Sondheim. Under the aegis of architects Bar-

A Chorus Line *(1975), Donna McKechnie as "senior" dancer Cassie performing one of the show's standout numbers, "The Music and the Mirror." When* A Chorus Line *transferred to the Shubert from the Off Broadway Public Theater in 1975, there was some talk of whether Broadway audiences would want to see a show about the lives and struggles of that often-ignored performer—the dancer in the chorus of a Broadway show. And with little in the way of scenery, sets, or costumes, this backstage musical drama did seem like a bit of a long shot. But pundits underestimated the commitment (financial, emotional, and otherwise) of producer Joseph Papp, the creative genius of director/choreographer Michael Bennett, and the public's growing interest in dance. The show would go on to win a number of awards including a Pulitzer Prize, run for 6,137 performances, and occupy the Shubert for almost fifteen years.*

Chicago (1996), Bebe Neuwirth as Velma Kelly and cast performing "All that Jazz." Begun as a staged concert that was part of City Center's "Encores" series of "Great American Musicals in Concert," this revival of the Kander and Ebb/Bob Fosse musical from 1975 moved in for a long run at the Shubert after a brief engagement at the Richard Rodgers Theatre. Neuwirth costarred with Ann Reinking (as Roxie Hart) who along with Gwen Verdon (the original Roxie in the 1975 production) re-created much of Bob Fosse's original choreography.

bara Campagna and Francesca Russo, the multimillion-dollar makeover of the interior employed a color scheme of green and gold and restored the venue to its original luster. It added some improvements, too. New, ergonomically correct seating was installed, and technical areas backstage were thoroughly upgraded and modernized. The theater is now equipped to handle the most complex productions imaginable. The backstage renovation, in fact, marks the first time that a completely new counterweight and gridiron system has been installed in a currently operating United States theater. At the dawn of the twenty-first century, New York's Sam S. Shubert Theatre stands ready to move forward into the future.

The Shubert Theatre is located at 225 West 44th Street.

*P*opular legend has it that if the Messrs. Shubert could not get in touch with someone on the telephone, all they had to do was send word down to Shubert Alley, where they could usually find whomever they were looking for. Since 1913, the geographical and sentimental center of the Broadway theater district has been the narrow strip of real estate that runs along the Shubert and Booth Theatres from 44th to 45th Streets. Though Shubert Alley, as the passageway has become universally known, has been the scene of glamorous opening nights and landmark moments in the history of the American theater, its origins are humble. During the construction of the Shubert and Booth Theatres in 1913, the city fire laws required that an uncovered passageway at least eight feet wide and ten feet high run parallel to the two venues. This "alley" would guarantee emergency egress from both houses and allow emergency equipment to access the theaters. While it is currently much wider than the requisite eight feet, that was not always the case. When the Astor Hotel backed on the Alley, its dimensions were much narrower. In fact, for a period of time, the hotel maintained a bus terminal and taxi stand on their side of the Alley, much to the consternation of Lee and J. J. Shubert.

While Shubert Alley is primarily a pedestrian thoroughfare, theatrical VIPs have often been permitted to park there. The Shubert brothers' chauffeur-driven automobiles were, of course, always allowed, as were those of such stars as the Lunts and Katharine Hepburn when they were appearing in Shubert houses. By law, the Alley must be completely closed once a year in order to retain its status as a private way, so for one day each year during the second week of August, neither pedestrians nor vehicles are allowed through.

The Alley has been used as the location for special events, including the 50th and 75th anniversaries of the Shubert and Booth Theatres, and the 1983 celebration marking the record-breaking performance of *A Chorus Line*. It has also hosted the annual Broadway Cares/Equity Fights AIDS flea market, and the "New York City's Salute to Theater"–week party held each year on the Wednesday preceding the Tony Awards. Shubert Alley has also been the site for various concerts and community events such as blood drives and mammogram testing.

With Shubert Alley, Lee and J. J. built much more than a shortcut between two busy New York streets—they created what is recognized worldwide as the symbolic heart of the theater district.

An early photograph of the Alley as seen from 45th Street looking south. It shows the original width of the Alley and the way it was divided with a wrought-iron fence from the Astor Hotel. The buses lined up to the left are servicing the hotel's terminal. The noise it generated must have been a constant concern for the shows playing in the Shubert and Booth Theatres.

Al Pacino exits the Booth Theatre
during the run of *American Buffalo*,
c. 1983. Barricades are often erected
outside stage doors when the crush of
well-wishers becomes too large. The
stanchions allow stars to get to their
waiting cars.

In recent years, Shubert Alley has become home every September to the annual Broadway Flea Market, a fundraiser for Broadway Cares/Equity Fights AIDS. Broadway shows and related support groups sponsor booths in the Alley. The day culminates with the Grand Auction (pictured), in which lots are offered that include costumes and props from productions, autographed memorabilia, and walk-on parts in shows.

The Booth Theatre

West Forty~fifth Street New York

B uilt by Lee Shubert and the producer Winthrop Ames, the Booth Theatre was actually the second playhouse in New York City to be named after the actor Edwin Booth (1833–1893). The first, built by Booth himself in 1869 and turned into a dry-goods store by 1883, was located on the southeast corner of 23rd Street and Sixth Avenue. An avid collector of Booth memorabilia, Oakes Angier Ames, Winthrop's father, had been devoted to preserving the actor's legacy, and had even had a financial stake in the old 23rd Street venue. Winthrop Ames's decision to name his theater after such a distinguished American actor not only honored Booth, but also connected his own family's interest with the actor's rich theatrical history. Ames intended to present the most challenging and prestigious productions possible. With several award-winning shows to its credit, the Booth has certainly met Ames's goals.

Ames had an extensive knowledge of the architecture and technical advances of contemporary European theaters and the types of productions they presented. His first attempt at forming an American repertory company resulted in the establishment of the New Theatre, located at the corner of Central Park West and 62nd Street. Lee Shubert had also been involved in this endeavor, which ultimately proved too difficult and expensive to sustain (see pages 79–80). Consequently, Ames realized that his kind of productions required smaller, more intimate venues. As a result, in 1912 he built the Little Theatre (now known as the Helen Hayes Theatre), and in 1913 he combined forces with Lee Shubert to build the Booth Theatre. Both were located in the Times Square area.

The Booth was designed by Henry Herts to be one of a pair of playhouses: the Booth and the Shubert Theatres abut each other along Shubert Alley in one seamless unit. Styled with a "restrained classicism," the Booth is the smaller, less extravagant of the two houses. The sgraffito that adorns the exterior of both theaters is the last known surviving example in New York of this decorating technique that was quite popular for a time (see also page 81).

Son of the actor Junius Brutus Booth and brother to the infamous John Wilkes Booth, Edwin Booth, seen here as Hamlet, is perhaps the best-known actor among this family of thespians. His 100 performances as the Brooding Dane during the 1864–65 season broke records, and adoring audiences were convinced that they were seeing him in his greatest role ever.

OVERLEAF, LEFT:
View of the auditorium toward house left
Inset:
Detail of wooden side panel

OVERLEAF, RIGHT:
Detail of lamps hanging along the balcony-level hallway

OPPOSITE:
Program cover from the early 1920s with three muses: two holding up traditional comedy/tragedy masks and the third representing the musical theater

OPPOSITE:
Exterior signage above the theater, night view

RIGHT:
Not So Long Ago (1920), Mary Kennedy (left) as Rosamond Gill and Eva Le Gallienne as Elsie Dover. Arthur Richman's play was about a seamstress in an aristocratic household who captures the heart of her employer's son. Le Gallienne as the seamstress charmed not only the son, but also audiences and critics alike. Already a stage veteran by the time she was twenty-one, Le Gallienne had yet to make a big splash on Broadway until her performance in this production. Producer Lee Shubert paid careful attention to details of the production, including the elegant costumes by designer Homer Conant.

BELOW:
You Can't Take It with You (1936). As one synopsis of the play describes the Vanderhofs' living room, in which much of the play's action takes place: "Here meals are eaten, plays written, snakes collected, ballet steps practiced, xylophones played, printing presses operated—if there were room enough there would probably be ice skating." Filled with joyful absurdities and eccentric characters, this Kaufman and Hart play was awarded a Pulitzer Prize.

The American premiere of Arnold Bennett's *The Great Adventure* inaugurated the Booth on October 16, 1913, and ran for 52 performances. In 1917, Arthur Hopkins produced Clare Kummer's *A Successful Calamity,* which marked William Gillette's return to the stage after an absence of several years. The Shuberts produced a number of fairly successful shows at the Booth, including Arthur Richman's romantic comedy *Not So Long Ago* (1920), in which Eva Le Gallienne starred with Sidney Blackmer; John Drinkwater's *Bird in Hand* (1929), another romantic comedy; and *Laburnum Grove* (1935), J. B. Priestley's comedy about a respectable and well-regarded man within his community who suddenly confesses to being a counterfeiter. The following year, George S. Kaufman and Moss Hart's *You Can't Take It with You* was a huge success. Produced by Sam Harris, this play about an eccentric family won its authors that year's Pulitzer Prize, and it remains extremely popular with audiences today.

In 1945, the Shuberts produced two shows at the Booth: Ralph Nelson's *The Wind Is Ninety,* featuring a young Kirk Douglas, and *You Touched Me!,* by Tennessee Williams and Donald Wyndham, starring Montgomery Clift. *Come Back,*

Come Back, Little Sheba *(1950).*
Shirley Booth and Sidney Blackmer
gave Tony Award–winning
performances as the stars of William
Inge's drama about a recovering
alcoholic, his disillusioned wife, and
the lost little puppy that continually
reappears in her dreams.

Little Sheba (1950), which showcased Shirley Booth and Sidney Blackmer, marked its author William Inge as an up-and-coming playwright, and won Tonys for both its stars. Eight years later, Henry Fonda appeared with Anne Bancroft in William Gibson's *Two For the Seesaw.*

John Shubert, J. J.'s son, presented Claudette Colbert in Howard Teichmann's *Julia, Jake, and Uncle Joe* (1961), but the show ran for only one performance. Murray Schisgal's *Luv* (1964) did much better. A big hit that ran for 901 performances, its powerful ensemble cast included Alan Arkin, Eli Wallach, and Anne Jackson in a production directed by Mike Nichols. Leonard Gershe's smash *Butterflies Are Free* (1969) closed out the 1960s with a cast that included Keir Dullea, Blythe Danner, Eileen Heckart, and Paul Michael Glaser. Danner won a Tony for her performance.

Jason Miller's *That Championship Season* arrived at the Booth in 1972 after a successful Off-Broadway run at Joseph Papp's Public Theater earlier that year. The play won a Pulitzer and a Tony, and its director, A. J. Antoon, also won a Tony. Another notable transfer from the Public was Ntozake Shange's *For Colored Girls Who Have*

LEFT:
Julia, Jake, and Uncle Joe *(1961).*
Claudette Colbert starred in this
play, coproduced by John Shubert
and written by Howard Teichmann,
based on a memoir by Oriana
Atkinson. Set against the backdrop of
Stalinist Russia, the story revolves
around Atkinson's experiences living
in Moscow with her husband, the
critic and New York Times *reporter*
Brooks Atkinson. This was one of
only a few shows that the Shuberts
would produce after Lee's death in
1953, and it would be the last to bear
the company name until 1972.

Butterflies Are Free (1969). In Leonard Gershe's play, Blythe Danner as Jill Tanner and Keir Dullea as Don Baker are two young neighbors with quite different backgrounds who meet and fall in love. As it happens, Don is blind, but this matters little to Jill, who treats him as she would any other guy. The playwright cited his friend Mia Farrow as the inspiration for Jill Tanner.

The Elephant Man (1979), Philip Anglim in the title role as John (né Joseph) Merrick. Without using prosthetics or makeup to alter his appearance, Anglim, by twisting and manipulating his body into a pose suggestive of Merrick's deformities, managed to convey both the suffering and essential humanity of this historical figure.

Sunday in the Park with George (1984), Act One, George (Mandy Patinkin) seated in the foreground with his sketchpad while his mistress Dot (Bernadette Peters), holding an open parasol, strolls with the baker at center. Stephen Sondheim based the first act of his musical on the life of artist Georges Seurat and the creation of the seminal pointillist painting entitled A Sunday Afternoon on the Island of La Grande-Jatte. This innovative production managed to evoke Seurat's work both visually and aurally and to explore the very nature of art itself.

Considered Suicide/When the Rainbow Is Enuf (1976). This "choreopoem," a heady mixture of music, song, dance, and poetry ran for 742 performances. Bernard Pomerance's The Elephant Man, a well-received British import that also transferred from Off Broadway, won the Tony Award for Best Play of the 1978–79 season.

In 1984, another Pulitzer winner graced the Booth stage: the Shubert-produced Stephen Sondheim/James Lapine musical Sunday in the Park with George. Georges Seurat's famous painting A Sunday Afternoon on the Island of La Grande-Jatte (1884–86) burst into colorful, tuneful, and light-filled life, with Mandy Patinkin as the painter and Bernadette Peters in the role of his model, muse, and mistress. The first act's scenic design closely echoed Seurat's original painting, while the musical compositions were intended as an aural equivalent of the artist's pointillist compositions. The following year, the Booth housed Herb Gardner's *I'm Not Rappaport* (1985), starring Judd Hirsch and Cleavon Little as two odd-couple oldsters who happen to share a park bench. Robert Morse's tour-de-force performance in Jay Presson Allen's *Tru* (1989) closed out the decade.

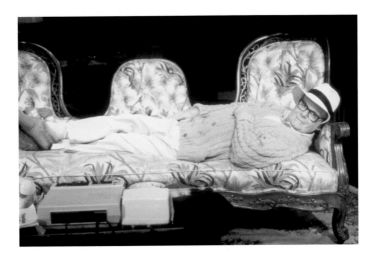

Tru (1989), Robert Morse as Truman Capote in Jay Presson Allen's portrait of the controversial author. Centered on a particularly trying period in Capote's life when he was shunned by the very friends about whom he was writing, Morse's one-man, Tony Award–winning performance depicted both Capote's active defiance and his painful bewilderment. The sofa upon which Morse lies in this photograph actually belonged to Capote.

The 1990s saw more Shubert productions take up residence: *Once on This Island* (1990), a musical by Lynn Ahrens and Stephen Flaherty about a peasant girl in the French Antilles and her love for an aristocratic boy; a well-received revival of Frank Loesser's *The Most Happy Fella* (1992) directed by Gerald Gutierrez; and Frank McGuinness's prison drama, *Someone Who'll Watch over Me* (1992), juxtaposing three incarcerated men—American, English, and Irish—to fascinating effect.

Emily Mann's adaptation of the Delany sisters' book, *Having Our Say,* transferred from the McCarter Theatre in New Jersey to the Booth in 1995. Mary Alice and Gloria Foster inhabited the roles of the two sisters who, having lived more than a century, shared with audiences their views of American social and cultural history as women of color and women of professional regard. A new kind of woman closed out the century when Barry Humphreys, playing his alter ego, the smashing Dame Edna Everage, brought his/her one-"woman" show, *Dame Edna: the Royal Tour* (1999), to the Booth's stage.

RIGHT:
Having Our Say (1995), Mary Alice (left) and Gloria Foster as Bessie and Sadie Delany, respectively. A dramatization of the autobiographical memoirs of the centenarian Delany sisters, Having Our Say *chronicles a century of living life in a world segregated by both race and gender. The sisters' remarkable personalities resound throughout Emily Mann's adaptation of their book. In addition, it was only appropriate that the play should run in a Shubert-owned playhouse, since Peggy Delany, the sisters' niece, currently works in the Shubert Organization's administrative offices.*

The Booth Theatre is located at 222 West 45th Street.

T he theater known today as the Golden was originally called the Theatre Masque and was built between 1926 and 1927 by real-estate magnates, the Chanin Brothers, as part of a three-theater complex that included the Royale (see page 190) and the Majestic (see page 64). An intimate house, the Theatre Masque was designed for "serious" or "artistic" drama, or those plays that producers were apt to try out before a relatively small audience in order to gauge their appeal before moving them to one of the larger theaters. The Theatre Masque opened on February 24, 1927, with the not-so-successful *Puppets of Passion*, by Rosso di San Secondo. By 1930, the Chanins had transferred ownership of the three-venue complex to the Shuberts.

Theatre Masque, exterior, c.1927, with its opening production, Puppets of Passion, *on the marquee. The playhouse was renamed in 1937 for producer John Golden.*

OPPOSITE:
View of arched ribs along the ceiling showing the theater's "modern Spanish"-style ornamentation, including spiraled columns, geometrically patterned panels, cameos, and decorative shields

OVERLEAF, LEFT:

ABOVE:
Closeup of a light fixture whose design reflects the "modern Spanish" style

BELOW:
Detail of seat standard

OVERLEAF, RIGHT:
View of the auditorium as seen from the stage

Lee and J. J.'s first years at the Theatre Masque were peppered with short-run shows. There were, however, several notable exceptions. *Louder Please* (1931) counted silent-screen siren Louise Brooks among its cast, and *Goodbye Again* (1932) marked a young James Stewart's second appearance on Broadway. Then, toward the end of 1933, *Tobacco Road*, a tale of an impoverished and downtrodden Georgia family, opened with Henry Hull as the family's patriarch. It was an enormous success that ran for a total of 3,182 performances. In 1937, management of the Theatre Masque passed to producer John Golden, who renamed the theater after himself.

There have actually been three playhouses bearing Golden's name: from 1926 to 1933, he occupied what later was known as the Fifty-eighth Street Theatre (202 West 58th Street); from 1934 to 1936, he took over the Royale and rechristened it the Golden; and then in 1937, he relocated to and renamed the Theatre Masque, which has retained the Golden name to the present.

A significant presence on the New York theater scene, John Golden enjoyed a varied career that encompassed acting, songwriting, directing, and producing. His first theatrical venture took place at New York University (NYU), where he was enrolled in law school. A fellow student, thinking him an actor because of his loud dress and long hair, approached Golden about putting on a show. The future producer set about organizing NYU's first theatrical production, which led to the establishment of its Drama Department. The production, a play by Frank Soul entitled *Nirvana, or the Spook, the Sage and the Sandwich,* was essentially a "burlesque on Theosophy." Young Golden managed to keep 10 percent of the profits, and NYU unwittingly turned out its first theater producer. Golden's lifelong ambition was to present only those plays that depicted clean, wholesome fun. The logo on one version of his business stationery consisted of a crowned heart-shaped face whose smile read: "COMICLEAN" Plays.

Unfortunately, however, John Golden's reign at the theater was not marked by long-running shows. The most notewothy production to play the house during his tenure was Patrick Hamilton's *Angel Street* (1941), a surprise hit that featured

Lee Shubert (left) and his wife, Marcella Swanson Shubert, at the Waldorf Astoria with John Golden in July 1952.

OPPOSITE, BOTTOM:
Waiting for Godot *(1956), with Bert Lahr (foreground) as Estragon, and (from left) Luchino Solito de Solis as the boy, Kurt Kasznar as Pozzo, Alvin Epstein as Lucky, and E. G. Marshall as Vladimir. Samuel Beckett's absurdist play about "two bums" waiting for a third party who never shows up was quite controversial. Lahr read it with great interest, if not a full understanding, sensing that it possessed a fantastic theatricality. The production's first trial run in Miami was a fiasco. One letter Lahr received in protest of the play read: "How can a man, who has charmed the youth of America as the lion in* The Wizard of Oz, *appear in a play which is communistic, atheistic and existential[?]" Yet the play continued to intrigue Lahr, despite the entreaties of his theatrical associates to drop the show. In the end, he agreed to a Broadway production that, with a new director and new cast, ultimately turned out to be a success. Everyone agreed that Lahr had an unmistakable feel for the work, which left the star emotionally drained after each performance. Audiences and critics were also deeply affected. Kenneth Tynan remembers that "when the curtain fell, the house stood up to cheer a man who had never before appeared in a legitimate play, a mighty and blessed clown whose grateful bewilderment was reflected in the tears that sparkled his cheeks. . . . Without him, the Broadway production of Mr. Beckett's play would be admirable; with him, it is transfigured. It is as if we, the audience, had elected him to represent our reactions, resentful and confused, to the lonely universe into which the author plunges us. . . . [It was] one of the noblest performances I have ever seen."*

Vincent Price, Judith Evelyn, and Leo G. Carroll. Formerly entitled *Gaslight*, the play had seen disappointing ticket sales in other locales, and expectations were so low for its New York run that the producers ordered only enough tickets printed for opening night and two performances thereafter. But the first-night audience loved *Angel Street*, and it went on to chalk up 1,293 performances.

John Golden's association with the theater ended in 1946. For the next two years, the Shuberts leased the house to the Supercinema Corporation, a foreign-film exhibitor. The Golden then reverted to legitimate use and hosted a number of significant productions, chief among them Samuel Beckett's *Waiting for Godot* (1956), which garnered a lot of attention due to Bert Lahr's portrayal of Estragon, a role perceived as radically different from his usual comedic work.

The 1960s began with laughs by way of *An Evening with Mike Nichols and Elaine May* (1960). The dynamic duo brought down the house with their characteristic wit. Comedy continued to grace the Golden with the British production of *Beyond the Fringe* (1962), whose nimble cast—Alan Bennett, Peter Cook, Jonathan Miller, and Dudley Moore—wrote and performed a show that left American audiences reeling from their particular brand of British humor. In 1966, a musical revue from South Africa entitled *Wait a Minim!* featured a variety of

SHEPARD TRAUBE
(in association with Alexander H. Cohen)
Presents

"ANGEL STREET"
by PATRICK HAMILTON
with

VINCENT   JUDITH   LEO G
PRICE   EVELYN   CARROLL

GOLDEN THEATRE
45th STREET WEST OF B'WAY., N. Y. C.   MATS. WED. & SAT.

Angel Street (1941), postcard. Vincent Price and Judith Evelyn played husband and wife in this eerie tale of murder and madness. An old-fashioned Victorian-style thriller originally entitled Gaslight, *the show owed much of its success to the special chemistry between its two stars and its effective staging.* Gaslight, *the 1947 film adaptation of the play, starred Ingrid Bergman and Charles Boyer.*

folklike tunes, played on a dazzling array of musical instruments, interwoven with South African social and political commentary.

David Rabe's *Sticks & Bones*, which moved to the Golden from Joseph Papp's Public Theater in 1972, was a harrowing account of a blinded young man's return from the war in Vietnam to his middle-American family. The show stunned audiences, impressed critics, and ultimately won a Tony for Best Play. In 1977, the Shuberts produced D. L. Coburn's *The Gin Game*, directed by Mike Nichols and starring Jessica Tandy and Hume Cronyn as two strangers in a home for the elderly, who gradually begin to discover each other's darker depths through

The Gin Game (1977). Hume Cronyn and Jessica Tandy gave memorable performances as Weller Martin and Fonsia Dorsey. Over a series of card games, these two crusty inhabitants of a home for the aged manage to get under each other's skin in a way that leads them down a psychological path that they later regret visiting.

a shared card game. Coburn's first play won the Pulitzer Prize that season, and Tandy was awarded a Tony for her performance.

Another Tony winner that made its way to Broadway from London, *A Day in Hollywood/A Night in the Ukraine* (1980), started the 1980s off with a bang. Tommy Tune directed this two-part musical extravaganza, the first half of which offered an homage to old Hollywood movies, while the second half recalled old Marx Brothers sketches. The Golden next played host to three Pulitzer-winning plays, two of them written by women. Beth Henley's *Crimes of the Heart* (1981) came to Broadway after an auspicious beginning in regional theater. With a cast that included Mary Beth Hurt, Mia Dillon, and Peter MacNicol, the production moved audiences with its depiction of a troubled family. In 1983 the Shuberts produced Marsha Norman's *'night, Mother* (1983), starring Kathy Bates as a woman who is determined to end her own life. The next year, the Shuberts brought to the boards David Mamet's *Glengarry Glen Ross* (1984), which made a big splash in London before arriving on Broadway. The show depicted the cutthroat world of real estate and boasted a terrific cast that included Robert Prosky, J. T. Walsh, James Tolkan, Mike Nussbaum, and Joe Mantegna. The production received several Tony nominations and an award for Mantegna's performance.

The 1990s were ushered in by *Falsettos* (1992), a musical combination of two Off-Broadway shows, *March of the Falsettos* (1981) and *Falsettoland* (1990), which told the story of Marvin, who leaves his wife and son for Whizzer, his male lover. James Lapine and William Finn won Tonys for the Best Book of a Musical, and Finn also won for Best Original Score. In 1995, Terrence McNally's *Master Class* presented Zoe Caldwell as the legendary opera diva Maria Callas, whose complex character is revealed through the open master classes she conducts. McNally won a Tony for his play, and Caldwell and Audra McDonald both won Tonys for their performances as teacher and student, respectively.

The Golden Theatre is located at 252 West 45th Street.

'night Mother *(1983), Kathy Bates (left) and Anne Pitoniak as Jessie and Thelma Cates. Marsha Norman's Pulitzer Prize–winning play told the heartbreaking story of a daughter who unwaveringly decides to end her life and her mother who futilely tries to stop her.*

Master Class *(1995). Zoe Caldwell (left) as the legendary Maria Callas coaches a student, played by Audra McDonald, who dares to stand up to the diva. Terrence McNally structured his play around the idea that the audience was witness to one of Callas's famous master classes.*

The Shubert Operetta

The Blue Paradise (1915), advertising flyer. The Shuberts asked Sigmund Romberg to contribute eight new compositions to this American adaptation of Viennese composer Edmund Eysler's operetta. The story involves a young European who travels to America to make his fortune and then returns to his homeland only to find that the girl he left behind is not all that he remembered. This was Romberg's first real operetta assignment, and it yielded one of the theatrical season's bigger hits, "Auf Wiedersehn," which was sung by Vivienne Segal making her Broadway debut.

Maytime (1917), an advertising flyer picturing star Peggy Wood. Maytime was Sigmund Romberg's first full original Broadway score and the first show to establish him as a composer of merit rather than a mere staff writer. As was the case with many operettas, the source of Maytime's story was a German musical, but with anti-German sentiment running high, the Shuberts decided New York City would provide a better setting for this story of lost and regained love over several generations. They hired Rida Johnson Young to adapt the piece, which turned out to be the hit of the year. It seemed to be especially popular with servicemen departing for the war. Peggy Wood, the show's ingenue, was a major Broadway star during the 1920s and 1930s, but she is perhaps best known for her portrayal of the Mother Abbess in the 1965 movie musical The Sound of Music.

PAGES 126–127:
The Student Prince (1924), Ilse Marvenga as Kathie singing "The Drinking Song." In 1902, the Shuberts presented the American premiere of Heidelberg, adapted from the original German play Alt Heidelberg. With actor Aubrey Boucicault in the lead, the show proved to be a disappointment. But Sam Shubert believed in the play and convinced the celebrated actor, Richard Mansfield, to revive the show as the opening attraction (October 12, 1903) at the Shuberts' new Lyric Theatre on 42nd Street. The play was a big success and helped Sam and his brothers gain credibility as producers in New York City. The Student Prince, a musical adaptation of Heidelberg, was an even bigger asset to the Shuberts. This story of royalty and thwarted love was immensely popular, and Romberg's score was considered his best to date. The show ran for more than 600 performances, and touring companies were sent across the United States to satisfy the public's demand.

Inset, page 126, left:
The Student Prince, window card for the Shubert Theatre, New Haven, one of the countless playhouses in which this perennial favorite appeared, n.d.

Inset, page 126, center:
The Student Prince, advertising flyer for the Maryland Theatre in Baltimore, n.d.

Inset, page 126, right:
The Student Prince, costume rental house shot for the character of Lutz. It is fairly well known that for more than thirty years the Shuberts operated the Century Library, which rented to professional and amateur theatrical companies the scores to hundreds of musicals, revues and operettas. One of the most popular of these shows was, of course, The Student Prince, which was presented in many places around the United States for decades. Less known is the fact that the Shuberts also operated a costume rental house called Stage Costumes, Inc., which kept a complete inventory of costumes for the most popular of the brothers' productions. Clients could peruse photographs of models wearing the costumes and make their choices based on them.

Inset, page 127:
Sigmund Romberg at the piano, undated. Hired by J. J. Shubert in the early teens, the Hungarian-born Romberg was the Shuberts' house composer for most of the teens and twenties. Although he worked on numerous revues including several editions of The Passing Show, The Show of Wonders (1916), Bombo (1921), and Artists and Models (1924), and musical comedies including Her Soldier Boy (1916) and The Dancing Girl (1923), it is his operetta scores that have earned him a rightful place among the major Broadway composers of the twentieth century. Blossom Time (1921) and The Student Prince (1924) were the longest-running shows of the 1920s, and the Shuberts toured road companies of the two musicals year after year. Along with The Blue Paradise (1915), Maytime (1917), My Maryland (1927), Nina Rosa (1930), and the non-Shubert-produced The Desert Song (1926) and The New Moon (1928), these shows would come to represent the apogee of American operetta of the time.

$\mathcal{A}$udiences enjoyed many forms of musical theater in the early twentieth century, but for Lee and, especially, J. J. Shubert, none had more appeal than operetta. This genre of popular entertainment traced its origins to mid-nineteenth-century France and, by 1900, was thriving in the United States. Imported works from Vienna (by composers like Johann Strauss II, Franz Lehar, Franz von Suppé, and Karl Millöcker), England (Gilbert and Sullivan, Sidney Jones), and France (Jacques Offenbach, Alexandre-Charles Lecocq, and Edmond Audran), along with the early works of American composers like Reginald De Koven and Victor Herbert, were great successes with audiences, not only in New York, but all over the country. Soon after arriving on the Great White Way, the Shuberts began to present operettas in their houses, and during the 1910s and 1920s they would play a crucial role in the golden age of American operetta. With their typically lush costumes, exotic European settings, romantic stories, melodic music, and large casts, these productions were, along with revues, the dominant form of musical theater in the pre-Depression era.

A number of factors contributed to the demise of this form of entertainment on the Broadway stage: the Great Depression, talking (and especially singing) motion pictures, World War II, and the advent of television. In 1948, J. J. attempted to resurrect the genre with a new production, *My Romance,* but the show was not a success. Even so, the Shuberts remained committed to operetta. In all, the brothers would produce dozens of operettas over the course of their careers.

Florodora (1920), the couples sextet performing "Tell Me Pretty Maiden." A London import, *Florodora* first played New York during the 1900–1901 theatrical season and ran for 505 performances at the Casino Theatre—up to that time, only the second musical to exceed the 500-performance mark. The show was not an immediate hit, but the sextet and its song, "Tell Me Pretty Maiden," struck a chord with audiences, and the show became famous on the Rialto. Recognizing the lure of the original sextet, J. J. Shubert made sure that his 1920 revival of the show had not one but three sextet numbers—one in modern dress, one in period costume, and a third composed of children (including a young Milton Berle). In addition, topical jokes and songs were added to the show to further freshen its appeal.

NUMÉRO 1   LES PREMIÈRES ILLUSTRÉES   PRIX: 10 FR

Rose-Marie

THÉÂTRE
MOGADOR
PARIS

*Cloé Vidiane
dans le rôle de
Rose-Marie*

ÉDITIONS ARTISTIQUES DE PARIS — 32, RUE LOUIS-LE-GRAND — PARIS

MESSRS. LEE AND J.J. SHUBERT PRESENT

OSCAR STRAUS'

MUSICAL MASTERPIECE

THE LAST WALTZ

with

ELEANOR PAINTER

OPPOSITE:

Rose-Marie, French souvenir program, n.d.
The original production of Rudolf Friml's
Rose-Marie, which opened at the Imperial
Theatre in 1924, was produced by Arthur
Hammerstein. The show turned out to be the
biggest moneymaker of the 1920s, and it had
long and prosperous runs throughout the
United States and Europe. When Hammerstein
filed for bankruptcy in 1931, he lost control of
the play, and the Shuberts soon obtained the
rights to it. It took its place in the stable of
operettas that Lee and J. J. would present and
also lease out to others (through their Century
Library) during the next few decades.

RIGHT, ABOVE:

The Last Waltz, advertising flyer, 1921.
Viennese composer Oscar Straus had enjoyed
great success in the United States with his
operetta *The Chocolate Soldier,* which had
premiered at the Shuberts' Lyric Theatre in
1909. For his international hit *The Last Waltz,*
Lee and J. J. devised a production with lavish
sets and costumes by Shubert house designer
Watson Barratt. The show, which told the
story of an American naval officer's romantic
and political entanglements in the Balkans,
included several national dances—Russian,
Egyptian, Spanish—that allowed Barratt to
show off his flair. Performer Eleanor Painter
starred in numerous operettas during the
1910s and 1920s.

RIGHT, BELOW:

The Love Song (1925), Allan Prior as
Offenbach. Hoping, no doubt, to
duplicate the success of *Blossom
Time* (see pages 212–13), the
Shuberts produced this musical
whose plot was suggested by the
life of Jacques Offenbach. Harry
B. Smith adapted the text and lyrics
from Hungarian and German source
material, while Edward Kunneke chose
and arranged selections of the great
composer's music to provide the show's score.
Despite a beautiful physical production,
however, *The Love Song* was no equal to
Blossom Time, and the show ran for a decent,
but far from spectacular, four months.

Naughty Riquette (1926), Cosmopolitan Theatre, New York, advertising flyer. The Shuberts hired prolific librettist/lyricist Harry B. Smith to adapt this German import for their star Mitzi. Hungarian-born Mitzi Hajos had first worked with Lee and J. J. in the opening production at the Winter Garden Theatre, *La Belle Paree* (1911), and went on to be featured in several of their shows. When at last her theatrical career waned, she retired from the stage and went to work in J. J. Shubert's office.

Nina Rosa (1930), drop-curtain design by Orry-Kelly. Set in the Peruvian Andes, this love story had a score by Sigmund Romberg, a libretto by Otto Harbach, and lyrics by Irving Caesar. It starred Ethelind Terry, who had triumphed three years earlier in Ziegfeld's *Rio Rita*. The operetta was moderately successful on Broadway, but, perhaps because of its exotic setting, it turned out to be immensely popular in France. Orry-Kelly (né Orry George Kelly) had an early career as an actor on Broadway before turning his attention to design. He worked on costumes and sets for many Broadway productions during the late 1920s, but he is better known for his work in motion pictures.

My Maryland (1927), Evelyn Herbert as Barbara Frietchie facing down Confederate spies. Sigmund Romberg and Dorothy Donnelly's musical adaptation of Clyde Fitch's play *Barbara Frietchie* began its theatrical life with a record-breaking forty-week run in Philadelphia, before moving on to Broadway, where it also proved to be a hit. Set during the Civil War, the operetta was a romanticized version of the real-life heroine Barbara Frietchie. Herbert, much younger than the historical figure, was considered to have had one of the finest singing voices of the time. The fact that *My Maryland* featured one of Romberg's strongest scores, coupled with a patriotic American theme, ensured a long life for the musical, which for many years was a favorite with stock companies, schools, and amateur theaters.

Countess Maritza (1930), (left to right) Harry K. Morton, Odette Myrtil, and Carl Randall. Although its plot, involving the loves and foibles of middle-European nobility, was typical of the genre, *Countess Maritza* featured an impressive Emmerich Kalman score that included what would become the popular hit of the show, "Play Gypsies, Dance Gypsies." Myrtil, especially celebrated for her violin playing, began her career with Ziegfeld and had subsequently enjoyed much success in Europe. In his opening-night review of the show, critic Brooks Atkinson said, "Miss Myrtil is volatile and spirited; and she plays the violin with skill. Her wanton destruction of that instrument . . . may indicate the tremendous overhead expense of all such operettas." And in fact, Lee and J. J. had a three-month supply of violins at the ready, just in case.

Imagine Ethel Merman belting, "There's No Business Like Show Business"; Zero Mostel fantasizing, "If I Were a Rich Man"; and Jennifer Holliday proclaiming, "And I Am Telling You (I'm Not Going)": as historian Mary Henderson noted, the Imperial Theater "can boast of more thrilling moments in American musical theater than any other on Broadway."

And that was Lee and J. J. Shubert's plan from the very beginning. Construction on the Imperial, the Shuberts's fiftieth New York venue, began in 1922 when the brothers leased the plot of land stretching from 45th to 46th Street, creating one of the few block-deep theaters in New York. The Shuberts hired architect Herbert Krapp, who employed his trademark Adam-style design here. The recessed ceiling and ornamental panels that grace the walls are elaborately decorated with a number of motifs, including florals and geometrics. The rectangular auditorium is wider than it is deep, which allows most audience members to feel "up close and personal" to the stage and with the performers, respectively.

All through December of 1923, passersby could glimpse workers toiling feverishly to meet the deadline for the Imperial's scheduled opening on Christmas night. On December 21, Mary Hay, star of the theater's first musical, *Mary Jane McKane*, officially christened the Imperial's marquee with champagne, and, four nights later, the show went on.

Opening-night critics were duly impressed. The *New York Herald* declared it "the very latest thing in playhouses," describing it as "one of the most tasteful of the latter-day theaters of the Shuberts." Wonder of wonders, the orchestra and single balcony could accommodate 1,650 people "without the faintest suggestion of overcrowding."

Over the years, the Imperial has witnessed a distinguished roster of hits. The operetta *Rose-Marie* opened on September 2, 1924, and became Broadway's biggest money grosser of the decade. Its most popular song, "Indian Love Call," would later become associated with Jeanette MacDonald and Nelson Eddy, who starred in the 1936 motion-picture version of the musical. The Imperial's next great success was George and Ira Gershwin's *Oh, Kay!* (1926). Set in Jazz Age Long Island and starring the

OPPOSITE:
View of the Imperial's chandelier, boxes, and mezzanine from house right

OVERLEAF, LEFT:
ABOVE:
Detail over the proscenium

BELOW:
Seat standard

OVERLEAF, RIGHT:
View of the stage and mezzanine from house right

Oh, Kay! (1926), Gertrude Lawrence as Kay. Having met with some success in a series of London revues, Lawrence first came to the United States as part of the cast of the British Charlot's Revue (1924). Oh, Kay! was her first American production, and the one that established her as a Broadway star. Of course, a dazzling score by George and Ira Gershwin contributed to her success with the show, which was set in the world of Prohibition and bootlegging.

luminous Gertrude Lawrence, this lighthearted, brassy story about bootlegging and love included classics like "Do, Do, Do," "Clap Yo' Hands," and "Someone to Watch Over Me."

The 1930s were a mixed bag for the Imperial. Milton Berle starred in his first book musical, *Saluta* (1934), which closed after a meager 40 performances, and Bob Hope fared little better that same year when he headlined the musical comedy *Say When*. But back-to-back successes filled the theater in 1935 and 1936. First up was Moss Hart and Cole Porter's *Jubilee*, with Mary Boland and Montgomery Clift, in only his second Broadway appearance. The standards "Begin the Beguine" and "Just One of Those Things" originated in this show. Rodgers and Hart's *On Your Toes* came next, with Ray Bolger, Monty Woolley, and Tamara Geva. The production's "Slaughter on Tenth Avenue" ballet, choreographed by George Balanchine, remains a benchmark in the annals of Broadway dance.

One of the rare nonmusical productions to play the Imperial was also one of its more prestigious: William Shakespeare's *Hamlet* (1936), starring and codirected by Leslie Howard. The bill soon reverted back to hit musicals, however, as Mary Martin scored a sensation singing "My Heart Belongs to Daddy" in Cole Porter's *Leave It to Me* (1938). Martin shared the stage with Sophie Tucker, Victor Moore, and a young chorus boy named Gene Kelly.

OPPOSITE:
On Your Toes (1936), Ray Bolger as Junior Dolan and Tamara Geva as ballerina Vera Barnova performing the show's most notorious musical number, "Slaughter on Tenth Avenue." The Shubert brothers declined an offer to invest in this show, which had director George Abbott collaborating with Rodgers and Hart and choreographer George Balanchine. Once the production proved to be a hit, however, the Shuberts opted to become financially involved in its presentation abroad.

Hamlet *(1936), Leslie Howard (center, left) as Hamlet dueling with Clifford Evans as Laertes. Two different productions of Shakespeare's great tragedy competed for audiences during the 1936–37 season: John Gielgud's reportedly masterful, but traditional, version, which opened at the Empire Theatre on October 8, and Howard's trimmed-down and more streamlined one, which opened at the Imperial about a month later, on November 10. Although most critics and audiences were respectful of the Hollywood star's production, they generally agreed that it suffered by comparison to its rival. After only 39 performances on Broadway, Howard toured his* Hamlet *across the United States, where he met with considerably more success.*

OPPOSITE, BELOW:

Jamaica *(1957), Lena Horne as Savannah. Horne's first starring role on Broadway found her playing a beautiful Jamaican native girl who longs to live in New York, but gives up her dream to marry a heroic local fisherman, played by Ricardo Montalban. Harold Arlen composed the score, E. Y. "Yip" Harburg wrote the lyrics, and Harburg and Fred Saidy supplied the libretto. Arlen had contributed songs to many Broadway shows during the early 1930s, including three Shubert productions, before he embarked on a successful career in Hollywood, where he composed the songs for, among other films,* The Wizard of Oz. *He returned to Broadway in 1941 with the show* Bloomer Girl, *starring Celeste Holm, which ran for 654 performances at the Shubert Theatre.* Jamaica *was the only other hit out of the four musicals that Arlen composed during the postwar period.*

One Touch of Venus (1943), Mary Martin as Venus. The story of a statue that comes to life and complicates things for a hapless man was not a new conceit. But with a book by S. J. Perelman and Ogden Nash, lyrics by Nash, music by Kurt Weill, direction by Elia Kazan, choreography by Agnes de Mille, and a beguiling performance by Mary Martin, One Touch of Venus was anything but your average run-of-the-mill musical. The Imperial was, in fact, proving to be a lucky theater for Martin. Her Broadway debut there in Leave It to Me (1938), in which she sang "My Heart Belongs to Daddy," had made her the talk of the town. Now, as the goddess Venus come down to earth, she established herself as a major star on the Great White Way.

Annie Get Your Gun (1946), Ethel Merman as Annie Oakley. Over the years numerous actresses afforded audiences at the Imperial many landmark musical moments, but perhaps none were as quintessentially "Broadway" as those of Ethel Merman in this great Irving Berlin musical. Belting out songs like "You Can't Get a Man with a Gun," "Doin' What Comes Natur'lly," "Anything You Can Do (I Can Do Better)," "I Got the Sun in the Morning," "They Say It's Wonderful," and the number that would become the anthem for performers all over the world, "There's No Business Like Show Business," Ethel as the great Wild West legend Annie Oakley earned a special place in the pop culture pantheon. The show ran for 1,149 performances, and except for several weeks of vacation, Merman stayed with Annie until the end of the run.

From 1940 onward, the Imperial hosted a constant parade of long-running musicals by an impressive array of composers. Included were four hits by Irving Berlin: *Louisiana Purchase* (1940), *Miss Liberty* (1949), and two starring the inimitable Ethel Merman—*Annie Get Your Gun* (1946) and *Call Me Madam* (1950). Other hits here were Herbert and Dorothy Fields's *Let's Face It* (1941), Cole Porter's *Silk Stockings* (1955), and Frank Loesser's *The Most Happy Fella* (1956). These musicals have provided some much-loved standards, such as Berlin's "Doin' What Comes Naturally" and "There's No Business Like Show Business," Porter's "All of Me," and Loesser's "Standing on the Corner."

The early 1960s saw big hits like *Carnival* (1960) and *Oliver!* (1963), but nothing could rival the Broadway history made by *Fiddler on the Roof* (1964), starring the singular Zero Mostel. Jerry Bock and Sheldon Harnick's musical about life in the shtetls of Russia won the Tony and Drama Critics Awards for the 1964–65 season. After moving to the Majestic in 1967, it went on to become the longest-running musical up to that time, logging 3,242 performances before it closed in 1972.

LEFT:
Too Many Girls (1939), Desi Arnaz as drum-beating football fullback Manuelito. Not the most memorable of Rodgers and Hart's shows, but with direction by George Abbott, sets by Jo Mielziner, dances by Bob Alton, costumes by Raoul Pène Du Bois, and the exotic Latin rhythms of Desi Arnaz, Too Many Girls was, nonetheless, a sizable hit. Arnaz, appearing here for the first time on Broadway, would, of course, become a household name twelve years later as television's Ricky Ricardo on the I Love Lucy show. Ironically, Vivian Vance, who would also later find fame on I Love Lucy as Lucy and Ricky's neighbor, Ethel Mertz, was performing just down the street at the Morosco Theatre in the hit comedy Skylark. The Imperial was a lucky theater for the Arnaz family. In 1979, Desi's daughter Lucie Arnaz garnered much acclaim for her performance there in Neil Simon's smash musical They're Playing Our Song.

Fiddler was a tough act to follow, but two consecutive John Kander and Fred Ebb musicals were up to the challenge: *Cabaret* (1967), based on the Berlin stories of Christopher Isherwood and starring Lotte Lenya, Jack Gilford, and relative newcomer Joel Grey, transferred from the Broadhurst; and *Zorba* (1968) starring Herschel Bernardi and Maria Karnilova followed. Bob Fosse's production of Stephen Schwartz's *Pippin* (1972) was the Imperial's most successful tenant in the 1970s. Possibly Fosse's most adventurous show, *Pippin* included Ben Vereen, Ann Reinking, Irene Ryan, and John Rubinstein. It played for four and one-half years at the Imperial before it moved to the Minskoff, where it completed its run of 1,944 performances. Back-to-back Neil Simon hits closed out the decade: *Chapter Two* (1977) and *They're Playing Our Song* (1979), the latter featuring Robert Klein and Lucie Arnaz, who followed in her father's footsteps: Desi had made his Broadway debut at the Imperial in 1939 playing his congas in *Too Many Girls*.

From the beginning, Imperial audiences have witnessed some amazing productions and performers, but in 1981 they were treated to the thrill of watching Jennifer Holliday bring down

LEFT:

Dreamgirls (1981), (left to right) Jennifer Holliday as E_ Melody White, Sheryl Lee Ra_ as Deena Jones, and Loretta Devine as Lorell Robinson performing "Heavy." Coproduced by the Shubert Organization along with Michael Bennett, Bob Avian, and Geffen records, Dreamg__ was an ultra-stylish and fast-paced look at the ups an_ downs in the personal and professional lives of a pop mu_ girl group. Audiences admire_ director/cochoreographer Michael Bennett's fluid—ma_ said cinematic—staging, but some felt that the heart of the show became lost in all the pyrotechnics. Although the musical ran for almost four ye_ the director was never quite satisfied with it, and he scale_ back the physical aspects of the show for a bus-and-truck production that toured the United States. In an unusual move, Bennett and company decided to bring the new Dreamgirls back to Broadwa_ in 1987, only two years after _ original production had close_ It was received enthusiasticall_ but Bennett was in no conditi_ to appreciate the acclaim. He died of complications from A_ on July 2, 1987, just four days_ after the show's opening.

the house each night in *Dreamgirls*, with her powerful rendition of "And I Am Telling You (I'm Not Going)." Later in the 1980s, the Shubert Organization produced two more musicals: *Chess* (1988) and *Jerome Robbins' Broadway* (1989). The latter is an excellent example of how Lee and J. J.'s initial hopes for the Imperial were realized: a "greatest hits" package, the show consisted of colorful and energetic numbers from Robbins's impressive body of work. Coming full circle, this show included material from *Fiddler on the Roof*, which had played the Imperial twenty-five years earlier. In 1990, *Les Misérables* moved to the Imperial from the Broadway (see page 265), and it has settled in for a long run.

The Imperial Theatre is located at 246 West 45th Street.

The Lyceum is the last remaining example of a repertory house in New York City. Built by producer-manager Daniel Frohman, its inaugural production, *The Proud Prince*, opened on November 2, 1903, and starred E. H. Sothern. Frohman saw this as a good omen, as Sothern had also starred in the first show at his old Lyceum, located on Fourth Avenue near Madison Square, which closed in 1902. Thirteen bricks from the former theater were laid into the foundation of the new Lyceum, further symbolizing the bridge between nineteenth- and twentieth-century theatrical traditions.

Designed in a Beaux Arts style by architects Herts and Tallant, the building boasts a handsome gray limestone facade with six ornate Corinthian columns. The elegant entrance is shaded by a marquee that extends to the street and was said to have been

Nighttime exterior of the Lyceum Theatre, probably shortly after opening

OPPOSITE:
The Lyceum Theatre, spring 2000

E. H. Sothern in The Proud Prince *(1903), the Lyceum's opening production. The play by Justin Huntley McCarthy was based on a poem by Robert Southey.*

*View of the auditorium
from house-left box*

Relief over proscenium showing Pallas Athena, the Goddess of Wisdom, flanked by the Muses of Music and Drama. Design by Herts and Tallant

large enough for eight carriages to discharge at once. Because the Lyceum was built so far north and on a side street, Frohman placed gas torches on top of the building, dramatically illuminating it so that theatergoers would be sure not to miss it. The drama continues once inside the foyer, which features two grand staircases leading to the mezzanine. Among its decorations are portraits by James Wall Finn of Sarah Siddons and David Garrick—again part of Frohman's desire to emphasize the continuity of tradition. The marble for the lobby has an eggshell finish that "approximates the marble of Athens."

The Lyceum's interior is elegant and intimate. Every critic mentioned how wide and shallow the orchestra was, which had the effect of bringing the audience closer to the stage than was typical at that time. There are two balconies and fewer than one thousand seats. One of its singular characteristics was the ventilation system; the auditorium was kept cool in the summer and warm in the winter as air was passed over either ice chambers or steam coils on its way into the house.

Cartouche with "L" for Lyceum over entrance to auditorium; the "L" is used as a decorative motif throughout the theater. The portrait of David Garrick is by James Wall Finn.

Due to Frohman's vision of the new Lyceum as a home for a repertory company, the structure includes a ten-story building behind the stage. Housed here were scene, carpentry, and costume shops, as well as dressing rooms with separate bathrooms—a true innovation for the time—and a comfortable greenroom where performers could meet and greet their well-wishers. Frohman took advantage of the latest technical improvements by installing elevators that descended thirty feet below the stage for scenery changes.

Ladies' room sign

Above the theater, Frohman built an apartment for himself—his "home away from home"—which included an office, a rehearsal studio, and a library modeled after David Garrick's. The penthouse's most notable feature is a small door that offers a bird's-eye view of the stage below and from which, over the years, countless auditions and performances have been secretly observed by producers and directors. One story that persists has Frohman waving a white handkerchief out the open door at his wife, the actress Margaret Illington, whenever he felt she was overacting. Frohman's sanctuary has been the home of the Shubert Archive since 1978, and it contains his massive monogrammed desk (a gift from friends upon the theater's opening) and a thronelike chair that Frohman, in his autobiography, aptly describes as "Napoleonic."

Although Frohman built such a striking example of a repertory theater, his dream of installing a permanent repertory company was not to be. The rise of the star system and the public's appetite for new plays rather than old standards led to the demise of the repertory system, and most theaters became "combination" houses, which brought in a new cast for each play. By 1903, Frohman was forced to follow the combination trend.

Nevertheless, the Lyceum's early years saw some of the best performances the American theater had to offer: William Gillette in J. M. Barrie's *The Admirable Crichton* (1903), the Lyceum's first original play; Lionel Barrymore in *The Other Girl* (1904); Ethel Barrymore in *A Doll's House* (1906); and Margaret Illington in *The Thief* (1907). Over the next three decades, the playhouse hosted such luminaries as Fanny Brice, Billie Burke, Humphrey Bogart, Walter Huston, Judith Anderson, Leslie Howard, and Bette Davis.

On May 28, 1940, the Lyceum was bought by a conglomerate of producers: George S. Kaufman, Moss Hart, Sam H. Harris, Max Gordon, Marcus Heiman, and Joseph M. Hyman. Frohman, then in his eighties, was allowed to remain in his penthouse for the rent of a dollar a year. That year the producers premiered Kaufman and Hart's new comedy, *George Washington Slept Here*, and continued with subsequent hits like *Born Yesterday* (1946), which brought Judy Holliday Broadway stardom.

The Thief, *Margaret Illington (at the time, Mrs. Daniel Frohman) and Kyrle Bellew. The show, which opened on September 9, 1907, ran for 281 performances. Mr. and Mrs. Frohman divorced amicably in 1909, and Illington later married Edward J. Bowes of* Major Bowes Amateur Hour.

The Shuberts took over the space in 1950. Their first big success came that same year with Clifford Odets's *The Country Girl* starring Uta Hagen. Other long runs of the decade included *A Hatful of Rain* (1955) with Shelley Winters and *The Happiest*

OPPOSITE, ABOVE:

George Washington Slept Here *(1940). After George S. Kaufman and Moss Hart bought the theater in 1940, the Lyceum became home to a number of their shows, including this one. The comedy tells the tale of Newton (Ernest Truax, center) and Annabelle (Jean Dixon, standing, center) Fuller, city dwellers who come to the country in search of greener pastures. Dixon, one of Kaufman's favorite actresses, won raves for her acerbic delivery.*

OPPOSITE, BELOW:

Morning's at Seven *(1980). This revival of a Paul Osborne play from the 1930s was more successful the second time around. The ensemble cast included (left to right) Nancy Marchand, Maureen O'Sullivan, Richard Hamilton, David Rounds, Lois De Banzie, Gary Merrill, Elizabeth Wilson (on porch), Teresa Wright, and Maurice Copeland.*

Born Yesterday *(1946), Paul Douglas and Judy Holliday in the famous gin rummy game. This was the show that launched Holliday to stardom.*

Millionaire (1956) starring Walter Pidgeon. Then the Lyceum hosted a British invasion, with Alan Bates in John Osborne's *Look Back in Anger* (1957); Shelagh Delaney's *A Taste of Honey* (1960) starring Angela Lansbury and Joan Plowright; and Harold Pinter's *The Caretaker* (1961) with Alan Bates, Robert Shaw, and Donald Pleasance.

In 1965, Frohman's vision of a Lyceum repertory company was finally realized, when the Association of Producing Artists (APA)–Phoenix Repertory Company took up residence. Although the alliance lasted only four years, a number of significant classic and modern plays were produced, including *You Can't Take It with You* (1965), *The School for Scandal* (1966), and *The Cherry*

Master Harold . . . and the Boys *(1982), Sam (Zakes Mokae, left) watching as Willie (Danny Glover) practices for the ballroom dance contest. Athol Fugard's drama about apartheid focuses on these two men, who work in a tearoom in Port Elizabeth, South Africa, and their disintegrating relationship with Hallie (Lonnie Price), the son of the tearoom's white owners. This award-winning show was coproduced by the Shubert Organization.*

Whoopi Goldberg in her eponymously named show directed by Mike Nichols in 1984. This one-woman multicharacter tour de force nicely highlighted the actress's versatility and was her springboard to success.

Orchard (1968). In 1988, hopes of a repertory company were revived when the Lincoln Center Theatre leased the Lyceum, intending to present a full season of productions. Its first show, *Our Town* with Spalding Gray, was a big (if controversial) success, but it remained the only play that the Lincoln Center team would produce in the space until 2000. Meanwhile, in 1992, Tony Randall's National Actors Theatre became the next repertory company to call the Lyceum home, where it produced more than a dozen shows. In spring 2000, Lincoln Center Theatre returned to the playhouse with Olympia Dukakis in *Rose*, Martin Sherman's one-person drama about the ups and downs in the complex life of an octogenarian Holocaust survivor.

Regarded by many as a crown jewel among New York's playhouses, Broadway's oldest continually operating legitimate theater is poised to mark its own centennial in 2003 and stands ready to entertain audiences well into the next century.

The Lyceum Theatre is located at 149 West 45th Street.

OPPOSITE:

My Romance *(1948), with Anne Jeffreys as Madame Cavallini, Lawrence Brooks as Bishop Tom Armstrong (right),and Melvin Ruick as Cornelius Van Tuyl. This was J. J. Shubert and Sigmund Romberg's final Broadway operetta.*

Inset:

Costume designer Lou Eisele's sketch and fabric swatch for the dress seen in the photograph. During the 1940s, Eisele designed extensively for Broadway, nightclubs, ice shows, and the circus. In addition he was the author of books on fashion, drawing, and illustration. This page is a rare example from the Archive in which a photograph exists that shows the realization of a costume design. The addition of a fabric swatch makes it even more unique.

Costume and Set Designs

MADAME CAVALLINI
ANN JEFFRYS
ACT 2 —
1895

Of the several Shubert-run ancillary companies that supported the brothers' production and theater management, their in-house design shops were perhaps the most colorful. House costume designers created playful attire for chorus girls and boys, as well as for the stars of the Shuberts' many revues, musicals, and dramas, while set designers provided scenes with equally inventive detail.

Many of the three thousand costume sketches in the Shubert Archive are by Cora MacGeachy and Homer B. Conant. Also well represented are designers Alfredo Edel, Caroline Siedle, Lou Eisele, Myra Butterworth, William Mathews, Alois Bohnen, William Weaver, Sam Zalud, and Ernest Schraps. Represented in less depth are designers Irene Sharaff, Orry-Kelly, Howard Greer, Charles LeMaire, Russell Patterson, Connie De Pinna, Basil Crage, and Yvette Kiviat. The Archive also holds set renderings by Watson Barratt, the Shuberts' scene designer from 1917 through the 1930s. Other set designers who worked on Shubert productions include Vincente Minnelli, Homer B. Conant, Orry-Kelly, Rollo Wayne, and Albert Johnson.

The most playful of all the designs are the costume sketches created for musical numbers in Shubert revues. These were often based on a given theme and amusingly depicted chorus girls dressed, for instance, as various cocktails, or as the components of a complete tea service. Flower girls, bird girls, butterfly girls, World War I girls, bathing-suit girls, automobile girls—it did not matter how silly or serious the song was, the costume designer devised a novel way to get the point across.

The designs were done in pencil and watercolor on either paper or board, materials so acidic that they are crumbling today. Some designers marked up the margins and backs of drawings with notes about what materials to use, how the costume should be constructed, and what show, scene, and/or performer the design was for. Sometimes sample fabric swatches were attached. Often the backs of costume designs included a listing of the names and measurements of the chorus girls who would wear the finished outfits. Some designers provided no extra information, only the unvarnished drawing.

Ultimately responsible for the look and feel of a show, these designers are among the unsung heroes and heroines of the Broadway stage.

ABOVE AND RIGHT:
Design for Mae West in *The Whirl of the Town* (the title of the show was later changed to *The Mimic World of 1921*; designer unknown) and (right) a costume by Cora MacGeachy for Adele Astaire for *The Passing Show of 1918*, "I Can't Make My Feet Behave." The Archive does not have many designs for stars. What is notable about these two designs is that each evokes the personality and style of the performer for which it was designed.

OPPOSITE:
These three sets of costume sketches—bathing-suit girls, nut girls, flower girls—are typical revue designs. The Archive contains many sketches that are not identified by production or performer. In addition, some of these designs may have been proposed for a show but not executed. In the examples seen here, designers Conant, Johnston, and Weaver left no clues on their respective drawings: no dates, no performers, no production title, no indication of a scene.

Bathing-Suit Girls, by Homer Conant. Shades of Mack Sennett's bathing beauties, these designs may well have been inspired by the popular Keystone motion-picture comedies. The movies exerted an influence on revue sketches and were used as fodder by the writers in much the same way that current dramatic offerings are spoofed.

Nut Girls, by Mabel E. Johnston. Chorus girls served as mannequins for many whimsical numbers—one, for example, featured girls dressed as various sorts of illumination (lantern, torch, chandelier, lighthouse beacon). Shown here are Miss P. Nutt (left) and Miss Chest-A-Nut (right). Designer Johnston designed frequently on Broadway in the 1920s when she worked on shows such as *Little Jessie James* (1923), *Earl Carroll's Vanities* (1928), and *Animal Crackers* (1929).

Flower Girls, by William Weaver. Chorus girls frequently appeared in specialty numbers dressed as various blossoms. Some of the more elaborate concoctions had them arranged into a bouquet or adorning a trellis. And, of course, there were the other woodland elements that included girls costumed as birds, bees, and butterflies. Seen here are Flag (left) and Peony (right). William Weaver designed on Broadway and for the Metropolitan Opera Company during the 1920s and 1930s. Shows he worked on included Irving Berlin's *Music Box Revue* (1923) and the Shubert operetta *Frederika* (1937).

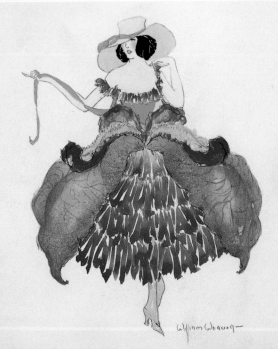

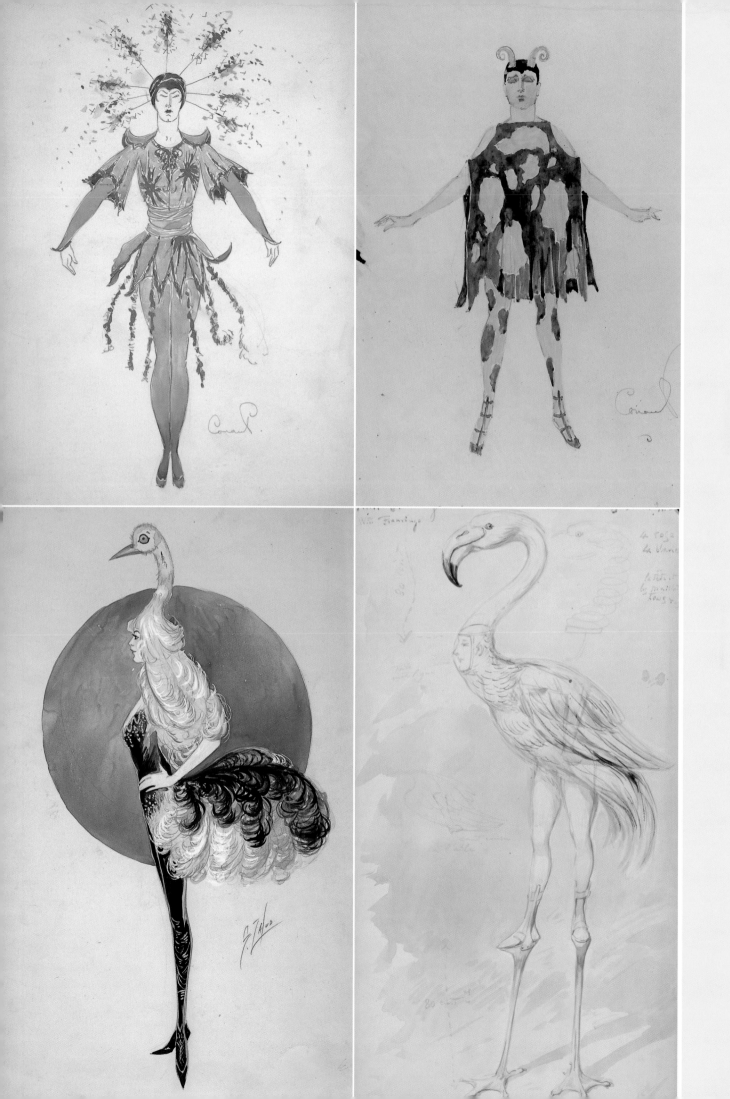

OPPOSITE, ABOVE LEFT:
Fireworks, male dancer, by Homer Conant, an in-house designer for the Shuberts. The design shows the influence of Les Ballets Russes, which had a major impact on the performing arts. Conant worked for the Shuberts from about 1914 until the mid-1920s. During World War I, he was drafted and assigned to the camouflage unit, where his artistic talents were put to a more utilitarian purpose. In Paris after the war, Conant was a theatrical spy for the Shuberts. He would attend shows at the Casino de Paris and other venues and jot down his impressions of acts, make rough sketches of sets and costumes, and send the information to J. J. Shubert.

OPPOSITE, ABOVE RIGHT:
Nijinski ("Najensky") Number (Faun for "Back to Nature"), by Homer Conant. This sketch for *Show of Wonders* (1916) was either a spoof or a tribute to the famous Ballets Russes dancer Nijinsky in "Afternoon of a Faun."

OPPOSITE, BELOW LEFT:
Ostrich, by Sam Zalud, is one of a series of bird girls, possibly for the "Birdland" scene in *The Passing Show of 1918.* The featured number of the scene was the unforgettable "Twit, Twit, Twit," with Fred and Adele Astaire and a flock of Dancing Birds. Other Shubert shows to which Zalud contributed set and/or costume designs included *Sinbad* (1918) and *Cinderella on Broadway* (1920).

OPPOSITE, BELOW RIGHT AND RIGHT:
The Hippodrome was a 5,000-seat house located on 44th Street and Sixth Avenue that featured spectacles and extravaganzas. Costumes were designed for large choruses and meant to bedazzle an audience from a distance. In the Pink Flamingo costume, for "The Land of the Birds" scene in *The Sporting Days* (1908), the performer is strapped onto stilts that are part of the bird's legs and leans forward for balance. She is able to see through a hole covered by a gauzy fabric in the base of the bird's neck. The height and breadth of the wingspan of the Black Butterfly (right) for *Around the World* (1911) must also have made a searing impression. Both were executed by Alfredo Edel, who had designed costumes for operas at La Scala and for productions at La Comédie Française, among other notable venues.

OPPOSITE, ABOVE:
Aeroplane girls (left), and Automobile girls (right), two sketches by William Mathews for a Hippodrome show, possibly *America,* (1913) which had a scene paying tribute to "Inventions." Designers and their audiences were obsessed with the automobile, and several designers turned the obsession into costumes. In this whimsical drawing on the right, note the headlamps as epaulets on the model's shoulders and the license-plate numbers on her gloves. The prolific Mathews, a native New Yorker, first designed on Broadway for *The Ziegfeld Follies* of 1907 and was active until the 1930s.

OPPOSITE, BELOW:
Tea Service, by Myra Butterworth. Two designs from a series drawn for an unidentified show. Shown here are a teacup with steam rising from the chorus girl's head and a teapot. Among the other sketches are a teaspoon, a sugar bowl and creamer, a serving tray, a bowl of orange marmalade, a butter dish, and a sugar cube with tongs. Virtually nothing is known about Myra Butterworth, but this set of designs, along with another depicting girls dressed as various denominations of currency, are among the wittiest in the Archive's collection.

RIGHT:
Combination costume design/backdrop, skyscraper with girl. Production and artist unidentified, possibly Conant or Orry-Kelly

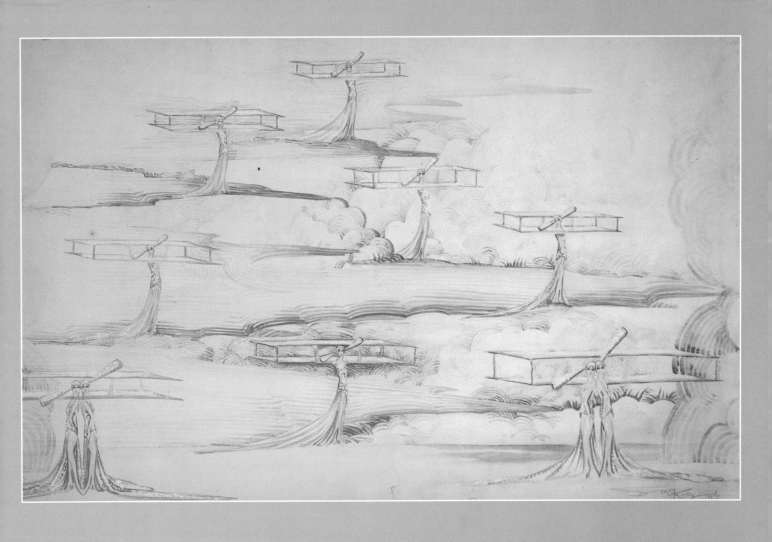

163 *Interlude: Costume and Set Designs*

ABOVE AND LEFT:
Artists and Models (1925).
Set design for knife-throwing
scene, probably by Watson
Barratt, and a photograph
illustrating the completed
set, which consists of a
painted backdrop and a
three-dimensional set piece.
This was probably the segment
titled "Oriental Memories,"
featuring the singer Harold
Stanton and the Gertrude
Hoffmann dancers. Barratt's
first Broadway design was for
A Night in Spain (1917). As
Lee and J. J.'s chief scenic
designer for many years, he
worked on such Shubert classics as *Blossom Time* (1921),
The Passing Show (several
editions) and *The Student
Prince* (1924). It is very rare
for the Archive to have a set
design and a photograph of
the realized sketch.

Sets and numbers inspired by the Orient frequently appeared in revues. The huge Chinese dragon in the background seems to have been conjured from an opium pipe, but how the set actually was meant to work is unclear. The design was by Jack Savage, about whom little is known.

OVERLEAF, ABOVE:
Airplane girls backdrop, by Orry-Kelly. Like the skyscraper backdrop with the girl (page 161), this is a combination set and costume design. There is no information on how to achieve the effect or what show inspired the design. Orry-Kelly was known as a costume not a set designer and had an illustrious Hollywood career at Warner Bros. and Fox. He won Academy Awards for costume design for *An American in Paris* (1951), *Les Girls* (1957), and *Some Like It Hot* (1959).

OVERLEAF, BELOW:
Vincente Minnelli's design is for a scene entitled "Parade Night," in Act One of the revue *The Show Is On* (1936). The scene is a spoof of *Uncle Tom's Cabin,* with Eliza (Gracie Barrie) ascending to heaven and Simon Legree (Andre Charise) brandishing a whip over Uncle Tom's body. The lyrics issued an invitation to the audience:

"Tonight's parade night. Come along, you'll see Uncle Tom's Cabin.
See little Eva fly up to heaven high up and join the angels in the sky.
Tonight's parade night. Join the throng. Weep at Uncle Tom's Cabin.
See poor Eliza racing, the bloodhounds chasing.
Just one misstep and she will die."

The Show Is On also parodied recent Shakespearean offerings such as *Hamlet, Romeo and Juliet,* and *Othello* and performers such as John Gielgud, as well as playwright Eugene O'Neill.

OVERLEAF, CENTER:.
A backdrop featuring pagodas silhouetted against a Chinese harbor. Unidentified production sketch by Endré

Lunette featuring a Mme Pompadour–type couple by Homer Conant. This might possibly have been a curtain or drop design for *The Century Revue* (1920).

Prize-fight ring, by Rollo Wayne, which is labeled *A Night in Spain* but does not seem to have anything to do with that 1927 Shubert revue. Wayne studied at Harvard University with George Pierce Baker and Workshop 47 before focusing on the Broadway stage. His twelve-year affiliation with the Shuberts included his revolving stage set for a 1926 revival of *HMS Pinafore*—the first use of a revolving stage set in the United States.

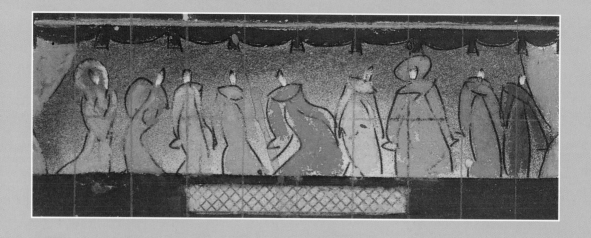

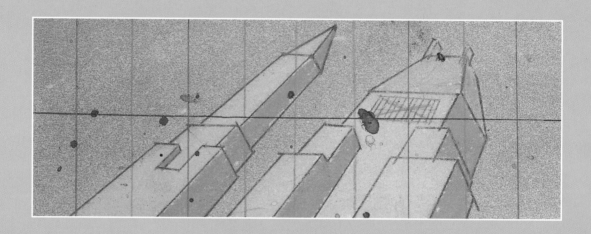

OPPOSITE:
"Fifth Avenue," *Ziegfeld Follies of 1934*. Four panels designed by Albert Johnson for the first *Follies* that the Messrs. Shubert
produced with Billie Burke after Ziegfeld's death. Johnson began his design career in 1929 and was active on Broadway until 1967.
He studied with Norman Bel Geddes and consulted on many projects including the 1939 New York World's Fair, Radio City Music Hall,
and the Ringling Brothers & Barnum and Bailey Circus. Among his other Shubert credits were *Life Begins at 8:40* (1934), *Between the
Devil* (1938) and *You Never Know* (1939).

ABOVE:
Drawing Room, a double design, by Raymond Deshays, a French designer who has only one American credit, the *Folies Bergère* (1939),
but who designed many productions for the Opéra Comique as well as the *Folies Bergère* in Paris. While it may seem inexplicable
that the Shubert Archive has a design in its collection by an artist who appears never to have worked for Shubert, one possible explanation
is that Deshays's drawing may have been tucked into a collection of costume designs and secondhand costumes from French revues
that the Shuberts bought after the war. World War II had a devastating effect on the French theater, which was still slowly recovering
in the late 1940s. Through their representative in Paris, the Shuberts learned about secondhand costumes that were going for a song
and decided to buy these handcrafted, elaborately beaded and bedecked items for future use.

T oward the close of 1919, the prominent theatrical producer Sam H. Harris made a proposition to his friend Irving Berlin: if the popular songwriter would devise a musical revue, Harris would find a theater for it. Berlin responded with *The Music Box Revue*, and in 1920 the Music Box Theatre was built to house the show. From the start the venue possessed an almost magical quality, especially for Berlin—it was, after all, quite rare for a theater to be built for a specific show. The great songwriter remained attached to the house long after his series of *Revues* ended, and to this day his estate retains half ownership of it.

At the time the theater was built, Berlin was at the peak of his tremendously successful career. He had the uncanny ability to compose songs the public loved to hear and musicians loved to play. His partnership with Sam Harris was highly anticipated and ultimately quite successful, for *The Music Box Revue* delivered on its promise of wonderful tunes, comic sketches, stunning girls, and extravagant spectacle.

TOP:
Auditorium and box chairs viewed from house left

ABOVE:
Detail of painted-glass panel indicating the Ladies' room at the orchestra level

OPPOSITE:
View of the half dome decorated with a pastoral mural and located above the box seats

View of auditorium toward house right

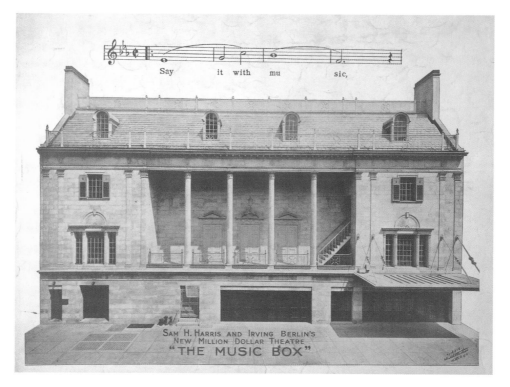

The Shuberts' affiliation with the Music Box Theatre began in 1926 when they purchased shares in the venue from Harris. In 1929 they acquired additional shares from Joseph Schenck, a film producer and chairman of the board of United Artists, who had initially joined his friends Harris and Berlin in financing the theater. Sam Harris died in 1941, and in 1950 his wife, China Marin, sold half of her late husband's shares of the Music Box to Berlin,

and the other half to the Shuberts. From that point on, Berlin and Shubert became equal partners in the ownership of the house.

Because of its dainty, jewel-like qualities, the Music Box Theatre is aptly named. With a maximum seating capacity of 1,010, it is known for providing both audiences and actors with an intimate setting. Designed by architect Charles Howard Crane in collaboration with E. George Kiehler, it was built in the neo-Georgian style, which many regarded as being fancifully domestic in the manner of a grand country manor. The contemporary architectural press hailed the Music Box as a beauty, and especially noted its elegant facade with its row of pillars and other adornment.

Music Box Theatre, program cover (c. 1922). This artwork aptly illustrates the charm of the Music Box Theatre, which has often been likened to an exquisite jewel-like box out of which emerges the most delightful music.

The Music Box Revue glamorously opened the theater on September 22, 1921. Each year for the next four years, Berlin created an entirely new edition of the show. Among the notable performers featured in the *Revues* were Charlotte Greenwood, Bobby Clark, Grace Moore, Fanny Brice, and Berlin himself. The house's first nonmusical production was a comedy entitled *Cradle Snatchers* (1925), which featured a young Humphrey Bogart in its cast. The next year, *Chicago* (1926), the play on which the Kander and Ebb musical is based and which starred Charles Bickford and Francine Larrimore, took up residence. Philip Barry's *Paris Bound* followed in 1927. The 1920s came to a close with two musicals, Cole Porter's *Paris* (1928) and the revue *The Little Show* (1929), which starred Fred Allen, Clifton Webb, and Libby Holman.

The 1930s began auspiciously with two George S. Kaufman and Moss Hart productions: *Once in a Lifetime* (1930) and *Of Thee I Sing* (1931). The latter, boasting music and lyrics by George and Ira Gershwin, became the first musical to be

The Music Box Revue *(1921–24), Irving Berlin surrounded by the chorus girls who constituted the octet known as the "Eight Little Notes." Berlin himself appeared in the 1921 edition of the* Revue *in a sketch that found him being "interviewed" by the Eight Little Notes, who played "reporters." No stranger to the stage, Berlin had made his first appearance in a musical production called* Up and Down Broadway *(1910) which the Shuberts had produced.*

awarded a Pulitzer Prize. Kaufman, this time with Edna Ferber, achieved another success with *Dinner at Eight* (1932), featuring Constance Collier, Sam Levene, Conway Tearle, and Cesar Romero among its cast. Not to be outdone, Moss Hart collaborated the following year with Irving Berlin on *As Thousands Cheer* (1933), which starred Ethel Waters, Clifton Webb, and Marilyn Miller. Kaufman again teamed up with Hart to do *Merrily We Roll Along* (1934; adapted as a musical by Stephen Sondheim in 1981), *First Lady* (1935), *I'd Rather Be*

Of Thee I Sing *(1931)*, *inauguration/wedding scene. This political satire, written by George S. Kaufman and Morrie Ryskind and featuring the musical talents of George and Ira Gershwin, became the first musical comedy to be awarded a Pulitzer Prize. In it, a presidential candidate, John P. Wintergreen, and his campaign committee conclude that what the American people care most about is love. Therefore, they decide to base the run for the presidency on this platform and endeavor to find the perfect all-American girl for Wintergreen to marry. Their strategy succeeds, and the candidate is sworn in as the president of the United States on his wedding day.*

RIGHT:

As Thousands Cheer *(1933), Clifton Webb as Mahatma Gandhi and Helen Broderick as Aimee Semple MacPherson. In this scene, called "Gandhi Goes on New Hunger Strike," the repartee between the nonviolent revolutionary leader of India and the charismatic American woman evangelist with the power to heal must have been quite interesting. This inspired musical revue was created by Irving Berlin and Moss Hart, and staged by Hassard Short. Berlin's score sparkled and included the hit "Easter Parade," sung by Marilyn Miller and Webb; Hart's sketches contained their customary bravura wit; and Short's staging was at its most impressive.*

Right (which opened at the Alvin Theatre in 1937 and moved to the Music Box in 1938), and *The Man Who Came to Dinner* (1939). Kaufman also teamed again with Ferber to do *Stage Door* (1936) and *The Land Is Bright* (1941), which featured a kid named Dickie Van Patten. In addition, the busy Kaufman directed John Steinbeck's *Of Mice and Men* (1937), winning the New York Drama Critics Circle Award.

Among the last of the revues to play the Music Box, two were notable for their extravagance, though their styles were distinctly opposite. Noël Coward's lavish *Set to Music* (1939)

starred Beatrice Lillie and was the height of sophistication and glamour. Mike Todd's *Star and Garter* (1942) featured Gypsy Rose Lee, Bobby Clark, and Georgia Sothern, included music by Irving Berlin, and was the epitome of burlesque—earthy, seductive, and fun.

In 1944, Rodgers and Hammerstein's production of John Van Druten's comedy *I Remember Mama* was a big hit, with a young Marlon Brando making his Broadway debut. Brando returned to the Music Box in Ben Hecht and Kurt Weill's *A Flag Is Born* (1946). Tennessee Williams's *Summer and Smoke* premiered in 1948, and Weill was back again the following year when he teamed up with Maxwell Anderson to create *Lost in the Stars* (1949).

Productions of note in the 1950s include three William Inge plays: *Picnic* (1953), *Bus Stop* (1955), and *The Dark at the Top of the Stairs* (1957); a revival of James Thurber and Elliott Nugent's *The Male Animal* (1952); Terrance Rattigan's *Separate Tables* (1956); Fay and Michael Kanin's adaptation of Ryunosu ke Akutagawa's *Rashomon* (1959) with Rod Steiger and Claire Bloom; and Peter Shaffer's *Five Finger Exercise* (1959).

Arthur Laurents's *Invitation to a March* kicked off the 1960s with a cast that included Celeste Holm, Eileen Heckart, Jane Fonda, and James MacArthur.

I Remember Mama *(1944), Mady Christians (second from the left) as Mama with the rest of the cast, which includes a young Marlon Brando (second from the right) as her son Nels. This Richard Rodgers and Oscar Hammerstein production was based upon Kathryn Forbes's collection of short stories entitled* Mama's Bank Account. *The stories first caught the attention of Rodgers's daughter Mary, who encouraged her mother to read them. She, in turn, recommended them to Mrs. Hammerstein, who then passed them on to her husband. Everyone agreed that the material should be dramatized, and they asked John Van Druten to adapt it. Meanwhile,* Mama's Bank Account *had also come to the attention of actress Mady Christians, who was sufficiently impressed with it to ask that Rodgers keep her in mind for the title role should he ever consider turning this material into a play.*

Henry Denker's *A Far Country* (1961) followed, and in 1964 Muriel Resnik's *Any Wednesday* brought Sandy Dennis and Gene Hackman to the Music Box stage. Harold Pinter's *The Homecoming,* with Ian Holm, Paul Rogers, and Vivien Merchant, premiered in 1967.

In the 1970s, the Music Box was shrouded in mystery. Anthony Shaffer's *Sleuth* (1970), starring Anthony Quayle and Keith Baxter, achieved a run of 1,222 performances—the venue's biggest hit to that date. This was not a long-lived distinction, however, because eight years later Ira Levin's *Deathtrap* (1978), with John Wood and Victor Garber, racked up a whopping 1,793 performances. Among nonmysteries, Alan Ayckbourn's *Absurd Person Singular* (1974), starring Sandy Dennis, Carole Shelley, Richard Kiley, and Geraldine Page, proved to be a great success, and the musical revue *Side by Side by Sondheim* (1977) presented a musical tribute to composer Stephen Sondheim.

Agnes of God (1982), for which Amanda Plummer won a Tony Award as Best Featured Actress, sparked controversy with its story involving a postulant accused of killing her newborn. In 1987, the Shuberts coproduced the Royal Shakespeare Company's *Les Liaisons Dangereuses* starring Alan Rickman and Lindsay Duncan. Another British import, the musical *Blood Brothers* (1993), was one of the more successful shows of the season. It was followed in 1995 by another musical, producer David Merrick's theatrical version of the Rodgers and Hammerstein film *State Fair* (1996)—it was to be the great showman's last production. The Music Box closed out the decade with two more British imports: Patrick Marber's intense *Closer* (1999) with Natasha Richardson, Rupert Graves, Anna Friel, and Ciaran Hinds; and a revival of Peter Shaffer's *Amadeus* (1999) starring David Suchet.

The Music Box Theatre is located at 239 West 45th Street.

Side by Side by Sondheim *(1977), window card. This revue of Stephen Sondheim's own songs, as well as those upon which he collaborated, came to Broadway from London, complete with its British cast. With this production, the revue format successfully returned to the Music Box, fifty-six years after Berlin's first show there.*

OPPOSITE, BELOW:
Bus Stop *(1955), Crahan Denton (left) as Virgil Blessing, Kim Stanley as Cherie, and Albert Salmi as Bo Decker in William Inge's comedy about the many vagaries of love. Cowboy Decker is head over heels for the disinterested nightclub chanteuse Cherie. When the two are stranded overnight in a café after their bus breaks down, Cherie performs the number that first made Decker fall in love with her. Having just won a Pulitzer Prize for* Picnic *two years earlier, Inge had already established himself as a playwright who wrote knowingly about the people and places of the American Midwest. The poignancy of his characters' search for some kind of connection with one another struck a chord with audiences.*

The Plymouth Theatre was built in 1917 by the Shuberts along with the contiguous Broadhurst (see page 48) on 44th Street adjacent to the existing Booth and Shubert Theatres. The Plymouth was architect Herbert Krapp's first independent commission and was clearly designed to complement its neighbors, which Krapp had worked on earlier while in the employ of Herts and Tallant. Design motifs of the theater's interior space subtly reflect those of the somewhat more ornate Booth and Shubert, while on the outside, the building has a rather plain facade with a rounded corner entrance that faces Broadway.

Detail of decorative molding

LEFT:
Detail of orchestra seat standard

OVERLEAF, LEFT:
The auditorium seen from the mezzanine, house left, showing box seats and the proscenium

OPPOSITE:
Detail of ceiling decoration

OVERLEAF, RIGHT:
View of the rear mezzanine

$3.00 a Year.   JUNE 1907   Vol. VII   NO. 9   25c. a Copy

THE THEATRE

Plain though it may be on the exterior, the Plymouth can nonetheless boast of having showcased some of the most exciting faces on Broadway. Credit for this goes largely to Arthur M. Hopkins, a much-respected producer/director to whom the Shuberts first leased the Plymouth. Hopkins, whose reputation was impeccable, claimed that his primary motivation for producing was to afford new talent the opportunity to hone their craft onstage. Throughout his career, he formed relationships with an impressive array of performers.

Though Hopkins opened the Plymouth on February 5, 1917, with a production of *A Successful Calamity* that had originally opened eight months earlier at the Booth, the producer went on in 1918 to bring three Henrik Ibsen plays to the new stage: *The Wild Duck*, *Hedda Gabler*, and *A Doll's House*, all starring Alla Nazimova. Further, Hopkins's relationship with the Barrymores was legendary: he first brought John Barrymore to the Plymouth in Tolstoy's *Redemption* (1918), later directed him together with his brother Lionel in *The Jest* (1919), and then again solo in the title role of a highly praised *The Tragedy of Richard III* (1920).

LEFT:

Alla Nazimova as Nora in Henrik Ibsen's A Doll's House, The Theatre *magazine (1907). A Russian actress of some renown, Nazimova first came to New York on tour with the St. Petersburg Players and eventually decided to remain. In 1906, Lee Shubert signed her to a contract that stipulated she receive English lessons on a regular basis—she became fluent in a matter of months. Nazimova was heartily praised as an actress who truly inhabited her roles. She is credited with having introduced Ibsen to American audiences, and Eugene O'Neill is said to have remarked upon seeing her performance in* Hedda Gabler, *"It gave me my first conception of a modern theater where truth might live." In 1918, under the direction of Arthur Hopkins, she reprised the role of Nora at the Plymouth Theatre, to much acclaim.*

BELOW:

The Jest (1919). Lionel Barrymore (far left), as Neri Chiaramantesi, points an accusatory finger at his brother, John (second from right), who plays Giannetto Malespini in an adaptation of Sem Benelli's "La Cena delle Beffe." Neri and Giannetto's rivalry develops into an extreme hatred for one another that eventually leads to a tragic end. Although the latter seems at first to be the morally stronger, but physically weaker, of the two characters, by the play's end circumstances have transformed him into the spitting image of his cruel tormentor. Arthur Hopkins directed the two Barrymores in what must have been a piquant study of sibling rivalry.

WHAT PRICE GLORY

25¢

ARTICLES BY: JOHN GOLDEN, RACHEL CROTHERS, GERTRUDE LAWRENCE CLARENCE BUDINGTON KELLAND AND HATTIE CARNEGIE

Susan and God *(1937), starring Gertrude Lawrence as Susan, souvenir program. Lawrence gave a stellar performance in John Golden's production of Rachel Crothers's play about a society woman's dramatically changed outlook on life. Although the show had quite a successful run on Broadway, it had a less than fortunate start. Just hours after the production's opening performance in Washington, D.C., its leading man, Osgood Perkins (father of actor Anthony Perkins), unexpectedly died of a heart attack. His understudy, Paul McGrath, took over as Susan's highly fallible husband, and he remained with the show in New York.*

PREVIOUS PAGE:
What Price Glory? *(1924), souvenir program. With its bracing depiction of soldiers at war, this play by Maxwell Anderson and Laurence Stallings upped the ante for the portrayal of unabashed, gritty realism on the stage. Its content and language were shockingly frank, yet audiences flocked to the production in droves, a testimony to their willingness to be challenged by thought-provoking, yet sometimes disquieting, material.*

In 1924, Hopkins staged Maxwell Anderson and Laurence Stallings's drama *What Price Glory?* at the Plymouth. The production was significant in its boldly realistic depiction of soldiers at war, complete with the unsparing use of rough language. With a run of 435 performances, it was the Plymouth's longest-running show to that date. Further highlights of the 1920s included a well-received show Hopkins cowrote with George Manker Watters called *Burlesque* (1927), which starred Barbara Stanwyck and Hal Skelly as two traveling burlesque actors struggling with alcohol and each other. Philip Barry's comedy *Holiday* (1928) brought real-life socialite Hope Williams to the stage as a young woman constrained by her position in high society. Her portrayal of carefree rebelliousness won audiences over, and she returned to the Plymouth the next year in Donald Ogden Stewart's comedy *Rebound* (1930), which he wrote specifically with the actress in mind.

Several notable productions appeared at the theater over the next decade: Elmer Rice's *Counsellor-At-Law* (1931), which starred Paul Muni; the French import *Tovarich* (1936) starring John Halliday and Marta Abba; Rachel Crothers's *Susan and God* (1937), in which Gertrude Lawrence was a standout; Robert E. Sherwood's *Abe Lincoln in Illinois* (1938), which featured an amazingly Lincoln-like Raymond Massey and was awarded a

Pulitzer Prize; and Clare Boothe's *Margin For Error* (1939), directed by Otto Preminger, who also played a character in the show. Another of the Plymouth's Pulitzer Prize winners was Thornton Wilder's *The Skin of Our Teeth* (1942) with Tallulah Bankhead, Fredric March, Montgomery Clift, and E. G. Marshall. Bankhead later returned in Noël Coward's *Private Lives* (1948).

The 1950s opened on a cheerful note with the Samuel Taylor comedy *The Happy Time*, starring Eva Gabor. The suspenseful *Dial M for Murder* (1952) followed, and in 1954 Herman Wouk's *The Caine Mutiny Court-Martial* brought Henry Fonda back to Broadway. Then it was a return to musical comedy as Marge and Gower Champion joined with Harry Belafonte in *Three for Tonight* (1955). Two comedies closed out the decade: Peter Ustinov starred in his own *Romanoff and Juliet* (1957); and Claudette Colbert, Julie Newmar, and Charles Boyer put a sexy spin on Leslie Stevens's *The Marriage-Go-Round* (1958).

Another musical, the racy *Irma La Douce* (1960) directed by Peter Brook, kicked off the 1960s. Paddy Chayefsky's *Gideon*

The Real Thing (1984), with Jeremy Irons and Glenn Close in their Tony Award–winning roles as Henry and Annie. Tom Stoppard's play centers around the relationship of these two long-term lovers who, when the play begins, are married to others. Accompanied by an array of significant period pop songs and a running commentary on the act of playwriting, the romantic entanglements of the characters become increasingly complex as the play progresses.

Equus (1974), starring Peter Firth as the disturbed boy in Peter Shaffer's controversial play based upon actual events in which a young man inexplicably blinded several horses. Shaffer focused on discovering the motivations behind such a grisly act. Anthony Hopkins played a psychiatrist called in to treat the boy, but who instead finds himself questioning the very notion of a "cure" that involves ridding a person of his utmost passion for the sake of societal normalcy. Shaffer was very explicit about how the play should look and feel, even including in his text detailed suggestions about staging and costuming. The play won a Tony Award that season, as did its director, John Dexter.

(1961), featuring Fredric March, was followed by two Sidney Michaels plays: *Tchin-Tchin* (1962) with Margaret Leighton, Anthony Quinn, and Charles Grodin; and *Dylan* (1964), for which Alec Guinness won a Tony Award for his portrayal of poet Dylan Thomas. The Plymouth then hosted a string of plays by Neil Simon: *The Odd Couple* (1965) starring Art Carney and Walter Matthau as perfectly mismatched men sharing an apartment; *The Star-Spangled Girl* (1966) featuring Anthony Perkins and Richard Benjamin competing for the attentions of Connie Stevens; *Plaza Suite* (1968) showcasing George C. Scott and Maureen Stapleton in a series of vignettes that take place within the Plaza Hotel; and *The Gingerbread Lady* (1970), for which Maureen Stapleton won a Tony for her performance as a witty, self-destructive alcoholic.

Three British imports were the Plymouth's highlights during the 1970s: Dudley Moore and Peter Cook's *Good Evening* (1973), a follow-up to their 1962 production, *Beyond the Fringe*; Peter Shaffer's controversial *Equus* (1974) with Anthony Hopkins and Peter Firth in the leading roles as a psychiatrist and the boy

he treats; and Simon Gray's *Otherwise Engaged* (1977) starring Tom Courtney. The British invasion continued into the 1980s. A dramatization of Charles Dickens's *The Life & Adventures of Nicholas Nickleby* (1981), a Shubert coproduction, swept the Tony Awards with wins for Best Play, for Roger Rees as Best Male Actor, and for directors Trevor Nunn and John Caird. In 1983 came David Hare's *Plenty* with acclaimed performances by Kate Nelligan and Edward Herrmann, who both won Drama League Awards. Another Shubert coproduction, Tom Stoppard's *The Real Thing* (1984), won every conceivable award, including Tonys for the show's stars, Jeremy Irons and Glenn Close, and director Mike Nichols.

The 1980s at the Plymouth welcomed American plays too, especially those written and performed by women. In 1981 the theater housed the Shubert production of Pam Gems's *Piaf*, which won Jane Lapotaire a Tony for her portrayal of the iconic singer. Then, in 1985, Lily Tomlin's one-woman show (conceived with Jane Wagner), *The Search for Signs of Intelligent Life in the Universe*, earned the performer a Tony and an Outer

The Life & Adventures of Nicholas Nickleby (1981). Roger Rees (seated at center), played the title role in The Royal Shakespeare Company's production of Charles Dickens's epic novel, adapted in its entirety by David Edgar. This eight-and-one-half-hour production stayed true to the novel's every subplot and managed to remain as faithful as possible to its original dialogue. Forty-two performers filled the play's 138 speaking roles in a truly ensemble endeavor. The Plymouth itself was transformed into multifarious versions of nineteenth-century England by means of cleverly used props and strategically placed catwalks. The show's success could be measured by the enthusiastic reception afforded it by critics and audiences alike and by the myriad awards it received.

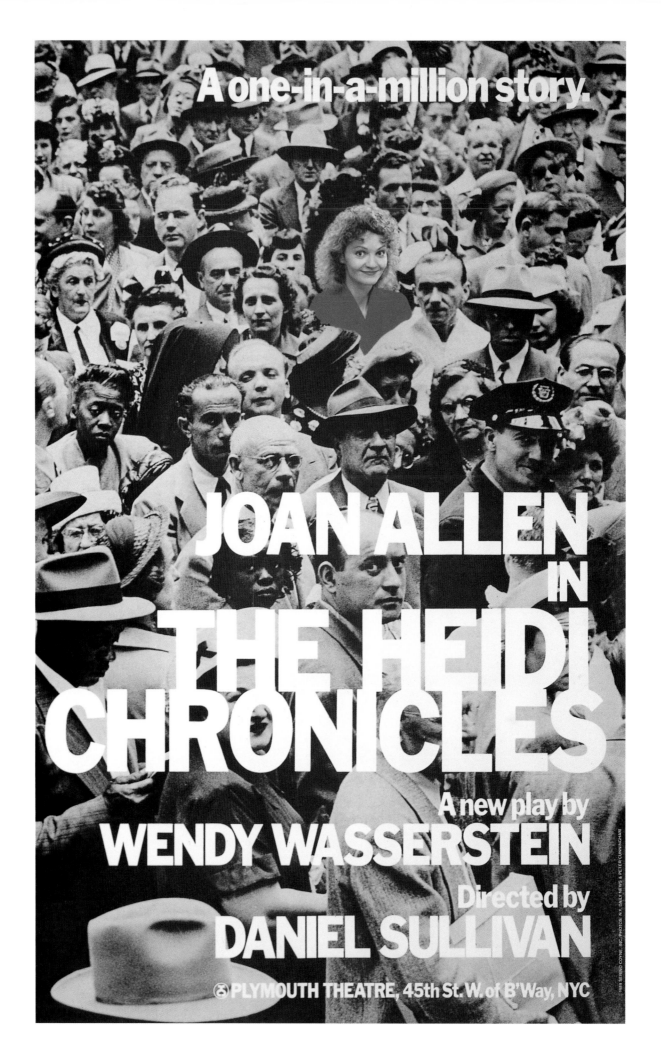

Passion (1994), featuring Marin Mazzie and Jere Shea as Clara and Giorgio. Based on Ettore Scola's motion picture Passione d'amore (1981), James Lapine and Stephen Sondheim's Tony Award–winning production was a compelling look at love, desire, and obsession.

Jekyll & Hyde (1997), Robert Cuccioli in the title's dual roles. Due in large part to Frank Wildhorn's pop-oriented score and dynamic performances by Cuccioli and Linda Eder, this production gave rise to an extremely loyal group of fans known as "Jekkies." Their enthusiasm for the show was such that during the entirety of its New York run, they are said to have bought out the first two rows of seats for nearly every performance. Some Jekkies claimed to have seen the show at least 150 times.

OPPOSITE:
The Heidi Chronicles (1989), window card. The vibrant Joan Allen played art historian Heidi Holland, who struggles both personally and professionally to find her place in a world that is still dominated by men. The beginning of the women's movement impacts on Heidi's college years and early professional life, creating conflicts that she must resolve. Wendy Wasserstein's insightful play won both a Pulitzer Prize and a Tony Award that year.

Critics Circle Award for Best Actress. Finally, in 1989, the Shubert-coproduced Wendy Wasserstein play, *The Heidi Chronicles*, also took home a slew of prizes.

In the 1990s the Plymouth was home to three plays by acclaimed Irish playwright Brian Friel: first the Tony Award–winning *Dancing at Lughnasa* (1991), followed by *Wonderful Tennessee* (1993) and *Translations* (1995). A new Stephen Sondheim–James Lapine musical, *Passion*, debuted in 1994. Coproduced by the Shuberts, this dramatic tale of love and obsession won Tonys that season for Best Musical, Score, and Book, as well as Best Performance by an Actress in a Musical (Donna Murphy). In 1996, a revival of Edward Albee's *A Delicate Balance* boasted a stellar cast that included Rosemary Harris, Elaine Stritch, Mary Beth Hurt, and George Grizzard. The decade closed with another new musical, Frank Wildhorn's *Jekyll & Hyde* (1997), an extremely popular adaptation of Robert Louis Stevenson's classic tale.

Given this high-caliber smorgasbord of stars and hit shows, it would seem that Arthur Hopkins's aim to produce new talent and quality productions has been realized on the Plymouth's stage.

The Plymouth Theatre is located at 236 West 45th Street.

I n the mid-1920s, the Chanin Brothers, New York real-estate developers, hired Herbert J. Krapp, the Shuberts' architect, to design a complex consisting of a hotel and three playhouses that included the Royale, the Majestic (see page 64), and the Golden (page 118). In his design, Krapp referred to his unifying theme as "modern Spanish style." The Royale, a one-

Light fixture, stairway to boxes, house left

LEFT:
Royale Theatre exterior, 1927. The playhouse's second production was Judy, *starring Queenie Smith and Charles Purcell.*

balcony house of 1,048 seats, features a groin-vaulted ceiling supported on either side by archways decorated with two murals, *Lovers of Spain*, by Willy Pogany. The original interior color scheme was cardinal red, orange, and gold.

The Royale opened on January 11, 1927, and was followed shortly by the opening of the other two venues. In 1930, the

OPPOSITE:
Drapery and chandelier in one of the boxes

OVERLEAF, LEFT:
The auditorium seen from the balcony, house right

OVERLEAF, ABOVE RIGHT:
Detail of Willy Pogany mural Lovers of Spain, *house right*

OVERLEAF, BELOW RIGHT:
Detail of Lovers of Spain, *house left*

ANGUS McBEAN

Christopher Fry's The Lady's Not for Burning (1950) was a romantic comedy in verse set in the fifteenth century. Pamela Brown played Jennet Jourdemayne, who is accused of witchcraft, and John Gielgud was Thomas Mendip, the soldier who loves her. The play marked Richard Burton's Broadway debut, and Gielgud, who also directed, regarded the play as one of the finest things Burton ever did. Gielgud's one complaint was that he had to chide Burton for yawning whenever he was hungry and tired.

OPPOSITE:
Two flyers (1931) and sheet music (center, 1928). Set in the Gay Nineties and written by and starring Mae West, Diamond Lil (1928) was the essential Mae West character—a salty, tough, saloon performer on the Bowery. West wore the corseted fashions of the period that suited her hourglass figure, and she delighted in her risqué songs and dialogue. She pushed the boundaries of what was acceptable on stage; her sexuality and easy good humor thrilled audiences while enraging the censors. She first worked for the Shuberts as early as The Mimic World of 1921 and later appeared on Broadway and toured in many shows that she wrote and tailored for herself, including The Constant Sinner. Her influence is felt down to the present with the recent revival of several of her plays and the homage offered by Claudia Shear in Dirty Blonde (2000), produced by the Shubert Organization.

Shuberts bought out the Chanins' stake in the three-theater complex, but during the brothers' period of bankruptcy, control of the Royale passed to John Golden, who renamed the playhouse after himself and ran it from 1934 to 1936. Almost immediately after regaining the property in 1936, the Shuberts restored the theater's original name and leased it to the Columbia Broadcasting System as a radio studio until 1940, when it reverted to legitimate theatrical use.

Because the Royale is a medium-size house, it has been home to both musicals and dramas. The musical *Piggy*, which underwent a title change to *I Told You So,* was the opening production, but it had a relatively brief run. Other early musicals included *Oh, Ernest!* (1927), a musicalized version of *The Importance of Being Earnest*, which was succeeded by a repertory of Gilbert and Sullivan's *The Mikado, Iolanthe*, and *The Pirates of Penzance* (1927). The Shubert musical *The Madcap* (1928) followed. It featured Mitzi Hajos, comedienne and later longtime Shubert office employee.

The Royale's first big hit was Mae West's *Diamond Lil* (1928), a drama set in a dance hall on New York's Bowery. Jack Linder was the credited producer, but the Shuberts had a 19¼ percent

A lively confection set in a girls' school on the French Riviera in the 1920s, The Boy Friend *(1954) was a bubbly piece of nonsense that introduced Julie Andrews (right) to the American public. She played Polly Browne, seen here with the headmistress of the school, Mme Dubonnet (Ruth Altman).*

investment in the show and, early in 1929, bought out all the production rights. Mae West, who was nobody's fool *and* ahead of her time, was not paid a performer's salary but instead received 52 percent of the net profits. As the author, under the standard Dramatists' Guild contract she was also entitled to royalties. In 1931 she returned to the house in *The Constant Sinner.*

In the 1930s, John Golden offered Rachel Crothers's *When Ladies Meet* (1932), a mildly risqué contemplation of a woman's affair with a married man. The Theatre Guild produced two prestigious dramas—Maxwell Anderson's *Both Your Houses*

(1933), a Pulitzer-winning political play focusing on Congress, and John Wexley's *They Shall Not Die* (1934), which was inspired by the story of the Scottsboro boys and was selected as a best play by critic Burns Mantle. Both were critical successes rather than box-office hits.

After the Royale's two-year interlude as a radio studio, it housed several long-running hits. Cole Porter's *Du Barry Was a Lady* (1940) moved from the 46th Street to the Royale and featured Gypsy Rose Lee, Bert Lahr, and Betty Grable. Ethel Barrymore appeared, in what some considered to be her greatest role, as the teacher in Emlyn Williams's semiautobio-

In John Osborne's The Entertainer *(1958), Laurence Olivier gave life to Archie Rice, a fifth-rate music hall song-and-dance man. Despairing and down on his luck, Archie fronts as a comedian for a show featuring nude chorus girls in a seaside backwater. This role was far from Olivier's usual establishment roles, but Osborne has said that Olivier captured the defeated Archie because Olivier felt himself "a deeply hollow man" who understood Archie's feelings of inadequacy. It was a tour de force for Olivier, who mastered the music-hall patter and delivered routines that gradually became less comic and more pathetic.*

The Night of the Iguana *(1961).*
Bette Davis was back on Broadway in
this Tennessee Williams play set in
Mexico. As Maxine Faulk, she played a
frowsy, lusty hotel keeper who has her
talons trained on Patrick O'Neal,
the defrocked Reverend Laurence
Shannon, an alcoholic and a predator
of young women. This physical
shoving match over the cocktail cart
between Shannon and Faulk matches
the emotional shoving match that the
two engage in from the start of the
action. Her designs on him are as
blatant as his need to escape her
clutches. Inadvertently stoking the
tension, Margaret Leighton played a
spinster gentlewoman artist whose
sympathetic connection to Shannon
sparks Maxine's jealousy.

graphical *The Corn Is Green* (1941), another production that
had transferred to the Royale. John Golden presented Paul
Muni in a revival of Elmer Rice's *Counsellor-At-Law* (1942), one
of three Rice plays to run at the theater in the 1940s—the oth-
ers were *Flight to the West* (1941) with Paul Henried and Betty
Field, and *A New Life* (1943) with Betty Field and John Ireland.
Additional notable productions were Mae West in *Catherine
Was Great* (1944), produced by Mike Todd; *The Glass Menagerie*
(1946), which transferred from the Playhouse; and Moss Hart's
Light Up the Sky (1948). During this period, John Gielgud
appeared in four shows at the Royale: *The Importance of Being
Earnest* (1947) with Margaret Rutherford, Pamela Brown, and
Robert Flemyng; *Love for Love* (1947) with Cyril Ritchard and
Sebastian Cabot; *Medea* (1947) with Judith Anderson; and *The
Lady's Not for Burning* (1950) with Pamela Brown and Richard
Burton.

OPPOSITE:
The Subject Was Roses *(1964),*
publicity photograph featuring Jack
Albertson (left), Irene Daily, and
Martin Sheen. The successful,
award-winning play by Frank D.
Gilroy focuses on the Cleary family,
who welcome their son, Timmy,
home after the war. Martin Sheen as
Timmy is at the center of the triangle
between his mother (Daily) and father
(Albertson). Although he loves both
his parents, he is powerless to make
their unhappy marriage work, and
his long absence because of the war
has given him a realistic perspective
on the family discord. The roses are
a reference to his grandfather's
custom of bestowing red roses on his
mother for her birthday—a gentle,
thoughtful practice that his father
has not continued. Its absence is a
symbol for what's missing in his
parents' marriage.

Over the next thirty years, the Royale hosted plays by writers ranging from Tennessee Williams to Neil Simon to Thornton Wilder. Some of the more successful runs include: *The Madwoman of Chaillot* (1949); *The Boy Friend* (1954), which introduced Julie Andrews to Broadway; *The Matchmaker* (1955) with Ruth Gordon; *The Night of the Iguana* (1961), in which Bette Davis played Maxine Faulk, "a rapacious and sloppily dressed Gorgon"; *The Subject Was Roses* (1964); *Cactus Flower* (1965); *The Man in the Glass Booth* (1968); and *Grease* (1972), which for a while earned the distinction of being Broadway's longest-running musical.

Not everything was a hit, although several unsuccessful productions at least featured interesting casts. *Nina* (1951) starred David Niven and Gloria Swanson, who was coming off a successful return to the screen as Norma Desmond in *Sunset Boulevard*; *The Immoralist* (1954) starred Geraldine Page, Louis Jourdan, and James Dean; and *From the Second City* (1961) provided Barbara Harris and Alan Arkin their Broadway debuts.

During the 1980s and 1990s, the Royale continued to feature a mix of plays and musicals. A return engagement of *Whose Life Is It Anyway?* (1980) saw the paralyzed protagonist's role switched from a man (Tom Conti) to a woman (Mary Tyler Moore). Directed and cochoreographed by Tommy Tune, *A Day in Hollywood/A Night in the Ukraine* (1980), which had moved from the Golden, was a zany spoof of the Marx Brothers' antics. Andrew Lloyd Webber's *Joseph and the Amazing Technicolor Dreamcoat* transferred from Off Broadway in 1982, and, in 1985, Lloyd Webber returned with *Song and Dance*, featuring a

OPPOSITE:
An Inspector Calls *(1994). The dynamic partnership of director Stephen Daldry and set designer Ian MacNeil breathed new life into J. B. Priestley's somewhat preachy mystery with its original claustrophobic one-set design. As the play begins, the Birling family is celebrating the engagement of their daughter Sheila to Gerald Croft when a mysterious inspector arrives to ask the family about a young woman who has committed suicide. The subsequent questioning reveals that each member of the family has been involved with the young woman and may have contributed to her sad end. Daldry and MacNeil updated the setting to World War II and built an almost doll's house version of a Victorian mansion on stilts set against a changing sky that reflected the moodiness of the piece. The mansion opened to reveal a cramped drawing room space, and much of the action and interaction with the inspector takes place outside the home. The house even self-destructs at the end with the crumbling of the family's honor; it tilts forward, spilling furniture and china onto the stage. The set was truly one of the stars, along with Philip Bosco, Rosemary Harris, and Jane Adams, who won a Tony Award as Best Featured Actress in a play.*

Song and Dance *(1985). In London, Andrew Lloyd Webber's* Song and Dance *featured two unrelated segments that were presented in concert. The first act, "Tell Me on a Sunday," was a song cycle about an English girl and her American lovers, and the second act was a dance piece set to "Variations on a Theme of Paganini." When the production crossed the Atlantic, the show was revised to integrate the two segments into a whole. In Act One, Bernadette Peters was the "Song" in a one-person star turn. She played Emma, an English designer, who comes to the United States to find success. In Act II, the "Dance" segment, Peter Martins, the codirector of the New York City Ballet, choreographed a piece that revolved around Bernadette as Emma and her male friends, including one played by Christopher D'Amboise. While the reviews were mixed, Peters took home her first Tony Award.*

Tony-winning performance by Bernadette Peters. The farce *Lend Me a Tenor* (1989), with a gifted ensemble of performers that included Philip Bosco, Victor Garber, and Tovah Feldshuh, struck a chord with audiences; Herb Gardner's *Conversations with My Father* (1992) starring Judd Hirsch got people talking; and the Shubert-coproduced *An Inspector Calls* (1994), which reimagined J. B. Priestley's old melodrama in a visually exciting way, had a Tony-winning run. In 1998, producers Sean Connery, David Pugh, and Joan Cullman brought Yasmina Reza's *Art* to the Royale, where it won the Tony Award for Best Play.

The Royale Theatre is located at 242 West 45th Street.

INTERLUDE

Herbert J. Krapp and the Architecture of Theaters

Architect of some thirty legitimate theaters and numerous other buildings for the Shuberts, Herbert J. Krapp played a key role in the growth and development of Shubert real-estate operations from 1916 until his retirement in the late 1960s. Born in New York City in 1887, Krapp received his professional training at the hands of noted designers Henry Herts and Hugh Tallant, whose staff he joined in 1903, and through attendance at drafting and technical courses at Peter Cooper Union. Early in his career, he often sought guidance and freelance work from other theater specialists, gaining a broad and thorough knowledge of the intricate mechanics of theater design in such areas as acoustics, stage-house construction, auditorium layout, entrance and egress planning, and fire prevention and safety.

During his tenure in the Herts and Tallant office, Krapp prepared working drawings of the Lyceum, New Amsterdam, Liberty, Gaiety (demolished), Folies-Bergère (later the Helen Hayes, demolished), and Longacre Theatres, all in Times Square, and the Brooklyn Academy of Music. When Herts and Tallant dissolved their partnership in 1911, Krapp was elevated to the role of associate architect in the reorganized firm. It was in this capacity that he came to the notice of the Shuberts in 1912, while overseeing the construction of the Herts-designed Shubert and Booth Theatres. The prospect of future architectural commissions from the Shuberts made it possible for Krapp to break with the difficult Herts and establish his own practice in 1916.

For the Shuberts, Krapp designed the Morosco and Bijou Theatres in 1916 (both demolished), the Plymouth and Broadhurst Theatres in 1917, and the Central Theatre in 1918 (demolished), all in New York City, and in Philadelphia, the Shubert Theatre and Office Building (now the Merriam Performing Arts Center) in 1918. The same period saw his rebuilding of the auditoriums of the Nora Bayes Roof Theatre (demolished), the Century Roof Theatre (demolished), and the Little Theatre (now the Helen Hayes). Simplified versions of the theaters he worked on while in the Herts office, Krapp's structures are often spartan in their exterior treatment and frugal with lobby space and other public amenities. They are also models of efficient and flexible playhouse design, ideally suited for the presentation of plays and musicals, factors that account for their continued viability and sought-after status three-quarters of a century after their construction.

In the years following World War I, Krapp and the Shuberts embarked upon a major building campaign, completing Broadway's Ambassador, Ritz (now the Walter Kerr), Jolson (demolished), and 49th Street (demolished) Theatres in 1921, the Imperial Theatre and an interior remodeling of the Winter Garden in 1923, the Forrest Hotel and Theatre (now the Eugene O'Neill) in 1925, and the Ethel Barrymore Theatre in 1928. During the same period outside of New York, Krapp designed the Shubert and Cox Theatres in Cincinnati (1921), the Shubert-Garrick Theatre in Washington, D.C. (1922), the Cass Theatre in Detroit (1925), and Philadelphia's New Forrest Theatre (1928). Among the five theaters, only the New Forrest remains.

In 1924, due to a joint booking agreement between the Shuberts and builder Irwin S. Chanin, Krapp designed the 46th Street Theatre (now the Richard Rodgers) for the Chanin interests. This

Herbert J. Krapp, portrait, 1905. In 1903, Krapp began a two-year apprenticeship with the architectural firm of Herts and Tallant, where he was involved in the company's designs for the New Amsterdam and Lyceum Theatres in New York City. He supplemented his apprenticeship with evening courses in architectural drawing and other subjects at Cooper Union. From 1905 until 1908, when he rejoined Herts and Tallant, he worked for other architects.

was quickly followed by the Biltmore Theatre in 1925, the Mansfield Theatre (now the Brooks Atkinson) in 1926, and in 1927, a three-theater complex that is now the Majestic, Royale, and Golden. For independent producers, Krapp undertook the Waldorf Theatre in 1926 (demolished), the Alvin (now the Neil Simon) in 1927, and Hammerstein's (now the Ed Sullivan) Theatre in 1928, as well as three movie houses in Queens. In contrast to his earlier works, these theaters display a markedly greater concern with exterior architectural treatment, ranging from the English Georgian and French Neoclassical styles to the more exotic Spanish Renaissance and French Gothic.

Along with his many playhouses, Herbert Krapp did nontheatrical projects for the Shuberts, including the 1927 Sardi Building (234 West 44th Street) with offices for the Shubert Organization and a rooftop penthouse for J. J. Shubert; the

Herbert J. Krapp standing across from the Winter Garden Theatre, October 29, 1948. Although the Shuberts were not building any new theaters at this time, Krapp was still their house architect and he continued to oversee renovations on all Shubert houses.

1,000-room Hotel Edison, built in 1929–30; and numerous storefronts, restaurants, apartment buildings, and parking garages throughout the Broadway district.

Once the Wall Street crash brought an end to the 1920s building boom, Krapp ceased designing theaters but continued to oversee the maintenance and upkeep of the Shubert real-estate holdings. He supervised numerous remodelings and alterations on Shubert venues throughout the country, and, when repairs were called for, he often forged the new fittings in his own shop. An inveterate creator, he also produced designs for furniture, fabrics and drapery, silver and flatware patterns, even his own sailboat. A design for a garden-hose coupling device he patented in the 1940s was later purchased by the Air Force and modified for aircraft in flight refueling. Following the death of J. J. Shubert in 1963, Krapp severed his connection with the Shubert Organization and retired to Florida. He died in 1973.

Text by William Morrison

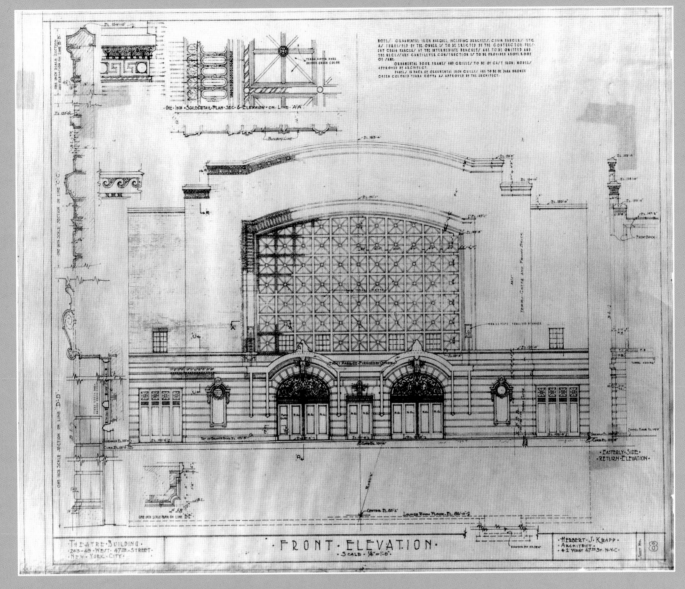

ABOVE:

Ethel Barrymore Theatre, rendering of exterior (1928). The Barrymore was the last playhouse that the Shubert brothers would build in New York City. Its exterior is unlike any of Krapp's other projects. The architect's design was inspired by a Roman bath and featured a single large grillwork screen, originally backlit, over an elaborate wrought-iron canopy. Krapp was a meticulous draftsman, and this pencil sketch drawn on tissue is an artwork in itself.

RIGHT:

Lyceum Theatre, design for proscenium arch (1903). One of the first theater projects that Krapp worked on when he apprenticed for Herts and Tallant was the Lyceum, which the architects were building on 45th Street for producer Daniel Frohman. Frohman wanted an intimate, but grand, house in the European Beaux Arts style. The elaborate proscenium is crowned by a sculpture of Pallas Athena, Goddess of Wisdom, surrounded by the figures of Music and Drama. It is almost certain that Krapp, at this early stage in his career, acted only as draftsman, transferring Henry Herts's design to paper, and had no real input in the design itself.

OPPOSITE:

Royale Theatre, rendering of interior: longitudinal section showing the proscenium, orchestra, boxes, balcony, and the mural over the balcony (1926).

The 47th, 48th, and 49th Street Theaters

After World War I, the Shuberts entered into a period of rapid expansion. Among their future plans was the construction of a new group of theaters on 48th and 49th Streets. In all, nine theaters were planned for this new "theater district," but only four were actually built: the Ritz (now the Walter Kerr), the Forrest (now the Eugene O'Neill), the 49th Street (demolished), and the Ambassador—the only one that still runs under the Shubert aegis.

The Shuberts leased the land at 215–23 West 49th Street in 1919 and began the process of clearing the property for a new venue. Construction began in the latter part of 1920 and was completed early the following winter. The plot of land for the Ambassador required that the auditorium be placed diagonally on its lot. This, combined with the relatively small acreage of the site, resulted in a lack of stage-wing space in the finished auditorium. The exterior of the building is simple, with little decoration other than some brick patterning. Most distinctive is the rounded corner on the entrance side that rises slightly higher than the rest of the facade.

OPPOSITE:
Ambassador Theatre, detail of dome and chandelier

RIGHT:
Ornamental detail, mezzanine wall

OVERLEAF, LEFT:
View of mezzanine and boxes from house right

OVERLEAF, RIGHT:
View of orchestra from house right

Blossom Time *(1921). One of the biggest hits ever to play the Ambassador and one of the Shubert brothers' biggest successes,* Blossom Time *was the fictional biography of composer Franz Schubert and his unrequited love for Mitzi Kranz. The operetta was also one of the longest-running shows in New York during the 1920s. Within a few months of* Blossom Time's *Broadway opening, the Shuberts sent out four road companies of the show, and in one form or another the musical toured for years.*

The interior spaces are more elaborate. Architect Herbert Krapp employed the Adam style for the plasterwork decorating the walls, ceiling, boxes, doorways, and arches. Cameo figures, swags, and circular patterns abound throughout the space, which contains a single balcony divided into two tiers. This design motif was a favorite of Krapp's—his interior for the now-demolished Cox Theatre in Cincinnati was a twin of the Ambassador's.

The playhouse opened on February 11, 1921, with *The Rose Girl*, a musical comedy produced by Lee Shubert that managed to eke out a run of 99 performances. *Blossom Time*, one of this theater's greatest hits, and one of the most successful Shubert operettas, opened on September 28, 1921. With music by Sigmund Romberg based on the work of Franz Schubert, and a book by Dorothy Donnelly, the production was a fictionalized account of Schubert's life. The show ran for 592 performances, toured around the world for many years, and played return engagements at the Ambassador in 1931 and 1943.

Musical comedies and operettas largely enjoyed the most success at this venue during the 1920s. These included such shows as *The Lady in Ermine* (1922) starring Walter Woolf King, *Queen High* (1926) starring Charlie Ruggles and Luella Gear,

and *Angela* (1928) starring Jeanette MacDonald. A few dramas from this period do, however, deserve mention. Popular playwright Owen Davis's adaptation of F. Scott Fitzgerald's *The Great Gatsby* achieved some success in 1926, as did a crime melodrama called *The Racket* (1927) with Edward G. Robinson. One of the most prestigious shows in the Ambassador's history, Leo Tolstoy's *Redemption* (1928), directed by Max Reinhardt, ran for a mere 20 performances.

The Great Depression hit the Ambassador hard. In the ensuing decade, the theater had few genuine hits. Ayn Rand's *Night*

Ambassador Theatre, exterior, early 1950s. After World War II the rapidly expanding television industry, which was centered in New York, desperately sought studio space from which to broadcast and film programming. Broadway theaters, with their commodious stages and backstage areas, offered a quick and ready solution—one that also appealed to many theater owners since legitimate theatrical production was on the wane and their venues could sometimes sit empty for months at a time. Between 1950 and 1956, the Shuberts leased the Ambassador, one of their more problematic theaters, to the Dumont Television Network.

Me and Bessie (1975), Linda Hopkins as Bessie Smith with musicians. Hopkins's tour-de-force performance singing the songs and narrating the tragic life of blues singer Bessie Smith made this small-scale revue popular with critics and audiences alike.

OPPOSITE:
The Straw Hat Revue (1939), Imogene Coca. This amalgam of comedy, song, and dance had its beginnings as an entertainment presented at Camp Tamiment in Bushkill, Pennsylvania, during the summer of 1939. Harry Kaufman, an assistant to Lee Shubert, had seen the show there and thought a Broadway transfer would be successful. Aside from the inimitable Coca, the revue featured other up-and-coming talents such as Danny Kaye and Jerome Robbins.

Eubie! *(1978), composer Eubie Blake onstage with the show's cast. This revue celebrated Blake's career through a sparkling evening of song and dance. Because of the show, the great jazz composer, then in his nineties, and his music enjoyed a new vogue around the world.*

of January 16 (1935) was a courtroom potboiler in which the audience became the jury that would each night decide the outcome of a trial. In 1939, Danny Kaye made his Broadway debut in a musical comedy called *The Straw Hat Revue,* which also starred Imogene Coca, Alfred Drake, and a new dancer named Jerome Robbins.

From 1936 through 1945, a few live attractions played the house, but the Ambassador served primarily as a venue for radio broadcasts and motion-picture exhibition. From 1945 to 1950, the theater was used exclusively for film exhibition, and, from 1950 to 1956, the Shuberts leased the Ambassador to the fledgling Dumont Television Network.

In 1956, J. J. Shubert (Lee had died three years earlier) decided to reclaim the Ambassador for legitimate theater use. The contract required the Dumont people to restore the house to the same condition it was in when they originally took up residency. Although Dumont maintained that they had fulfilled the terms of their lease agreement, the repairs they made did not satisfy J. J. Upset by the state in which Dumont had left the building, he vowed never to lease out another theater unless it was for the sole purpose of live production. He wrote to his son John: "These people who take the theatres for the purpose of television and that kind of things [*sic*] destroy the theatre, and it must not happen again under any circumstances. There are not to be any more leasing of our theatres on the basis of prominent names. Anybody leasing our theatres will have to put up a suitable bond to take care of restoring the theatre at the expiration of their lease.

That is what I insist upon doing in the future, and I hope you will carry our [*sic*] this same procedure."

In any case, J. J. refurbished the Ambassador to his liking and reopened it for legitimate stage production in October 1956, with the moderately popular drama *The Loud Red Patrick* starring Arthur Kennedy and David Wayne. For the next ten years, however, the theater had only a few successes: Lawrence and Lee's *The Gang's All Here* (1959) with E. G. Marshall, Melvyn Douglas, and Arthur Hill; *A Passage to India* (1962) with Gladys Cooper and Donald Moffat; *Calculated Risk* (1962) starring Joseph Cotten; *Absence of a Cello* (1964) with Ruth White and Charles Grodin; and *The Lion in Winter* (1966) with Robert Preston, Rosemary Harris, and Christopher Walken.

In 1967, the Ambassador housed the biggest hit it had seen in many years: *You Know I Can't Hear You When the Water's Running.* Composed of four one-acts, the show starred George Grizzard, Eileen Heckart, Martin Balsam, and Melinda Dillon. Aside from the Tom Jones and Harvey Schmidt musical *Celebration* (1969), a revival of *The Boy Friend* (1970) starring Judy Carne and Sandy Duncan, and Paul Sills's *The Story Theater* (1970) starring Melinda Dillon, Paul Sand, and Valerie Harper, the theater fared poorly in the late 1960s and early 1970s. During most of 1973 and 1974 it was dark.

Late in 1974, Jim Dale shone in a revival of Molière's *Scapino*, and in 1976 Linda Hopkins triumphed in *Me and Bessie.* After *Godspell* (1977) and *Miss Margarida's Way* (1977) found favor with audiences Off Broadway, they enjoyed runs at this venue on Broadway. *Eubie!* (1978*)*, a musical tribute to Eubie Blake, rekindled interest in the composer and helped establish Gregory Hines as a star.

The 1980s and 1990s were also a mixed bag for the Ambassador. The modest hits that did play here were composed of return engagements and revivals: *Your Arms Too Short to Box with God* (1980), *A View from the Bridge* (1983) starring Tony Lo Bianco, *Dreamgirls* (1987) starring Lillias White, *Ain't Misbehavin'* (1988), and *You're a Good Man Charlie Brown* (1999), for which Roger Bart and Kristin Chenoweth won Tonys. The Ambassador's most significant hit during this period was the dance/funk sensation *Bring in 'Da Noise, Bring in 'Da Funk* (1996). It ran for nearly three years after transferring from a successful Off Broadway run at the Public Theater.

The Ambassador Theatre is located at 215 West 49th Street.

Bring in 'Da Noise, Bring in 'Da Funk *(1996), starring Savion Glover. George C. Wolfe directed this musical revue, which he conceived with choreographer and star Savion Glover at the Public Theater in the fall of 1995. The show, which examined the evolution of tap and hip-hop through the lens of the African-American experience, sold out its initial run and transferred to the Ambassador the following spring. Glover's virtuosic mastery of tap won him a Tony Award for best choreography that year, while Wolfe's deft handling of the material netted him a Best Director Tony.*

Barrymore Theatre

The idea of naming a theater after a performer is certainly not a new one, and Lee and J. J. Shubert embraced the practice. Between 1908 and 1928, they built five New York City theaters named for performers affiliated with them: Maxine Elliott's Theatre (1908), Nazimova's 39th Street Theatre (1910), Weber and Fields's New Music Hall (1913), Jolson's 59th Street Theatre (1921), and the Ethel Barrymore Theatre (1928). Of this group, only the Barrymore survives.

When Ethel Barrymore signed with the Shuberts in 1928, she was already forty-nine years old. A member of the renowned Barrymore dynasty, she had scored her initial New York stage success while under the management of producer Charles Frohman in the early twentieth century. The show that had signaled the arrival of this new star on Broadway was Frohman's *Captain Jinks of the Horse Marines* (1901). Ethel Barrymore's tremendous popularity in New York and London society established her as a household name in the United States and England.

Barrymore's professional devotion to Frohman ended with the producer's death on the *Lusitania* in 1915. Subsequently, she

OPPOSITE:
Exterior of the Barrymore, 1931. The two-story terra-cotta grillwork that dominates the theater's facade is perhaps architect Herbert Krapp's most distinctive Shubert exterior. The vertical marquee seen in the center of the photograph is a design submitted by Strauss & Co. (now Artcraft Strauss) for new signage for the Barrymore. There is no evidence that the marquee as pictured was ever erected. (See also page 205.)

Ethel Barrymore, c. 1930. Often referred to at the time as "the First Lady of the American Theater," Barrymore was already forty-nine years old and had enjoyed international acclaim when the Shuberts decided to build a playhouse in her honor. Her tenure under Shubert management was, however, fairly short-lived. She would appear at her theater in only four productions, none of them particularly successful.

worked with Frohman's successors until 1928, when playwright Zoë Akins told Barrymore that the Shuberts wanted to build a theater and name it after the actress. They also had a play for her, called *The Kingdom of God*, which Barrymore loved, and so she decided to sign with the brothers.

After demolishing the existing buildings on the 47th Street site chosen for the new playhouse, the Shuberts once again selected Herbert Krapp to design the building. The Barrymore was to be the last theater Lee and J. J. would build. Of all the architect's projects, this venue's exterior is perhaps his most distinctive. It features a large two-story terra-cotta grillwork screen, supposedly modeled on the design of public baths in Rome. At night, the backlit grill is especially impressive. Two ornate bronze and glass canopies (not extant) framed the entrance. Inside, the decor combines Elizabethan, Mediterranean, and Adamesque styles. The most elaborate interior element are the boxes, which feature a sunburst pattern expressed by a series of concentric circles over a columned portico. The curved ceiling encompasses a thirty-six-foot dome from which hangs a chandelier of cut glass.

Chandelier detail as seen from directly below

Opening night, December 20, 1928, was a gala affair replete with celebrities anxious to see the new home of the "First Lady of the American Theater." The *New York Times* reported that "[w]hen Miss Barrymore made her first entrance on the stage she was warmly received and was compelled to bow several times before she was allowed to speak her lines. At the conclusion of the performance the star received seven curtain calls. After acknowledging them, she made a short speech. 'I want to thank Lee Shubert,' she said, 'for the courage of his convictions in building this theater. Also for allowing me to act the play as I wanted to.'" The newspaper went on to say that the new theater was a "striking addition to the list of Broadway houses."

Detail of sconce, house right

In *The Kingdom of God*, the star played a nun in three different stages of life, successfully aging from a novice to a mother superior. The play ran for 93 performances and turned a profit. In April another Barrymore vehicle, *The Love Duel*, opened, but it managed only 88 performances and lost money. A successful national tour of the two plays followed. In fact, in November 1929, Lee Shubert announced that Barrymore would be extending the tour until June 1930, thereby postponing her next planned production, *Scarlet Sister Mary*. The Shuberts' newspaper, *The New York Review*, reported that "the success of Miss Barrymore's tour has exceeded anything of the kind in recent years. . . . Miss Barrymore, who has always taken her successful New York productions on extensive road tours, recognizes her

OPPOSITE:
View of orchestra and boxes from house left

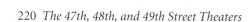

Facade detail

OPPOSITE, ABOVE:
Death Takes a Holiday (1929),
Philip Merivale (center) and cast.
Despite the stock market crash that
had occurred only two months before
the show's opening, Death Takes a
Holiday enjoyed a healthy run of
180 performances. The show's basic
premise—Death disguised as a
mysterious and seductive mortal
visits a human so as to summon him
to the great beyond—has, in fact,
proved consistently intriguing to
writers and audiences alike. Several
variations of the theme preceded Lee
Shubert's Broadway production, and
many followed, as well—the most
recent being the 1998 motion picture
Meet Joe Black starring Brad Pitt
and Anthony Hopkins.

OPPOSITE, BELOW LEFT:
Gay Divorce (1932), Fred Astaire
as Guy dancing with Claire Booth
as Mimi. Fred Astaire appearing
for the first time on Broadway
without his sister and longtime
dancing partner, Adele, took some
getting used to, but glorious Cole
Porter numbers like "Night and
Day" helped audiences make the
transition. The show ran for 232
performances and marked Astaire's
last appearance on Broadway before
moving on to Hollywood stardom.

OPPOSITE, BELOW RIGHT:
Design for Living (1933), Noël
Coward (top left) as Leo and
Alfred Lunt as Otto, peering at Lynn
Fontanne as Gilda. Coward wrote
this daring ménage-à-trois comedy
expressly for himself and his friends
Lunt and Fontanne. Scheduled for a
limited run, the demand for tickets
began months before an actual
theater was booked, and the show
was sold out for most of its
135-performance run.

RIGHT:
A Raisin in the Sun (1959),
Claudia McNeil as Lena Younger
and Sidney Poitier as her son
Walter Lee Younger. Lorraine
Hansberry's poignant play about an
African-American family's attempt
to raise themselves from poverty
won the Drama Critics' Circle Award
for the Best Play of 1959. In addition
to McNeil and Poitier, the stellar
cast included Ruby Dee, Diana
Sands, and Lou Gossett.

responsibility to the road and is anxious that her present two plays be seen in every important city of the United States and Canada." *Scarlet Sister Mary* finally opened on November 25, 1930. The show, which called for the actress to don blackface, was a flop and ran only 23 performances. It did, however, mark the stage debut of Barrymore's daughter, Ethel Barrymore Colt.

In October 1931, the Shubert Theatre Corporation went into receivership. The following month, Barrymore once again took the stage of her theater in a revival of *The School for Scandal*, but this production, too, ran for only 23 performances, although it made a profit on its subsequent tour. In 1932, the actress ended her association with the Shuberts. Ethel Barrymore would appear in her theater only one more time, in an unsuccessful play called *An International Incident* (1940). The biggest triumph of her later years, if not of her entire career—the role of schoolmarm Miss Moffat in *The Corn Is Green* (1940)—would ironically take place at another theater: the National.

If Broadway success eluded Ethel Barrymore during her brief tenure with the Shuberts, she could have been proud of several hits that did prosper at her namesake theater. These include: *Death Takes a Holiday* (1929); Cole Porter's *Gay Divorce* (1932) starring Fred Astaire and featuring the now-classic song "Night and Day"; two Noël Coward shows starring Alfred Lunt and Lynn Fontanne, *Design for Living* (1933) and *Point Valaine* (1935); Emlyn Williams's *Night Must Fall* (1936); Clare Boothe Luce's *The Women* (1936); *Key Largo* (1939) starring Paul Muni, Uta Hagen, and José Ferrer; *Pal Joey* (1940) starring Gene Kelly; Tennessee Williams's *A Streetcar Named Desire* (1947; revived in 1992 with Alec Baldwin and Jessica Lange); *The Fourposter*

Pal Joey (1940), starring Vivienne Segal as Vera Simpson and Gene Kelly as Joey Evans. This controversial Rodgers and Hart musical about a charming but self-centered and manipulative gigolo divided the critics, but Gene Kelly's performance, along with musical numbers like "I Could Write a Book," "Bewitched, Bothered and Bewildered," and "Zip," made the show a hit anyway.

OVERLEAF, LEFT AND RIGHT:
A Streetcar Named Desire (1947), director Elia Kazan visiting star Jessica Tandy backstage. One of the most compelling plays of the twentieth century, A Streetcar Named Desire, Tennessee Williams's follow-up to his wildly successful The Glass Menagerie, won the Pulitzer Prize in 1948. Elia Kazan, who earlier had been an actor with the Group Theatre, was America's preeminent theatrical director during the 1940s and 1950s. He helped found the Actors Studio in the same year that he directed this play. Equally adept in theater and film, Kazan would go on to helm the film version of Streetcar in 1951, to much acclaim.

A Streetcar Named Desire (1947), Marlon Brando as Stanley Kowalski and Jessica Tandy as Blanche DuBois. The smoldering sexuality and hyper-masculine stance that Brando brought to this role would mark this as one of his signature performances. He reprised the role in the 1951 motion picture. Jessica Tandy's indelible portrait of the southern belle slowly losing her grip on reality had a great impact on critics and audiences, and she won a 1948 Tony Award for Best Actress in a Play.

Indiscretions (1995),
Roger Rees as George,
Kathleen Turner (center)
as Yvonne, and Eileen Atkins
as Leonie. The Shubert
Organization imported this
new adaptation of Jean
Cocteau's Les Parents
Terribles from London's
Royal National Theatre.
Aside from its dynamic cast,
which also included Jude
Law and Cynthia Nixon, the
show boasted a distinctive
design—including this
spiral staircase—by Stephen
Brimson Lewis.

BELOW:
Lettice & Lovage (1990),
Maggie Smith (standing)
as Lettice Douffet and
Margaret Tyzack as Lotte
Schoen. Originally staged
on London's West End,
the Shubert Organization
brought Peter Shaffer's
comedy to New York
complete with its leading
ladies. Smith's star turn as
the flamboyant tour guide
prone to fantasy and
exaggeration was a
highlight of the 1989–90
theater season.

The Sisters Rosenzweig *(1993)*, *Madeline Kahn as Gorgeous Teitelbaum. Wendy Wasserstein's warm comedy about three sisters ran for 149 performances, beginning in October 1992 at the Mitzi Newhouse Theater under the auspices of Lincoln Center Theater, before transferring to Broadway in March 1993. Although the show featured a strong ensemble composed of Jane Alexander, Christine Estabrook, and Madeline Kahn, it was Kahn in her pink Chanel suit who stole the show.*

Amy's View *(1999), Judi Dench as Esme Allen. High expectations awaited Dame Judi Dench as the star of David Hare's* Amy's View*, a play about the difficult personal and professional life of a veteran stage actress. Dench certainly did not disappoint with her truly memorable performance, for which she won a Tony Award.*

(1951) starring Hume Cronyn and Jessica Tandy; *Tea and Sympathy* (1953); *Look Homeward, Angel* (1957) with Anthony Perkins; *A Raisin in the Sun* (1959) starring Sidney Poitier and Ruby Dee; *Wait Until Dark* (1966) with Lee Remick; David Mamet's *American Buffalo* (1977) starring Robert Duvall; August Wilson's *Joe Turner's Come and Gone* (1988); Peter Shaffer's *Lettice & Lovage* (1990); Wendy Wasserstein's *The Sisters Rosenzweig* (1993); *Indiscretions* (1995) featuring Kathleen Turner and Jude Law; and David Hare's *Amy's View* (1999) starring Dame Judi Dench.

The Barrymore Theatre is located at 243 West 47th Street.

SONG OF LOVE
THE MESSRS SHUBERT PRESENT
BLOSSOM TIME
A MUSICAL PLAY IN THREE ACTS

DANGER IN THE DARK
Lyric by AL DUBIN
Music by JIMMY McHUGH
MESSRS. SHUBERT in association with OLSEN & JOHNSON
Present a New Broadway Stage Production
STARRING
BOBBY CLARK
LUELLA GEAR · ABBOTT & COSTELLO
A New Parisian Revue
STREETS OF PARIS
and
JEAN SABLON
Music by JIMMY McHUGH and AL DUBIN

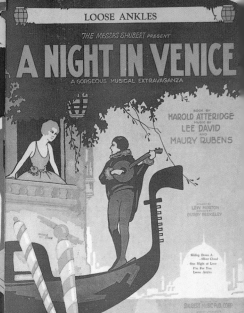

LOOSE ANKLES
THE MESSRS SHUBERT PRESENT
A NIGHT IN VENICE
A GORGEOUS MUSICAL EXTRAVAGANZA
BOOK BY
HAROLD ATTERIDGE
MUSIC BY
LEE DAVID
AND
MAURY RUBENS

OF THEE I SING

SAM HARRIS PRESENTS
OF·THEE·I·SING
A MUSICAL COMEDY
BOOK BY GEORGE KAUFMAN AND MORRIE RYSKIND
LYRICS BY IRA GERSHWIN
MUSIC BY GEORGE GERSHWIN

MICHAEL TODD'S
HOT MIKADO
with BILL ROBINSON
STAGED BY HASSARD SHORT

THERE IS NOTHIN' LIKE A DAME
RICHARD RODGERS & HAMMERSTEIN 2nd.   OSCAR
in association with
LELAND HAYWARD & JOSHUA LOGAN present
South Pacific
music by RICHARD RODGERS
lyrics by OSCAR HAMMERSTEIN 2nd.
book by OSCAR HAMMERSTEIN 2nd & JOSHUA LOGAN
adapted from "Tales of the South Pacific"
by JAMES A. MICHENER
directed by JOSHUA LOGAN

JUNE IS BUSTIN' OUT ALL OVER
THE THEATRE GUILD presents
CAROUSEL
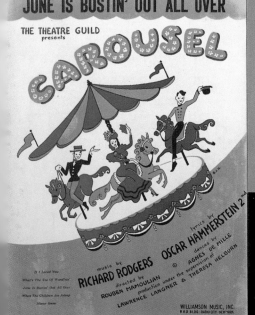
music by RICHARD RODGERS
lyrics by OSCAR HAMMERSTEIN 2nd
dances by AGNES DE MILLE
directed by ROUBEN MAMOULIAN

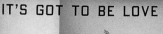

IT'S GOT TO BE LOVE
DWIGHT DEERE WIMAN PRESENTS

On Your toes
BOOK BY RODGERS AND HART AND GEORGE ABBOTT
LYRICS BY LORENZ HART   MUSIC BY RICHARD RODGERS

THERE CAN ONLY BE ONLY ONE FOR ME
THE MESSRS. SHUBERT PRESENT
NINA·ROSA
A New Musical Play
BY OTTO HARBACH
MUSIC BY SIGMUND ROMBERG
LYRICS BY IRVING CAESAR
ENTIRE PRODUCTION STAGED BY J.C. HUFFMAN

INTERLUDE

Sheet Music

The story of American popular music is inextricably bound to the Broadway stage. Not only were songs from Tin Pan Alley frequently interpolated into stage musicals and revues, but the Broadway shows themselves often featured numbers that became popular standards known throughout the country. The sheet music for these songs was the equivalent of the phonographic single record that would become popular during the 1940s and 1950s. Sold to promote a particular show or star, or to further popularize a hit song, they could be purchased not only in music stores, but in theater lobbies as well. Images of stars as well as scenes from shows were frequently featured on the covers. Design trends, too, were reflected in the artwork used on these musical mementos. Covers produced in the early decades of the twentieth century, for example, often showed a strong Art Nouveau or Art Deco influence.

The Shuberts themselves were involved in the sheet-music business. Through the Shubert Publishing Company and the Trebuhs (Shubert spelled backward) Publishing Company, they published much of the music that was featured in their many productions.

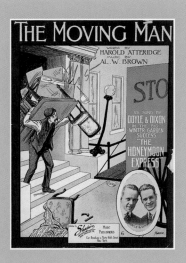

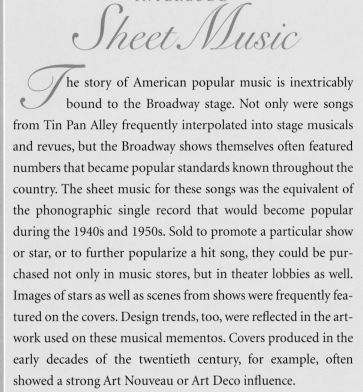

T he Cort Theatre was built by and named for John Cort (1862–1929), general manager of the Northwestern Theatrical Association, a theater circuit centered in Seattle with theaters scattered throughout the western United States and British Columbia. A fugitive from a vaudeville comedy team called Cort and Murphy, Cort moved from performing to management in the 1890s. An early member of the Theatrical Syndicate, he later joined the Shuberts and the Independents. The Shuberts acquired his theater on May 2, 1927.

The Cort is the only surviving, still active, legitimate theater designed by Thomas Lamb. Its classic exterior was inspired by the eighteenth-century French Petit Trianon at Versailles. The marble facade consists of four Corinthian columns. Architecture from the period of Louis XVI also inspired the interior. The lobby is constructed of Pavanozza marble with panels of Marie Antoinette plasterwork, while the metalwork of the box office is bronze with gold leaf and enamel relief. Tiffany Studios was responsible for the design and execution. The original color scheme of the auditorium was rose and gold with plasterwork in champagne and sienna, and a carpet of pale

OPPOSITE:
Interior of the Cort Theatre, from house left

Cort Theatre, at opening

Detail of ceiling cove

Detail of the house boxes, with gold inlay and cameo decorations

green Wilton. A Wurlitzer Hope–Jones "Unit Orchestra" organ was installed to serve as a one-man orchestra. The proscenium arch was constructed in perforated plaster treated with art glass that could be lit during performances; this arch still exists but is not operational today. In keeping with the stylistic treatment of the theater, a marble bust of Marie Antoinette rests in an alcove in the lobby. On opening night, the critics commented on the beauty of the theater, and one even noted that the ushers' costumes would not be out of place in the gardens of Versailles.

The Cort opened on December 20, 1912, with *Peg o' My Heart* starring Laurette Taylor and produced and directed by Oliver Morosco. Taylor's husband, J. Hartley Manners, wrote the play, which became an enormous hit and one of the longest-running shows of its day. The first show that John Cort produced himself at this theater was an operetta, *The Princess Pat* (1915), by the Irish-American composer Victor Herbert. It ran for 158 performances and was the first of only a handful of musicals to play the Cort. Of the eleven musicals that ran at the house, four were produced by John Cort in the venue's early years. It wasn't until 1974, when *The Magic Show* opened, that the Cort had a long-running musical (1,920 performances), a show remembered for Doug Henning's astounding magic. The three most recent musicals to play the Cort were *Sarafina* (1988), the story of South African students who create a show about Nelson Mandela; *Marlene* (1999) featuring Sian Phillips as Marlene Dietrich; and *Kat and the Kings* (1999), based on the rise and fall of a black South African doo-wop group.

For most of its life, the Cort has been home to plays, and since its opening production, as Mary Henderson notes in *The City and the Theatre*, it has been referred to as a "lucky" house. Roi Cooper Megrue had his first big hit, *Under Cover* (1914), at the Cort. Other early hits include two plays featuring Mr. and Mrs. Charles Coburn (the actress Ivah Wills)—*The Yellow Jacket* (1916) and *The Better 'Ole* (1918). In 1919, John Drinkwater's *Abraham Lincoln* was praised for Frank McGlynn's stunning performance as the fallen president.

In the 1920s, the Cort had many hits. George S. Kaufman and Marc Connelly's *Merton of the Movies* (1922) satirized country bumpkin Merton Gill, who goes to Hollywood seeking fame. The long-running comedy made a star of Glenn Hunter, who reprised his role on-screen in 1924. *The Blonde Sinner* (1926) with Enid Markey, *The Little Spitfire* (1926) with Sylvia Field, and *A Most Immoral Lady* (1928) with Alice Brady closed out the decade. The Cort also featured stars such as Ethel Barrymore and Henry Daniell in *The Second Mrs. Tanqueray* (1924), Judith Anderson in *Behold the Bridegroom* (1927), and

OPPOSITE:
Peg o' My Heart *(1912), flyer. Guthrie McClintic recounts how Lee Shubert inadvertently introduced Laurette Taylor to her husband, playwright J. Hartley Manners. Lee had seen Taylor performing in a melodrama in Kansas and was transfixed by her performance. He told her to come and see him when she was in New York. When she finally made it to New York, she had two children and desperately needed work but could not get past Lee's secretary. Furious, she created a scene just as J. Hartley Manners arrived for his appointment. He mentioned to Lee that there was a young woman in the reception area who had the right spirit for a role in* The Great John Ganton. *She got the part and later married the playwright, who wrote* Peg o' My Heart *for her. Taylor was an actress who was magical on the stage, and anyone who saw her never forgot her. Often better than the plays in which she appeared, she had one last triumph at the end of her career when she created the role of Amanda Wingfield in* The Glass Menagerie *(1945).*

ETHEL! — "PLEASE DON'T, IT'S SO HOT THIS MORNING!"

Katharine Hepburn in *These Days* (1928). This was her first appearance on stage under the name "Hepburn"; earlier that season, she had debuted as Katherine Burns in *Night Hostess* at the Martin Beck.

The decade of the 1930s was not a time for big hits, but the Cort featured short runs of interesting plays with celebrated performers. Jed Harris produced a notable *Uncle Vanya* (1930) with Lillian Gish, Osgood Perkins, and Walter Connelly; Ruth Gordon played in *The Three-Cornered Moon* (1933); and Laurence Olivier joined his wife Jill Esmond in *The Green Bay Tree* (1933). John Howard Lawson's *Gentlewoman* (1934) was

Katharine Hepburn in The Big Pond *(1928). She wrested the role of Barbara away from Lucile Nikolas, opened in Great Neck, New York, and then promptly was fired and replaced by the original leading lady. Hepburn then debuted on Broadway as one of the "other hostesses" in* Night Hostess *(1928), under the name Katherine Burns. Finally, in October 1928, she made her first actual appearance on a Broadway stage as Katharine Hepburn, in Arthur Hopkins's* These Days *at the Cort. She played a schoolgirl who spoke only a few lines. The show closed after eight performances.*

notable both for its extremely short run (12 performances) and its prestigious cast: Morris Carnovsky, Stella Adler, and Lloyd Nolan.

Many of the shows that played at the Cort through the 1940s were revivals of classics. The Theatre Guild presented *The Winter's Tale* in 1946, and in the same year Katharine Cornell presented *Antigone* and *Candida* in repertory with a company that included Wesley Addy, Sir Cedric Hardwicke, and Marlon Brando. The final production that year was a popular revival of *Lady Windermere's Fan* with Penelope Ward, Estelle Winwood, Henry Daniell, Cornelia Otis Skinner, and Cecil Beaton. In 1948, Eva Le Gallienne translated and appeared in repertory in two Ibsen plays, *Ghosts* and *Hedda Gabler*. Strindberg's *The Father* ran the following year with Raymond Massey, Mady Christians, and Grace Kelly in her Broadway debut.

The 1950s and 1960s continued the Cort's run as a "lucky" house. The Theatre Guild presented Katharine Hepburn and William Prince in *As You Like It* (1950), followed by *Saint Joan* (1951) with Uta Hagen. Other notable productions include: Pulitzer Prize winner *The Shrike* (1952) with José Ferrer; Darren McGavin and Geraldine Page in *The Rainmaker* (1954); *The Diary of Anne Frank* (1955); *Advise and Consent* (1960); *Purlie Victorious* (1961) with Ossie Davis and Ruby Dee; and *Sunday in New York* (1961) with Conrad Janis, Robert Redford, and Pat Stanley. The Cort's luck was occasionally better for the actors than for the productions themselves—*One Flew Over the Cuckoo's Nest* (1963) had a short run of only 82 performances but bolstered the careers of Kirk Douglas and Gene Wilder, and Jane Fonda made her stage debut here in *There Was a Little Girl* (1960), which logged only 16 performances.

In 1969, the Cort became the location for television's *The Merv Griffin Show*. It returned to legitimate production in 1972, and its biggest hit since then has been *The Magic Show* (1974). Still, the Cort continued to present many interesting, if not always successful plays with a variety of stars: Al Pacino in *Richard III* (1969); Geraldine Page as Zelda Fitzgerald in

Antigone (1946) with Katharine Cornell in the title role in Jean Anouilh's version of the classic tragedy. This modern-dress staging of Sophocles' drama played in Paris during the Nazi occupation, and Anouilh walked a fine line in depicting the despotic state versus the rights of the individual. The production received mostly negative reviews, and many critics felt the interpretation did not work. Even Miss Cornell did not fare well. Only the villain—Cedric Hardwicke as Creon—earned kudos. Actress/ manager of her own company, Cornell performed many classic roles, including Candida and Juliet. Called the "First Lady of the Theater," Cornell's most memorable role was as Elizabeth Barrett in The Barretts of Wimpole Street *(1931).*

The Shrike *(1952)*, José Ferrer, *Judith Evelyn. This was a banner year for Ferrer, who won Tony Awards for Best Actor in a Play and Best Director for his staging of three plays*—The Shrike, The Fourposter *and* Stalag 17. *The setting for* The Shrike *was a mental ward in a city hospital, to which Jim Downs (Ferrer) is taken after an unsuccessful suicide attempt. As the doctors extract information from Downs and his wife, Ann, from whom he is separated, Downs begins to feel trapped. He can never leave the hospital without his wife's consent, and she holds complete power over him.*

OPPOSITE, ABOVE:

Sarafina *(1988) was an unexpected musical hit from South Africa that featured a cast of 32 nonprofessional dancers, singers, and musicians who played students putting on a play about Nelson Mandela. The joyous Mbaqanga music and the fresh, young energetic cast made this musical, which dealt with serious issues such as apartheid and violence, uplifting.*

OPPOSITE, BELOW:

The Grapes of Wrath *(1990). The Steppenwolf Theatre Company dramatized John Steinbeck's novel about the Joad family's tribulations during the Depression and succeeded in bringing a major American literary work to the stage in much the same way that the Royal Shakespeare Company reworked Charles Dickens's* Nicholas Nickleby *for the stage. The production featured an ensemble of company members in key roles, including Gary Sinise as Tom Joad and Terry Kinney as Jim Casy, on a simple, almost stark set. The Joads' car was the only large-scale piece of scenery. Lois Smith played Ma Joad. Nominated for eight Tony Awards,* Grapes *took home Best Play and Best Director medallions for its coproducers, the Shubert Organization, Steppenwolf Theatre Company, Suntory International Corporation, and Jujamcyn Theaters.*

Tennessee Williams's *Clothes for a Summer Hotel* (1980); Glenda Jackson and Jessica Tandy in *Rose* (1981); and Zoe Caldwell and Judith Anderson in *Medea* (1982). In the 1990s, audiences' imaginations were captured by such shows as *The Grapes of Wrath* (1990); *Twilight, Los Angeles 1992* (1994); *The Heiress* (1995); *An American Daughter* (1997); *Freak* (1998); and *The Blue Room* (1998).

The Cort Theatre is located at 138 West 48th Street.

OPPOSITE:

The Heiress (1995). The timid, plain, and rich Catherine Sloper succumbs to Morris Townsend's blandishments, but her physician father shatters her self-esteem and any illusions she might have about Morris. Based on Henry James's Washington Square, this well-received revival of Ruth and Augustus Goetz's play brought together a wonderful ensemble that included Philip Bosco, Jon Tenney, and Tony Award winners Cherry Jones and Frances Sternhagen. This is the pivotal moment of the play, when Catherine (Cherry Jones) ascends the stairs and firmly shuts Morris out of her life. Catherine was first played on Broadway in 1947 by Wendy Hiller; Peggy Ashcroft played her in London, and Olivia de Havilland onscreen.

RIGHT:

The Blue Room (1998). One of the hottest tickets of the 1998–99 season was the David Hare adaptation of Arthur Schnitzler's La Ronde, and among the drawing cards were nudity and the opportunity to see Hollywood celebrity Nicole Kidman onstage. Kidman and Iain Glen each played five parts in the ten sexually charged vignettes, and it opened to good reviews. The Shubert Organization coproduced the Donmar Warehouse production with Scott Rudin, Robert Fox, Roger Berlind, and ABC.

The Longacre Theatre was designed by Henry B. Herts, architect of several Shubert theaters. Boasting a French Neo-classical-style exterior and a Beaux Arts–style interior, this two-balcony house with seating for 1,080 was named for Longacre Square (later Times Square), the district at the center of the horse and carriage trade. Producer/manager H. H. Frazee built the Longacre, but about a year after it opened in 1913, he ran into financial problems and effectively lost the theater. Ownership became complicated at that point. The Shuberts had an interest in the property from 1914, initially in partnership with L. Lawrence Weber, F. Ray Comstock, and Gilbert M. Anderson. The Longacre changed hands several times but in 1919 was sold to Astor Theatre Incorporated, a Shubert subsidiary, and remained under Shubert ownership from then on.

After a slow start, the Longacre featured several notable shows, such as A. H. Woods's *Kick In* (1914) starring John Barrymore and Katherine Harris. Also in 1914, Frazee had his first real hit with *A Pair of Sixes,* which he followed up with

Counterweight system

OPPOSITE:
Ornamentation on the ceiling of the Longacre Theatre

RIGHT:
Exterior. The Longacre Theatre had already had an opening production and was now awaiting its second offering, A Silver Wedding *(1913), which would have only a short run.*

OVERLEAF, ABOVE LEFT:
Detail of proscenium

OVERLEAF, ABOVE RIGHT:
Detail of ceiling ornamentation

OVERLEAF, BELOW:
Auditorium showing house right with balcony overhang

OVERLEAF, RIGHT:
View from house left showing ornamentation over the boxes and details of the proscenium (at far left)

Little Jessie James *(1923),*
sheet-music cover. L. Lawrence
Weber's musical hit starred
Nan Halperin as Jessie Jamieson
and featured Miriam Hopkins,
at the start of her stage and
film career, as Juliet.

James Montgomery's *Nothing But the Truth* (1916), starring William Collier. F. Ray Comstock, one of the investors in the Longacre and a producer of the Princess musicals, had a successful run with *Leave It to Jane* (1917), by Guy Bolton, P. G. Wodehouse, and Jerome Kern. In the 1920s, Ethel Barrymore made three appearances at the playhouse in *Rose Bernd*, *Romeo and Juliet,* and *Laughing Lady.* The other big hit of that era was George S. Kaufman's comedy *The Butter and Egg Man* (1925).

For the remainder of the 1920s and throughout the 1930s, with a few exceptions, the Longacre was home to a host of short runs of often unexceptional plays brightened by exceptional performers. In 1930, Jessica Tandy made her New York stage debut in *The Matriarch.* Other stars who graced the Longacre's stage during this period include Basil Rathbone, William Faversham, Joan and Richard Bennett, Sylvia Sidney, Miriam Hopkins, Thelma Ritter, Lillian Gish, Shirley Booth, Sybil Thorndike, and Fay Wray. An unknown actor, Clark Gable, played in *Hawk Island* (1929). The exceptions to the largely forgettable fare at the Longacre were the Group Theatre's productions of Clifford Odets's *Waiting for Lefty, Till the Day I Die,* and *Paradise Lost,* all in 1935. The cast for *Lefty* featured Odets, Elia Kazan, and Bobby Lewis, while that of *Paradise Lost* included Kazan, Stella Adler, Morris Carnovsky, and Sanford Meisner.

From 1943 to 1953, the Longacre was leased to WOR as a radio and television playhouse. In 1953, it reopened with a short-lived Dorothy Parker piece, *The Ladies of the Corridor*, with Edna Best, Betty Field, and Walter Matthau, as the up-and-down production history of the Longacre continued. Being a standard, or medium-size house, the theater was home mainly to plays and comedies of manners. Julie Harris appeared in the unsuccessful *Mademoiselle Colombe* (1954), with Robert Redford, and in *Little Moon of Alban* (1960), then triumphed as Joan of Arc in Anouilh's *The Lark* (1955) and as Emily Dickinson in *The Belle of Amherst* (1976). More star turns included Zero Mostel in *Rhinoceros* (1961), Ossie Davis in *Purlie Victorious* (1961, a transfer from the Cort), and Hal Holbrook in *Mark Twain Tonight* (1966). Other notable productions included *The Tender Trap* (1954); *The Pleasure of His Company* (1958); *A Case of Libel* (1963), starring Van Heflin and Sidney Blackmer; Lorraine Hansberry's *The Sign in Sidney Brustein's Window* (1964); Robert Anderson's *I Never Sang for My Father* (1968); Terrence McNally's *The Ritz* (1975); Harold Pinter's *No Man's Land* (1976) featuring John Gielgud and Ralph Richardson; and a revival of David Rabe's *The Basic Training of Pavlo Hummel* (1977) with Al Pacino. The two biggest hits to play the Longacre were the long-running, Tony Award–winning musical *Ain't*

Waiting for Lefty (1935) was a one-act play conceived to raise money for the radical New Theatre *magazine. The play moved to Broadway and was staged as a union meeting of cab drivers who were protesting working conditions and a corrupt union. At the meeting, the drivers sound a cry to strike! The vitality and rawness of the play introduced audiences to Clifford Odets and to the acting style of the Group Theatre whose impact on American stage and film acting still reverberates today. Among the ensemble cast, Elia Kazan is third from left.*

Jean Anouilh's The Lark
(1955), with Julie Harris
(center stage) as Joan of
Arc. Lillian Hellman
adapted Anouilh's play,
which had a successful
run and featured Boris
Karloff, Christopher
Plummer, Joseph
Wiseman, and Theodore
Bikel in pivotal roles.

OPPOSITE, ABOVE LEFT:
Children of a Lesser God
(1980). The Shubert
Organization coproduced
this Mark Medoff play
from the Mark Taper
Forum, Los Angeles. It
featured Phyllis Frelich as
Sarah Norman, deaf since
birth, and John Rubinstein
as James Leeds, her
teacher. Frelich herself was
the inspiration for the
main character, who does
not perceive her deafness as
a disability. The play and
the two featured actors
won Tony Awards.

OPPOSITE, ABOVE RIGHT:
No Man's Land (1976),
Sir Ralph Richardson (left)
and Sir John Gielgud. A
Harold Pinter play in two
parts, it confused the critics
with its enigmatic plot
but allowed audiences to
experience the verbal
parrying of these two
giants on stage. Gielgud
delighted in the role of the
seedy Spooner, which he
chose over that of Hirst
because it was unlike any
that he had played before.
His visual inspiration
for the part was W. H.
Auden but he based his
characterization of the role
on his older brother Lewis.
One critic referred to
Richardson and Gielgud
as the new Lunt and
Fontanne.

OPPOSITE, BELOW:
Ain't Misbehavin' (1978).
The lively revue's ensemble
cast kept the "joint
jumpin'" with their
colorful costumes, sassy
manners, and energetic
delivery. Ken Page was the
visual reincarnation of
Fats Waller, the composer/
pianist whose music was
the inspiration for the
show. Here, he is backed by
(left to right) Armelia
McQueen, Nell Carter,
whose insouciant song style
won her a Tony Award,
and Charlaine Woodard.
Andre de Shields was also
part of this talented group.

Rhinoceros (1961),
Eli Wallach (left) and
Zero Mostel. In Eugene
Ionesco's absurdist
comedy, Mostel plays
a character who
gradually turns into a
rhinoceros while Wallach
fights to remain human
and not to join the herd.

Medea (1994). Diana Rigg, in the monstrous title role of Euripides' tragedy, appears at the play's climax on the stunning metal set by Peter J. Davison, which is demolished just as Medea's entire world collapses around her. Rigg won a Tony Award for Best Actress, although some critics thought her performance too chilly. First presented by the Almeida Theatre Company in London, this modern translation by Alistair Elliot won kudos for its poetic language. Among the unforgettable past Broadway Medeas were Judith Anderson (1947) and Zoe Caldwell (1982).

Misbehavin' (1978), based on the music of Fats Waller, which ran for 1,604 performances, and the Tony Award–winning play *Children of a Lesser God* (1980), with 887 performances. Both of these shows were coproduced by the Shubert Organization.

The Longacre Theatre is located at 220 West 48th Street.

The Shuberts and the Movies

WORLD PICTURES

WORLD PICTURES
PRESENT
KITTY GORDON
IN
"MANDARIN'S GOLD"
WITH IRVING CUMMINGS
STORY BY PHILIP LONERGAN
DIRECTED BY OSCAR APFEL

Lobby card for *Mandarin's Gold*
(1919). This World Films picture
was directed by Oscar Apfel. Among
its mostly unmemorable and
forgotten cast were Kitty Gordon;
Irving Cummings, who later
directed Shirley Temple movies;
and Warner Oland, who achieved
fame as detective Charlie Chan in a
series of B movies.

By 1912, motion pictures were no longer a novelty but an accepted form of entertainment. In the United States, movies were about to graduate from one or two reels to the longer, four-reel feature-length format. The longer length allowed for the further development of plot.

Hollywood had not yet become the center of the film industry, and movies were still being shot largely on the East Coast. There was a lot of cross-pollination between theater and motion pictures—stars on the stage became stars on the screen, and theater producers looked upon plays as potential movie vehicles.

The Shuberts made forays into the film business on many fronts. Their initial excursion might have been incited by the announcement on June 21, 1913, that their chief theatrical rivals, Klaw and Erlanger, were forming the Protective Amusement Company for the purpose of making film versions of the 104 plays they controlled. Before long, the duo had merged with the Biograph Company, which, because of the directorial skill of D. W. Griffith, was considered the most prestigious American film company at that time. Part of their business strategy was to get theater owners who wanted to exhibit Klaw and Erlanger movies to buy franchises that would give them exclusive access to Klaw and Erlanger product and also help fund the production of films. Or the Shuberts' entry into motion pictures might have been defensive because they were worried that the proliferation of movie theaters was a threat to the legitimate stage. Operating a movie theater was certainly less risky and costly than producing a play. In 1912, Adolph Zukor had presented Sarah Bernhardt in *Queen Elizabeth* at Daniel Frohman's Lyceum Theatre. The success of this venture led to the founding of the Famous Players Film Company and later to Paramount Pictures. Everyone, it seemed, was jumping on the motion-picture bandwagon.

Not wanting to be left out in the cold, the Shuberts formed the Shubert Feature Film Booking Company to show movies in their theaters. They became allies of Marcus Loew and supported him in his various enterprises. In the early 1910s, Lee became a major investor in Loew's, Inc., and later was instrumental in fostering the merger that became M-G-M. With Broadway producer William Brady, the Shuberts invested in World Films Corporation, which had movie studios in Fort Lee, New Jersey. By 1916, Brady and the Shuberts were managing World, which produced films based on Shubert and Brady plays. Initially successful, the company eventually encountered financial problems and ran out of steam. The final World Films were released at the end of 1919.

An example of the early film industry's symbiotic relationship with the legitimate stage can be seen in the history of Broadway's Longacre Theatre. In its early days that venue had producer/managers who were actively and simultaneously involved in the film industry. After H. H. Frazee surrendered control of the house in 1918, the Shuberts took over along with L. Lawrence Weber, F. Ray Comstock and G. M. Anderson.

Weber (nephew of Joe Weber of Weber and Fields fame) worked predominantly as a producer/manager but had a well-rounded entertainment career—he booked acts for a vaudeville circuit, served as secretary for the Producing Managers Association (a precursor of the League of American Theatres and Producers), and was associated with a number of motion-picture development companies, including Popular Plays and Players, Inc.; Producing Theatrical Plays with Stars in Motion Pictures, Sigmund Lubin's company situated in Philadelphia; Metro Film Company which merged into M-G-M in 1924; and L. Lawrence Weber Photo Dramas, Inc. (Super Films), of which corporation Lee Shubert was listed as a director. The Shuberts were investors in Lawrence Weber's Photoplay Company and helped him comb through scripts in search of likely candidates for the screen. All of these companies listed the Longacre as their address. Numerous memos exist during this period from Lee Shubert to Weber introducing performers, authors, or other individuals, like Shubert brother-in-law William H. Weissager, who "up to now has been practising law [but] . . . is very desirous of getting into the picture game in the distributing end of it . . ." In 1917, Weber Photodramas produced *Raffles, The Amateur Cracksman,* with John Barrymore, and *The Passing of the Third Floor Back*, with Sir Johnston Forbes-Robertson.

Another Longacre partner, Gilbert M. Anderson, came to New York looking for a career on stage but achieved his greatest success on film. Working as a model, he was hired to work in Edison pictures in 1902 and achieved a spot in the history books when he appeared the next year in Edwin S. Porter's *The Great Train Robbery*. Anderson also worked for Selig and Vitagraph before forming Essanay ("S" and "A") Films with George K. Spoor in 1907. At Essanay, he created the character of Broncho Billy, who appeared in almost four hundred shorts beginning in

...ends to see me in my two best pictures—
...geously beautiful, and charming 'Miss Pet-
...erpieces."

Alice Brady

...sed me as a play everyone should see, but
...'riday the 13th' is the triumphant note in
...rama. If anyone should doubt the supe-
...TURES, BRADY-MADE, I should re-
...ays, and also the forthcoming release 'The

Robert Warwick

...to educate my child, I have shown my
...eedom. In 'The Crucial Test' I have tried
...hould appeal to every woman the world

Kitty Gordon

...rady-Made are good pictures, but there is a
...Susan' that held me in its fascinating grasp
...ry friend of mine will go to see what made
...e."

Clara Kimball Young

...n the success of 'What Happened at 22'
...rary.' These two pictures afforded me an
...est work, and they will be especially enjoy-
... something novel."

Arthur H. Ashley

...s fall in plays like 'Sally in Our Alley'
...ap more than it is. The wonderful children
...the heroine does, will appeal to the public
...ve. I hope the thousands of little children
...the past will see this darling play."

Muriel Ostriche

"I was happy indeed to begin my work in WORLD-PICTURES—
BRADY-MADE, with so excellent a picture as 'His Brother's
Wife.' It is one of the most novel and exciting pictures I have
ever been associated with, and we are now making one that is
even better—'A Woman's Way.'"

Ethel Clayton

"It would afford me eternal pleasure to work always in pictures like
'His Brother's Wife' and 'A Woman's Way,' because I am sure they
will increase my popularity and stamp World-Pictures — Brady-
Made as par-excellent."

Carlyle Blackwell

"Mercy, I am too busy to write. 'Tangled Fates' everyone should
see, but every sweetheart, old or young, and every bachelor or
bachelor-girl, will agree that 'Mary, Quite Contrary' is one of the
sweetest plays ever written."

Mollie King

"You may make a permanent record of this—'The Velvet Paw' is
going to create a sensation, because it surpasses in thrills, settings
and everything that goes to make it more than a mere picture.
'The Velvet Paw,' I dare say, will have no competitor, unless it be
'The Other Sister,' which follows in the line of release."

Gail Kane

"World-Pictures can never fail under the able direction of William
A. Brady, so long as pictures of such high quality as 'The Weak-
ness of Man' and season successes like 'Husband and Wife' are
released in the regular program."

Holbrook Blinn

"So many things happened in 'What Happened at 22' that I think
folks are going to sit in their seats and wonder 'What Next?' It is
a play that attracted my most earnest efforts. Now I am working
in 'The Country Girl,' and it is just as sweet as country lassies, and
just as thrilling as a drop in an elevator from the Woolworth
Tower."

Frances Nelson

see them IN
PICTURES BRADY-MADE

A promotional flyer for World Films
featuring the stars of the company

1907 and was probably the first screen cowboy. In addition, Essanay Films produced the first of
the Charlie Chaplin shorts after Chaplin left Keystone. By becoming a partner in the Longacre,
Anderson was returning to his true love, the theater. Weber and Anderson produced and
Anderson himself staged *Yes or No* (1918), which had a respectable run of 147 performances.
They also produced *Nothing But the Truth* (1916) and *Nothing But Lies* (1918). Anderson did
not appear on stage, however, and he returned to filmmaking after the Longacre was sold to the
Shuberts. By the mid-1920s, he had drifted into obscurity, but in 1957 he was awarded an hon-
orary Oscar for his pioneering contributions to motion pictures.

The 50th and 51st Street Theaters

The Broadway Theatre has been home to the likes of everyone from Mae West to Mickey Mouse. The arc of the Broadway's seventy-six-year history from movie palace to premier musical house has made it one of the theater district's most fascinating venues. One of only five playhouses that actually front on the street named Broadway, it opened in 1924 as B. S. Moss's Colony, a premier film house. It went "legit" from 1930 to 1934, when it was rechristened the Broadway. From 1934 to 1940, the house was once again dedicated to motion-picture exhibition. In 1940, however, it returned to legitimate stage production and, except for a brief stint as a Cinerama movie theater in the 1950s, has remained in the business of showcasing live theater ever since.

B. S. Moss was the owner of a chain of movie theaters, many of which also housed vaudeville. He commissioned architect Eugene DeRosa to design the Colony, and the resulting venue

OPPOSITE:
Detail of ceiling and columns in the lobby of the Broadway Theatre

Exterior of the theater, c. 1959, at Broadway and 53rd Street, when the hit musical Gypsy *starring Ethel Merman was in residence*

The renovated exterior of the Broadway, c. 1991, after it was incorporated into a new office building at Broadway and 52nd Street. Miss Saigon *was the first production to grace the new marquee and facade.*

PREVIOUS PAGES, LEFT TO RIGHT:
Interior as seen from the orchestra level, showing the front of the balcony, the center dome and chandelier

View of the orchestra pit toward the end of the run of Miss Saigon. *At the top of the photograph are the house right boxes.*

Cabinet for fire-hose storage

was a spacious 1,765-seat house—a size that would later make it ideal for the production of musical comedy. The most notable film that played in the early years was Walt Disney's *Steamboat Willie,* which premiered here in 1928. The benchmark cartoon short introduced American audiences to an adorable rodent named Mickey Mouse.

The New Yorkers, which opened on December 8, 1930, marked the Broadway's debut as a legitimate theater. Written by Cole Porter and Herbert Fields, the musical was the sophisticated story of a Park Avenue doyenne who dreams she is in love with a bootlegger. Jimmy Durante very nearly stole the show from Hope Williams, Fred Waring and his Pennsylvanians, and Ann Pennington. The show ran for twenty weeks and introduced two classics: "I Happen to Like New York," and "Love for Sale," which was considered too scandalous to receive airplay on the radio. Next, the Broadway housed a new edition of Earl Carroll's popular *Vanities* (1932), starring Milton Berle, Helen Broderick, and Harriet Hoctor. Vincente Minnelli's modern scenic design was punctuated with neon, and the hit tune "I've Got a Right to Sing the Blues," by Harold Arlen and Ted Koehler, was introduced.

The transfer in 1940 of Rodgers and Hart's hit musical *Too Many Girls* from the Imperial Theatre would be the first of many long-running shows to move to the Broadway. Other notable transfers include *My Sister Eileen* (1942) from the

Biltmore; the Gertrude Lawrence tour of *Lady in the Dark* (1943) from the road; *South Pacific* (1953) from the Majestic; *The Most Happy Fella* (1957) from the Imperial; *Funny Girl* (1966) from the Winter Garden; *Cabaret* (1968) from the Broadhurst; *Mame* (1969) from the Winter Garden; *Fiddler on the Roof* (1972) from the Imperial; and *The Wiz* (1977) from the Majestic.

But the Broadway had its own share of significant premieres, too. On July 4, 1942, at the height of World War II, Irving Berlin opened the hugely popular *This Is the Army*. All proceeds from the show were earmarked for Army Emergency Relief. Berlin reprised his famous World War I number, "Oh, How I Hate to Get Up in the Morning," in addition to the spirited title tune. The cast was made up of professional actors who were in the service and their wives.

Billy Rose wowed the critics when his production of *Carmen Jones* opened on December 2, 1943. It was Oscar Hammerstein II's idea to cast an all-Black *Carmen* and situate it in a southern parachute factory during World War II. Another modern update, *Beggar's Holiday* (1946), was Duke Ellington's adaptation of *The Beggar's Opera*. John Latouche contributed book

Sheet-music cover from the Broadway's opening production as a legitimate house on December 8, 1930. The New Yorkers was a sophisticated musical by Cole Porter and Herbert Fields.

Sandra Church, Ethel Merman, and Jack Klugman in the landmark production of Gypsy, *which opened at the Broadway on May 21, 1959.* Gypsy *told the story of Gypsy Rose Lee and her sister June Havoc. Merman played their mother, Rose, and her performance of "Rose's Turn" was equally thrilling and horrifying.*

and lyrics, and Alfred Drake and Zero Mostel starred. In 1956, Sammy Davis, Jr., made the Broadway his home in the popular musical *Mr. Wonderful*, about a struggling nightclub singer whose friends convince him to audition for the posh Palm Club in Miami Beach. In the show's second act, Davis performed his actual nightclub act with his father and uncle.

Soon after, the Broadway was the site of a theatrical milestone. On May 21, 1959, Ethel Merman, starring in *Gypsy*, introduced the world to the formidable Mama Rose. The backstage saga of Gypsy Rose Lee and her family featured music by Jule Styne, lyrics by Stephen Sondheim, a book by Arthur Laurents, and choreography and direction by Jerome Robbins. The show was an immediate hit, and Mama Rose became one of Merman's signature roles.

A revised version of *Candide* transferred to the Broadway from Brooklyn's Chelsea Theater Center in 1974. The earlier 1956 production of the Voltaire classic had been a spectacular flop, but the Leonard Bernstein score had developed a cult following. Harold Prince, who directed the new version, gutted the theater so that the action could take place throughout the auditorium on various levels connected by ramps, runways, and trapezes. The year 1979 brought one of the Broadway's biggest hits, Andrew Lloyd Webber and Tim Rice's *Evita*, which told the story of Argentina's most glamorous first lady, Eva Perón. Starring Patti LuPone and Mandy Patinkin, with direction by Harold Prince, the show won seven Tony Awards.

Stage version of Candide *(1974). Based on Leonard Bernstein's 1956 musical, which had a cult following, the newly revised* Candide *was directed by Harold Prince at the Chelsea Theater Center in Brooklyn. The response was so positive that it was moved to the Broadway. The action took place on platforms, ramps, gangplanks, and other playing spaces all over the house for an audience that was placed on grandstands, stools, and platforms scattered throughout the theater.*

The Broadway was a busy theater in the 1980s and 1990s, with a hit revival of *Zorba* (1983) starring Anthony Quinn, Yul Brynner's farewell performances of *The King and I* (1985), and

Patti LuPone in the Andrew Lloyd Webber and Tim Rice production of Evita *(1979). LuPone played Eva Perón, the corrupt first lady of Argentina, in a tour-de-force performance. Harold Prince's brilliant direction resulted in a Tony Award for Best Direction of a Musical and six other Tonys, including one for LuPone's performance.*

Gerald Schoenfeld, chairman of the Shubert Organization (left), and Bob Fosse in the rehearsal room for Fosse's last Broadway musical, Big Deal *(1986), based on the film* Big Deal on Madonna Street. *Reviews for* Big Deal *were mixed at best. Soon after the closing, Fosse collapsed on the streets of Washington, D.C., while working on a revival of* Sweet Charity.

Bob Fosse's final Broadway show, *Big Deal* (1986). Just before *Big Deal* opened, the Shubert Organization undertook a major renovation of the house, which transformed it into the glittering jewel that it is today.

On March 12, 1987, the megahit *Les Misérables* opened at the Broadway. The epic musical by Alain Boublil, Claude-Michel Schönberg, and Herbert Kretzmer, adapted from Victor Hugo's classic novel, won seven Tony Awards, including Best Musical. In 1991, the show transferred to the Imperial Theatre to make room for another Boublil-Schönberg collaboration, *Miss Saigon,* an updated version of *Madama Butterfly,* set during the Vietnam War. Major structural changes had to be made backstage prior to the show's opening to accommodate the helicopter that landed onstage every night during the evacuation of Saigon.

The Broadway Theatre is located at 1681 Broadway.

OPPOSITE, ABOVE:
Act One of Les Misérables *(1987) concludes with the revolutionaries promising defiance in "One Day More." The longrunning hit inspired by the classic Victor Hugo novel opened at the Broadway Theatre on March 12, 1987, and has since moved to the Imperial Theatre.*

OPPOSITE, BELOW:
Jonathan Pryce as the Engineer extols the virtues of "The American Dream" in Miss Saigon, *which opened at the Broadway on April 11, 1991. The* Madama Butterfly–*inspired megaproduction, set during the Vietnam War, opened amid a swirl of hype and controversy. The hype had to do with the installation of a helicopter, which landed on the stage during the evacuation of Saigon at every performance. The controversy had to do with Pryce's being cast in an Asian role. Minority actors protested outside the theater on opening night.*

S hubert has owned the Winter Garden longer than any of its other venues. The organization's third-largest musical house (1,513 seats), the theater occupies a site that was originally a Dutch farm owned by the Hopper family. William K. Vanderbilt bought the property for $200,000 in 1883 and razed the farmhouse. Two years later, he erected the American Horse Exchange, which was rebuilt in 1896. At that time Longacre Square (now Times Square) was the center of the horse and carriage trade. By 1911, when the Shuberts leased the American Horse Exchange from Vanderbilt, horses had given way to the automobile and the legitimate theater was making inroads north of 42nd Street.

OPPOSITE:

Detail from the Winter Garden's restored ceiling dome, 2001. When Cats' phenomenal record-breaking run of eighteen years ended in 2000, its oversized junkyard set came down to reveal the theater's former splendor. The Shubert Organization immediately embarked on a multimillion dollar restoration of the glorious old playhouse.

RIGHT:

Early photograph of the Winter Garden showing its unadorned front and its clean classical lines, just one step beyond its origins as a stable. Note the sign on the adjoining building for "O.E. Short, Wholesale, Carriages."

Winter Garden program cover, 1911

Lee and J. J. Shubert hired architect William Albert Swasey to convert the existing horse exchange building into a theater. Swasey's idea was to turn the showring into an auditorium with only one balcony and decorate it with a garden motif. The existing space dictated that Swasey design a playhouse that was unusually wide; the proscenium arch, measuring approximately forty-five feet, was wider than any other Broadway house of its day, and the breadth of the auditorium brought the audience closer to the stage. Swasey left the American Horse Exchange's

La Belle Paree *(1911). The opening production was billed as "A Jumble of Jollity in One Act and Several Scenes." It featured a Parisian setting, Al Jolson in his first Broadway show—as Erastus Sparkler, "a colored aristocrat from San Juan Hill cutting a wide swath in Paris"—and a plot that revolved around a widow. This photograph probably shows the "Widow Number," which, despite its melodramatic tone, spoofs the lonely fate of widows:*

"It's queer how men avoid the weeping widow
Their coldness to us passes all belief,
Though we've powdered and we've painted,
Had hysterics and then fainted,
They respect our bitter grief."

trusses exposed, giving the interior the look of a giant erector set. He covered the ceiling in sky blue canvas and trimmed both ceiling and walls with latticework. The overall color scheme was ivory and gold. Garlands and leaves entwined the box fronts and proscenium arch. The curtain was constructed of heavy rose-pink plush; the floors were covered with red Pompeian tile; and the wall spaces were decorated with Pompeian pottery, statuary, shrubs, and flower boxes. The new theater opened on March 20, 1911, with a double bill of *Bow Sing* and *La Belle Paree*, featuring Al Jolson in his Broadway debut.

The Winter Garden boasted some unusual features that generated quite a buzz among audiences. A tank was installed onstage for Australian swimming champion and vaudeville performer Annette Kellerman, who was signed to appear in *The Passing Show of 1912* but who walked out after a week because her name was not positioned above the title. Inspired by Max Reinhardt's Asian fantasy *Sumurun* (1912), which employed a Kabuki ramp, or "flower way," as a part of the set, a runway was built over the orchestra pit, extending from the stage to the rear of the auditorium, for *The Whirl of Society* (1912), in which Al Jolson sings "My Sumurun Girl," a burlesque of Reinhardt's production. The runway was a big hit with Winter Garden audiences, who dubbed it "The Bridge of Thighs" because of the dancing chorus girls who promenaded down the ramp. But economic considerations (the runway killed twenty-one seats for eight performances a week) forced its removal in 1922. For *Pacific Overtures* (1976), Stephen Sondheim and John Weidman's Kabuki-like musical, set designer Boris Aronson wanted to restore the runway, but director Harold Prince vetoed the idea.

OPPOSITE, ABOVE:
Audience of schoolchildren saluting the flag, 1917

OPPOSITE, BELOW:
Orchestra and mezzanine, 1922

Both photographs display the Winter Garden auditorium from two different periods. The photograph above captures W. Albert Swasey's executed design for the Winter Garden interior in its original incarnation. From the stage, the runway which extended down the center aisle, is discernible. Other embellishments—such as the trellis effect on the rear wall of the orchestra, the garlands and flower motifs on the front of the mezzanine, and the exposed steel trusses that support the mezzanine and allow for clear sight lines—are also visible. The photograph below shows the exact same view in 1923, twelve years after the theater opened, and after Herbert J. Krapp's major renovation. Krapp eliminated the runway and the center aisle, reconfigured the seating in the auditorium, lowered the ceiling, and covered the trusses. Using an Adamesque style, he decorated the theater in gold and cream tones for an elegant effect.

On November 15, 1923, the Shuberts bought the Winter Garden building and annex outright from Vanderbilt for $915,000. Between 1922 and 1923, architect Herbert J. Krapp remodeled the theater using the more traditional Adamesque style. For the renovation, he replaced the ceiling, covered the exposed trusses, and added elegant ornamentation on the trusses, boxes, and proscenium.

The Winter Garden has traditionally been the home of revues and musicals. *The Passing Show* (the Shuberts' answer to Ziegfeld's *Follies*) and almost every Al Jolson musical played the Winter Garden. Among Jolson's vehicles were *Honeymoon Express* (1913); *Dancing Around* (1914); *Robinson Crusoe, Jr.* (1916); *Sinbad* (1917); and *Big Boy* (1925). After Ziegfeld's death, the Shuberts and Billie Burke, Ziegfeld's widow, presented Ziegfeld's *Follies* at the Winter Garden (in 1934, 1936, 1943, and 1947) featuring artists such as Fanny Brice, Bobby Clark, Bob Hope, Eve Arden, Gypsy Rose Lee, Josephine Baker, and Willie Howard. In 1964, *Funny Girl*, a musical about Fanny Brice, a perennial *Ziegfeld Follies* headliner, made Barbra Streisand a major star. In 1971, Harold Prince unveiled *Follies*, the Stephen Sondheim/James Goldman tribute to the era of spectacular revues and beautiful showgirls.

OPPOSITE, ABOVE:

Palace of Americus/Salome for The Passing Show of 1918. *In this production shot, one can clearly see the trellis work over the proscenium, which architect W. Albert Swasey used to enhance the garden effect. Also visible at center stage is part of the runway over the orchestra pit.*

OPPOSITE, BELOW:

Stage, proscenium, curtain, and boxes. In the 1923 renovation, Krapp lowered and narrowed the proscenium arch and added graceful Adamesque decorative details to the proscenium, the ceiling over the stage, and the boxes.

Winter Garden exterior (1923). While the house's legitimate stage hosted the new Paris edition of the revue Artists and Models, *Florence Mills was featured at the upstairs nightclub, the Plantation. The restaurant space in the Winter Garden is one of the oldest cabaret locations in Manhattan. In 1911, the Palais de Danse opened there and fed the craze for ballroom dancing. In 1914 it gave way to Club Doraldina, named for the proponent of the Hula and the Hawaiian craze. From 1916 to 1917, Clifford C. Fischer managed what was then called the Montmartre, which in turn, metamorphosed into Bal Tabarin and featured violinist Jack Harris and up-and-coming comic Joe Frisco. By 1918, the club transformed into the Folies Bergère, with clarinetist/bandleader Ted Lewis ("Is Everybody Happy?") as the attraction. From 1921 to 1925, the Plantation Club flourished and presented Broadway's first all black revue—Ethel Waters, Florence Mills, Will Vodery's band, Josephine Baker in chorus, and Paul Robeson. Other clubs occupied the space—the Ross-Fenton Club (c.1926–27), Les Ambassadeurs, Chez Fischer, Casa Lopez, The Rendezvous, the New Montmartre (1928–34), Beachcomber, Midnight Sun, New Beachcomber, Mother Kelly's, the Mardi Gras, Benny Davis' Frolics, and, in 1943, the Café Zanzibar. More recently the space was home to a theme restaurant, the Hawaii Kai. Closed for about a decade, the space now houses the seafood restaurant Lundy's.*

Ziegfeld Follies of 1934. *The first Follies, presented by the Messrs. Shubert and Mrs. Florenz Ziegfeld after Ziegfeld's death, paired the Shuberts' comedian Willie Howard with Ziegfeld's star Fannie Brice, playing the precocious Baby Snooks.*

Funny Girl *(1964). The musical biography of Fanny Brice's life made a star of Barbra Streisand pictured here as a very pregnant Fanny on the arm of her gambler husband, Nick Arnstein (Sydney Chaplin). Jean Stapleton played Mrs. Strakosh, a friend from the old neighborhood. Although* Funny Girl *was nominated for multiple Tonys, the show came up empty-handed against the Hello, Dolly!* juggernaut *that year. Streisand won the 1968 Best Actress Oscar for portraying Fanny onscreen.*

Sons o' Fun *(1941) sheet music. The zany comedy duo, Olsen and Johnson, were a smash hit at the box office in their Shubert shows:* Hellzapoppin' *(1938),* The Streets of Paris *(1939),* Sons o' Fun *(1941), and* Laffin' Room Only *(1944). Their crazy humor influenced generations of comics and inspired presentations like the television show* Laugh-In *(1968–73). Carmen Miranda, who was introduced in* The Streets of Paris, *was the icing on the cake with her Brazilian sambas, her Bahian costumes of bright colors, her bare midriff and fruit-bedecked hats, and her enchanting bigger-than-life personality. A hit the minute she stepped on the stage, Miranda and her band also played nightclubs before heading to Hollywood and knocking the film world on its ear.*

OPPOSITE:

Al Jolson as Pierrot

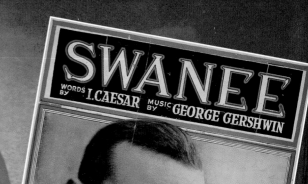

SWANEE

WORDS BY I. CAESAR   MUSIC BY GEORGE GERSHWIN

Successfully Introduced BY AL JOLSON in "SINBAD" at the Winter Garden New York

6

T. B. HARMS
FRANCIS, DAY & HUNTER
NEW YORK

*Panoramic photograph of Al Jolson
and New York Winter Garden
Company in* Robinson Crusoe, Jr.
*(Season 1916–17–18). Where is Al?
Hint: he appears more than once.
Because the camera moved slowly to
capture the entire touring company,
Al was able to get into the picture
three times.*

AL JOLSON AND NEW YORK WINTER GARDEN COMPANY IN

orn in Lithuania, the son of a rabbi, Al Jolson was the proverbial black sheep who wanted nothing of school or religious studies and longed to go on stage. From the time they were children growing up in Washington, D.C., he and his older brother, Harry, were forever running away from home to join a burlesque company, a circus, or a vaudeville show. A talented singer and comedian, Jolson developed a comedy act in which he played a blackface character in burlesque and vaudeville. In 1908, he joined Lew Dockstader's Minstrels and received excellent reviews for his comic delivery, his timing, and his singing of "coon songs." The Shuberts spotted him and hired him for the show *La Belle Paree*, which opened the Winter Garden in 1911. From then on, Jolson became associated with the Winter Garden,

NSON CRUSOE JR.   SEASON 1916-17-18

where in every revue he played a comic sidekick character in blackface, who was often named Gus and was always fast-talking, clever, and able to outsmart anyone. The loose format of the revues allowed for plenty of comedy and melody, and Jolson became such a dynamic interpreter of songs that songwriters deluged him with new material that they begged him to introduce.

Jolson was nearly the last major performer of a minstrelsy tradition that was dying. While it is sometimes hard for contemporary audiences to accept or understand his immense popularity, Jolson's blackface persona was quick-witted, never mean-spirited or intentionally denigrating. His Gus represented a complex character deeply entrenched in the roots of American popular entertainment.

Rocky Mt Photo Co.
Denver,

J. J. Shubert (left) and Al Jolson, two difficult personalities who somehow got along. Unlike many Shubert stars who wandered off to greener pastures, Jolson stayed with the Shuberts for his entire stage career until he went off to film The Jazz Singer *(1927).*

BELOW:

Jolson's first contract, February 7, 1911, for $325 per week. Jolson was making this much in vaudeville but wanted to play Broadway. Henceforth, his salary would continue to go up until 1913, when the Shuberts paid him a $10,000 bonus to sign a seven-year contract at $1,000 a week.

OPPOSITE:
Mary Martin in Peter Pan *(1954), the role that made her as much a part of everyone's childhood as Judy Garland's Dorothy in* The Wizard of Oz. *The collaboration between Jule Styne and Comden and Green, and a cast that included an impish Cyril Ritchard as Captain Hook, Margalo Gillmore as Mrs. Darling, Sondra Lee as Tiger Lily, and Martin's daughter Heller Halliday as Liza, captured the magical fairyland of the story. Both Martin and Ritchard won Tony Awards, but it was the television production with the original cast that turned this show into legend.*

ABOVE AND RIGHT:
West Side Story *(1957) was a musical retelling of the Romeo and Juliet story set on New York City's West Side as a battle between two gangs—the Anglos (the Jets) versus the Puerto Ricans (the Sharks)—which featured a cast of newcomers. The creative partnership included major names in the American musical theater— Jerome Robbins, Arthur Laurents, Leonard Bernstein and Stephen Sondheim, and producers Robert E. Griffith and Harold Prince. The only Tony Awards went to Robbins for choreography and Oliver Smith for sets. In the photograph above, director/choreographer Robbins (second from left) rehearses (from left) Chita Rivera (Anita), Larry Kert (Tony), and Carol Lawrence (Maria). Below, the Jets display their "cool."*

Mame *(1966). In "The Man in the Moon" sequence, Angela Lansbury as Mame rides the crescent before completely upstaging Bea Arthur's Vera Charles.*

There were two periods during which the Winter Garden departed from legitimate stage productions. From 1928 to 1933, J. J. Shubert leased the theater to Warner Brothers for the presentation of Vitaphone Talking Pictures. *The Singing Fool*, the opening Warner Brothers presentation, featured long-time Winter Garden favorite Al Jolson. Later, on October 1, 1945, United Artists leased the Winter Garden as a venue for its films as well as those of British producer J. Arthur Rank. Among the Technicolor films debuting there were *Blithe Spirit* (1945), *Tomorrow Is Forever,* and *Caesar and Cleopatra* (both 1946).

Other live theatrical hits that have played the Winter Garden include *West Side Story* (1957*), The Unsinkable Molly Brown* (1960), *Mame* (1966), *Gypsy* (with Angela Lansbury, 1974), *Beatlemania* (1977), *Gilda Radner—Live from New York* (1979), and *42nd Street* (1980). The theater was home to *Cats* from 1982 until its final performance on Sunday, September 10, 2000, a period during which it logged 7,485 performances and became Broadway's longest-running musical.

The Winter Garden Theatre is located at 1634 Broadway.

ABOVE:

Follies *(1971). Gene Nelson in* "Buddy's Folly," "I've got those 'God-why-don't-you-love-me-oh-you-do-I'll-see-you-later' Blues," *a comic vaudeville number that tragically underlines Buddy's love for his wife, Sally.* Follies *was Stephen Sondheim and James Goldman's lavish, nostalgic, and bittersweet tribute to the type of revue that Florenz Ziegfeld produced. Directed by Harold Prince and Michael Bennett, the show centered on a reunion of showgirls at midlife who were looking back and taking stock of their lives.*

BELOW:

A succès d'estime rather than a hit, Pacific Overtures *(1976) was Stephen Sondheim and John Weidman's look at the opening of Japan to the West by Commodore Matthew Perry. They structured the play as a Kabuki performance (including an all-male cast) with the score composed of a pastiche of styles reflecting traditional Japanese music as well as popular music from each invading country. The music and lyrics were delicate and witty and the theme probably ahead of its time. This is the satiric "Welcome to Kanagawa," in which a madam and her geishas are perhaps the only Japanese who are happy to see Perry.*

At Cats' record-breaking performance, Andrew Lloyd Webber sat at the piano, flanked by his creative team (from left to right): producer Cameron Mackintosh, choreographer Gillian Lynne, and director Trevor Nunn. Laurie Beecham, who played the role of Grizabella more times than any other performer, is on the far left, surrounded by other Cats from various periods in the show's history. By the time it closed on September 10, 2000, Cats had racked up a whopping total of 7,485 performances.

Winter Garden exterior. Celebration of Cats' record-breaking performance—number 6,138, June 19, 1997. The special invitation-only performance brought back former cast members together with the creative team, who performed for an enthusiastic audience. The street on the Seventh Avenue side of the Winter Garden was closed for a special ceremony and for a fireworks display.

The Shubert Revues

TO·NIGHT AFTER THE PLAY
VISIT THE

CENTURY PROMENADE
at
11:30 P.M

MIDNIGHT
ROUNDERS
of
1921

DINING and
DANCING

GREATEST (AFTER HOURS)
SHOW in the WORLD

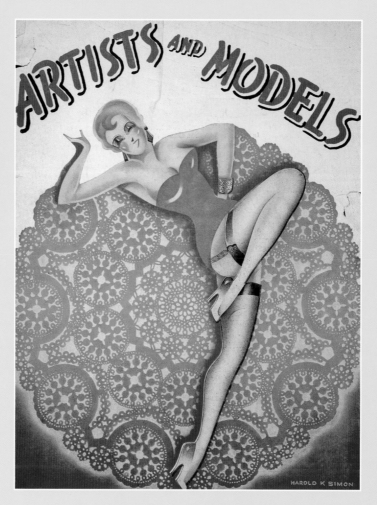

PREVIOUS PAGE:
Flyer for *Midnight Rounders of 1921*, at the rooftop playhouse of the Century Theatre. Many Broadway theaters had smaller venues on their roofs in which revues were offered as late-night presentations. They were especially popular in the summers before air conditioning made theaters comfortable year-round.

ABOVE:
The cover of a souvenir program for *Artists and Models*, a revue that capitalized on scantily attired showgirls as its main draw. At least five editions of this popular title were produced beginning on August 20, 1923.

RIGHT:
Flyer for *A Night in Spain* (1927). Exotic locales were often used as a motif for stringing together material for revues. *A Night in Spain* opened at the 44th Street Theatre. The loading docks for the *New York Times* currently occupy the space where the theater once stood.

The revue, a major influence in the development of the musical-comedy format, has its roots in vaudeville and burlesque. While those shows were composed of a series of specialty numbers or unrelated acts, revues were usually organized around a single theme. Stars performed dialogue, sketches, songs, and dance numbers, which were written specifically for the show.

As the themes of revues became more refined and focused, the boundaries between them and what came to be known as the book musical became increasingly blurred. Despite the huge success and subsequent domination of book musicals like *Show Boat* and Rodgers and Hammerstein classics like *Oklahoma!, South Pacific*, and *Carousel,* the revue format endured and is still popular on Broadway today.

The first Shubert-produced revue, presented on the monumental stage of the Hippodrome in 1906, was composed of three parts: *Pioneer Days*, a spectacular drama of western life; various circus events; and *Neptune's Daughter*, which featured an elaborate aquatic ballet called "Under the Sea." After Shubert rival Florenz Ziegfeld's *Follies of 1907* met with tremendous success, Lee and J. J. lost no time in jumping on the revue bandwagon, first with *The Mimic World* in 1908 and then with their extremely successful *The Passing Show* in 1912. Annual editions of *The Passing Show* continued until 1924. Other well-known and popular Shubert examples of the genre include the *Greenwich Village Follies, Artists and Models, Hellzapoppin'*, and four of their own *Ziegfeld Follies*, produced after the death of Ziegfeld.

In all, between 1906 and 1943, the Shubert brothers produced a staggering 104 revues. At their most basic, these shows featured lots of scantily clad chorus girls, vernacular popular songs, and colorful sets and costumes. At their best, they represented the height of wit, glamour, and sophistication.

ABOVE, LEFT:
Program cover for *The Passing Show of 1914,* the third edition of the Winter Garden extravaganza. Marilyn Miller was one of its stars.

ABOVE, RIGHT:
Proposed artwork for the program cover for *The Passing Show of 1916.* J. J. Shubert gave his approval by initialing the design. The Shuberts produced at least a dozen editions of *The Passing Show* at the Winter Garden Theatre beginning in 1912. The popular revue was the Shuberts' answer to the better-known *Ziegfeld Follies* after which they were patterned.

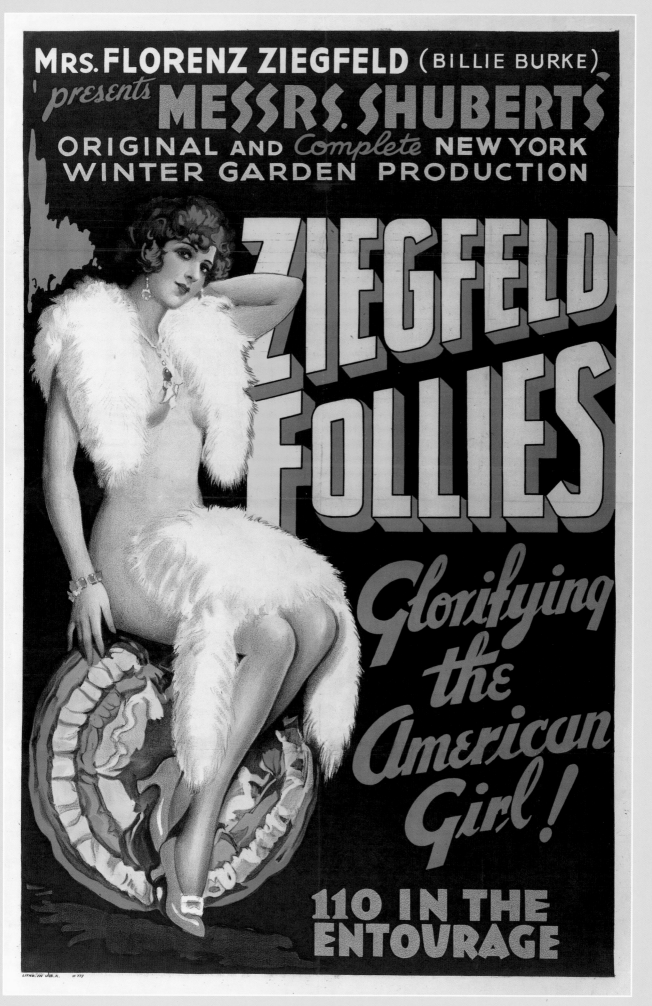

A rare one-sheet promoting one of the Shubert-produced editions of the *Ziegfeld Follies* after the death of Florenz Ziegfeld. He left his widow, Billie Burke, destitute, and the Shuberts seized the opportunity to cash in on the most famous of all revues. The company still owns the rights to the title "Ziegfeld Follies."

Rehearsal shot from *Keep Off the Grass* (1940) at the Broadhurst Theatre. Cast members included (left to right) Jimmy Durante, Jackie Gleason, Ray Bolger, Ilka Chase, and an unidentified man. Kneeling is director Fred deCordova, a boyhood friend of John Shubert's, who later became a well-known television producer in California; he was the longtime producer of *The Tonight Show* starring Johnny Carson.

Josephine Baker, the scintillating American export to France, in a production shot from Paris in the 1920s. The Shuberts lured her back to New York in 1936 for the second edition of their *Ziegfeld Follies*. The New York critics were vicious to her and she fled back to the French, who adored her.

In addition to featuring attractive girls, revues often used elaborated scenic devices to attract audiences. The second edition of *The Show of Wonders* in 1917 included a twenty-minute sketch called the "Submarine F-7 Scene," in which spectacular stage effects and film were used to depict the sinking and ultimate rescue of a submarine crew. According to Shubert Archive founding director Brooks McNamara, "At the end of the sketch, when the rescue was complete, an American flag was lowered into the scene and the audience stood up to sing the national anthem, accompanied by the theater orchestra."

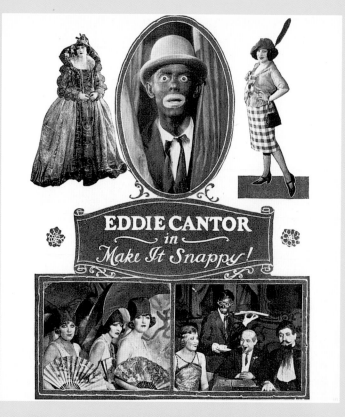

Flyer for Eddie Cantor in *Make It Snappy!* at the Winter Garden in 1921. Cantor first worked for the Shuberts after Ziegfeld fired him in 1919, when Cantor walked out on the *Ziegfeld Follies* in support of the actors' strike. Some years after the strike, he and Ziegfeld reconciled and Cantor never worked for the Lee and J.J. again.

Hellzapoppin', which opened at the 46th Street Theatre, was one of the productions that saved the Shuberts after the disastrous effects of the stock market crash and resulting Depression. The show was headed by the zany comedy team of Olsen and Johnson, whose antics convulsed audiences. Here, John Garfield's wife is being presented with a string of sausages. Other oddball prizes included loaves of bread, hot-water bottles, and toilet seats.

Cover of the souvenir program for *Sons o' Fun,* starring (left to right) Ole Olsen, Carmen Miranda, and Chic Johnson. *Sons o' Fun* was Olsen and Johnnson's follow up to their hugely successful run of *Hellzapoppin'*. It boasted a cast of one hundred fifty (including "Fifty U.S. Lovelies"), and it was Carmen Miranda's final Broadway appearance before relocating to Hollywood and the movies.

Showgirls from *New Priorities of 1943* at the 46th Street Theatre. Close inspection of the photograph reveals elaborate costumes crafted from whisk brooms, calendar pages, pencils, throw rugs, dish towels, and scrub brushes. There was a war going on, so everything was recycled!

Eleanor Powell and the male chorus of *At Home Abroad* at the Winter Garden Theatre in 1935. *At Home Abroad* was created by Vincente Minnelli and starred Beatrice Lillie, Ethel Waters, Powell, and Reginald Gardiner. Minnelli used the concept of the revue as a travelogue in order to "visit" a number of foreign destinations.

Chorus girls from *The Mimic World* (1908) at the Casino Theatre. This was the Shuberts' first attempt to duplicate the success of Florenz Ziegfeld's *Follies.* Although patterned closely after the hit show of 1907, *The Mimic World* lacked the famous showman's polish and class. The Shuberts finally found success in a similarly styled revue, *The Passing Show,* in 1912.

The Paris edition of *Artists and Models* was produced in 1925 and included the Gertrude Hoffman Girls as a box of pastels.

OPPOSITE, ABOVE:
Two costume designs by Homer Conant for *The Passing Show of 1917* in which showgirls were depicted as cocktails. Pictured here are Manhattan (left) and Horse's Neck (right).

OPPOSITE, BELOW:
Two costume designs by Howard Greer for an edition of *Greenwich Village Follies.* Greer left Broadway for Hollywood and enjoyed a successful career designing for films.

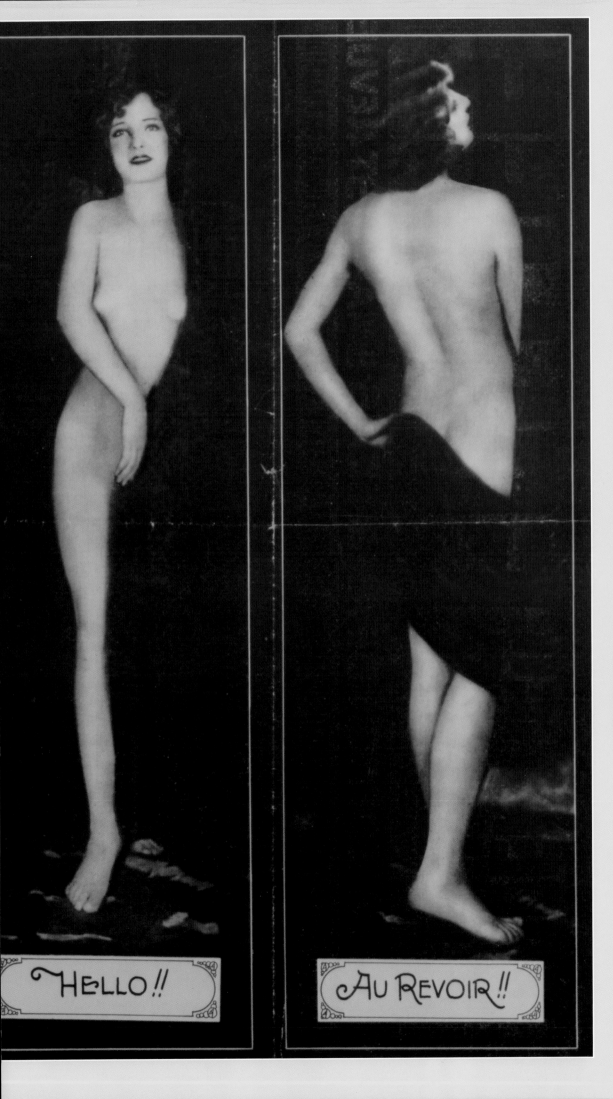

Poster for the eighth edition of *Greenwich Village Follies,* which was on tour in Philadelphia. The show began as *Greenwich Village Nights* and was actually originally produced in the Village. Ever watchful for new productions, the Shuberts moved *Greenwich Village Follies* to the Shubert Theatre in 1921. Like *Artists and Models, Greenwich Village Follies,* showcased as much female flesh as was legally allowed and portrayed the Village as a bohemian playground.

FORMER AND OUT-OF-TOWN THEATER

Broadway, North from 38th St., New York.

oday the Shubert Organization owns sixteen and one-half theaters on Broadway (including a half ownership, along with the Irving Berlin Estate, of the Music Box Theatre), making it by far the largest owner of legitimate theaters in New York City. Still, this number pales in comparison to the more than thirty venues that Lee and J. J. Shubert had under their control at the peak of their influence in the 1920s.

The Shuberts' first playhouses in the city, the Herald Square, the Casino, and the Princess—all of which they leased—no longer exist. The Lyric, the first venue the brothers built (in conjunction with composer Reginald DeKoven) survives in part as a component of the Ford Center for the Performing Arts. Later houses, such as the Maxine Elliott, the Nazimova (a.k.a. the Thirty-ninth Street Theatre), the Jolson, the Central, and the Century, do not survive. Other theaters, such as the Ritz (now the Walter Kerr) and the Forrest (now the Eugene O'Neill), endure but are no longer part of the Shubert chain, having been sold either for economic reasons or in compliance with the government's antitrust actions against the company during the 1950s.

Many of these former theaters were state-of-the-art facilities, and some were architecturally distinguished. From the Moorish grandeur of the Casino to the Rococo splendor of the Century, these houses reflected a time when theatergoing was the dominant leisure activity in the city.

PREVIOUS PAGE:
Assembling the troops of advertising personnel in front of the Shubert Crescent Theatre in Brooklyn. The sandwich boards highlight various headliners on the bill. The Shuberts' second foray into vaudeville occurred in the early 1920s. The witch hats adorned with jack-o'-lanterns and the pumpkins on the upper marquee suggest the photo was taken on or around Halloween. The automobile (far left) contains a cameraman and his equipment. The sign on the rear of the vehicle reads in part: "Shubert Crescent Vaudeville Theatre, To-day . . . Cash Prize Contest, All motion pictures taken will be shown at the theatre, Will You Be There?"

OPPOSITE:
Postcard (1919) showing a view of Broadway looking north, from 38th Street. At right is the Casino Theatre (demolished 1930), at Broadway and 39th Street across from the old Metropolitan Opera House (demolished 1966). The Casino, along with the Herald Square Theatre, at 35th Street and Broadway, were the neophyte producers' first acquisitions in New York City. Signage for the Maxine Elliott's Theatre (demolished 1959), a house the Shuberts built at 109 West 39th Street for the famous actress, is visible just to the left of the Casino marquee, and an advertising billboard for the Shubert-produced Monte Cristo, Jr., *at the Winter Garden can be seen above that.*

The box office of the Casino Theatre during the 1914–15 theater season. The Moorish design of the exterior was continued indoors. The sign to the right in the photograph lists the attractions at other Shubert venues, including Suzi *at the newly opened Shubert and* Wars of the World *at the mammoth Hippodrome.*

The roof venue above the Century Theatre on Central Park West. The Century had opened as the New Theatre in 1909. It was the pet project of a number of influential New Yorkers, including J. P. Morgan, John Jacob Astor, and Cornelius Vanderbilt. From the opening, the main playhouse, which seated more than 2,000, had acoustic problems. The edifice never became the theatrical pinnacle it was envisioned to be. By 1911, the theater had been renamed the Century. In 1920, the Shubert brothers took over the management of the spaces. Chauve-Souris, a Russian import, moved from the Forty-ninth Street Theatre to the Century Roof in 1922. When this photograph was taken, the interior had been completely redecorated in a mock-Moscow decor to accommodate the production.

The Hippodrome, New York City.

A hand-tinted period postcard indicates the enormity of the Hippodrome, which was built as a spectacle house in 1905 on Sixth Avenue between 43rd and 44th Streets. It literally took up all of the westernmost end of the block and seated 5,200. The Shuberts managed the gigantic playhouse from 1906 to 1915 and took advantage of the huge stage by using it to reenact a realistic battle between a tribe of Indians and fully mounted infantry. They also flooded the tank under the stage to present scenes of sea battles with functioning warships.

Exterior of the Ritz Theatre, which the Shuberts built in 1921 in a record-breaking sixty-six days. The theater passed in and out of Shubert ownership. It was also used as a radio studio and movie theater. When its current owners, Jujamcyn, undertook a major renovation and renamed it the Walter Kerr, in honor of the esteemed theater critic, in 1990 the Shubert Archive provided the design team with original blueprints.

Exterior of Erlanger's Theatre (now the St. James) on 44th Street across the street from the Majestic and Broadhurst Theatres, c. 1927. The Shuberts bought the theater when their former archenemy Abe Erlanger could not afford its upkeep during the Depression. However, in a 1950s ruling by federal courts, the Shuberts were forced to divest themselves of a number of theaters and the St. James was one that they chose to hand over. While it must have been a hard decision for the brothers to make, the St. James, with two balconies and a mezzanine as large as its orchestra, also must have been an obvious choice.

The Lyric Theatre, on 42nd Street between Broadway and Eighth Avenue, c.1902–3. Built by the composer Reginald DeKoven, it was under the operation of the Shubert brothers and was the site of their offices. The facade, which has been incorporated into the Ford Center, is the oldest extant Shubert-related property in the city.

The Kirchner Paintings

Pierrot's Dream

Pride

Temptation

In 1916, Florenz Ziegfeld, Jr., teamed up with Charles B. Dillingham to manage the Century Theatre, located near Columbus Circle. They realized that it was a difficult house to fill because of its inconvenient location and hoped that a remodeled interior and spectacular revues would draw audiences. Joseph Urban was hired to produce sets for the shows and to create a fantasy "Coconut Grove" decor for the Century's Roof Garden. He recommended that Raphael Kirchner, a fellow Austrian designer, be brought over from Europe to help with the theater's redecoration. Kirchner was also put in charge of the costume department. In addition to designing costumes for the Century revues, he did program illustrations, decorated the curtains, and, in his spare time, painted portraits, including one of Mrs. Charles Dillingham.

One of Kirchner's most important contributions to the Century's 1916 renovation was a series of ten paintings that were hung in the lobby. Called *Les Amours de Pierrot*, the series depicts Ziegfeld showgirls as the various loves of Pierrot. According to a companion poem, the series begins with *Pierrot's Dream*, in which a woman in a white gown is sniffing a white flower. Pierrot, with eyes closed, seems contented. But Pierrot's dream of innocence takes a different turn in the following paintings as a series of temptresses appear. The first seven represent the Deadly Sins—*Temptation, Envy, Gluttony, Sloth, Covetousness, Pride,* and *Anger*. These are supplemented by *Luxury*. Finally, in the painting entitled *Expiation,* Pierrot pays for his dalliances as we see a dancing bejeweled Salome holding his head on a platter. The Shuberts acquired these works when they took over management of the Century in 1920. After the theater was razed in 1930, seven of the panels were hung in the rear aisle of the Winter Garden Theatre, and the other three were hung in the Longacre. The series became part of the Shubert Archive in 1977. —Text by X. Ted Barber

Anger

Envy

Sloth

Expiation

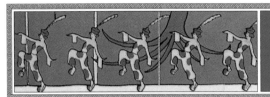
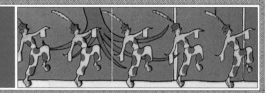
T heater outside of New York City has always been a significant part of the Shubert enterprise. After all, Lee, Sam, and J. J. began their theatrical careers out-of-town, in Syracuse and other upstate New York cities. But even after their success on Broadway was assured, they viewed touring companies and out-of-town properties as crucial ingredients of their business.

The Shubert Organization currently owns or operates four theaters outside New York—in Boston, Philadelphia, Los Angeles, and Washington, D.C. During the heyday of the road, however, the Shubert brothers owned more than one hundred venues and booked shows into nearly a thousand, including properties in London. Before radio, television, and movies came to dominate popular culture, it was not unusual for even the smallest of towns to have at least one theater or opera house. In the early years of the twentieth century, business across the United States was robust, and the Shuberts aggressively pursued it. In fact, Sam Shubert had been on his way to Pittsburgh to acquire the Duquesne Theatre when the train on which he was traveling met with the accident that ended his life. At the same time, Lee was in London supervising the completion of the brothers' first foreign theater, the Waldorf.

The Shuberts' greatest expansion across America took place in the decade after Sam's death. As a tribute to their late brother,

OPPOSITE:

Waldorf Theatre, London, England, interior, 1905. The Shubert brothers were just establishing themselves in New York City when they realized that Europe, especially England, could serve as a valuable source of theatrical properties. Eventually, productions or specialty numbers from overseas would make up a large percentage of the Shuberts' Broadway repertoire. A London theater under Shubert control, they reasoned, not only could serve as a European base from which they could make forays to the Continent in search of materials that might play well in America, but it could also be a potentially profitable theatrical venture. Thus, in 1904, the brothers negotiated a twenty-one-year lease for the Waldorf Theatre, which was then under construction in the Aldwych section of London. Instead of proving to be an auspicious beginning to a long and prosperous European career, however, the new playhouse turned out to be a disaster. Sam Shubert, who had played a large role in the Shuberts' European affairs, died ten days before the theater opened, and none of the attractions that Lee and J. J. subsequently booked caught on with British audiences. In 1909, the Shuberts gave up the theater, which still operates today as the Strand.

Shubert Theatre, Boston, Massachusetts, postcard showing exterior, c. 1910. The Shuberts had a very strong presence in Boston where they owned much property, theatrical and otherwise. Their theatrical holdings at one time or another included the Plymouth, the Majestic, the Wilbur, the Boston Opera House, the Colonial, the Columbia, and the Selwyn, but the Shubert was always their flagship house there. For several decades, Boston was a major tryout city, and many Broadway hits enjoyed pre–New York runs at the Shubert, including The Petrified Forest *(1936) with Leslie Howard and an unknown Humphrey Bogart; Ethel Merman in* Call Me Madam *(1950);* The Entertainer *(1958) starring Laurence Olivier; and* Camelot *(1960) with Richard Burton, Julie Andrews and Robert Goulet. The Shubert Organization still owns the 1,600-seat playhouse, but the Wang Center for the Performing Arts, Inc., books and manages the Shubert under the terms of a forty-year lease that began in 1996.*

OSITE, ABOVE:

jestic Theatre (a.k.a. Shubert Theatre) and office
lding, Chicago, Illinois, exterior, undated. Chicago
s another important city for the Shuberts. By 1924
y had an involvement with eight theaters, but the
ajestic was not one of these. Opened on New Year's
y, 1906, the Majestic was the Windy City's first new
yhouse since the tragic Iroquois Theatre fire in 1903.
was also the first Chicago theater to cost more
n one million dollars to build, due in part to the
merous fire-safety precautions that were incorporated
o its design. In addition, the theater, which was
voted exclusively to vaudeville, was elegantly and
borately outfitted. One critic called it "a theater of
ceptional beauty, comfort, safety, and completeness,"
ile another said it was "a superbly unique structure."
vertheless, the Majestic fell victim to the declining
pularity of vaudeville, and by the late 1920s it was
oked by the Shuberts for legitimate production.
e playhouse closed in 1934 and was dark until
45, when Lee and J. J. Shubert purchased it and
hristened it the Sam S. Shubert Theatre. For many
ars it thrived, and it was the Shubert's sole remaining
ece of theatrical real estate in Chicago when the
mpany sold the building in 1991. The current
ner, the Nederlander Organization, has decided to
tain the Shubert name in a nod to the theater's rich
eatrical past.

OSITE, BELOW:

m S. Shubert Memorial Theatre, Kansas City,
issouri, interior, 1906. Opened in 1906, the Shubert
heatre in Kansas City was the first of many theaters
at Lee and J. J. built in memory of their brother
m, who died in 1905. In 1923, the Shuberts took
t a lease on a second Kansas City venue, the Century
heatre (built in 1900), which they renamed the
ubert Missouri and managed until 1932.
he Shuberts' last tenant was The Ziegfeld Follies
1935; the playhouse was demolished in 1936,
uring the midst of the Depression. As for the Shubert
issouri, operated today as the Folly Theater by
nonprofit organization, it is the only extant
neteenth-century theater in Kansas City.

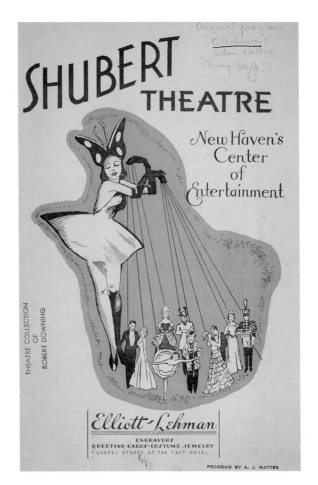

THEATRE COLLECTION OF ROBERT DOWNING

Shubert Theatre, New Haven, Connecticut,
program cover, Away We Go [Oklahoma!],
1942. Yet another monument to the memory
of Sam Shubert, this theater, opened in 1914,
was designed by W. Albert Swasey, Lee and
J. J.'s chief architect at the time. Greeted by
the local community as a "beautiful,
ultra-modern playhouse . . . which New
Haven people can refer to with justifiable
pride," the Shubert was an instant success.
Its proximity to New York City made it an
ideal venue for out-of-town tryouts, and
throughout its history it played host to more
than six hundred pre-Broadway tryouts,
including over three hundred world premieres
and fifty American premieres. Lee and J. J.
gave up the theater in 1941, but the Shubert
moniker remained. Maurice H. Bailey took
over management for the next thirty-five
years. Today the venue operates as the
nonprofit Shubert Performing Arts Center.

Shubert Theatre, St. Louis, Missouri,
program, c. 1920s; Majestic Theatre, Boston,
Massachusetts, program, 1924; and Shubert
Rialto Theatre, St. Louis, Missouri, program,
1929. Although generic in the sense that it
does not relate to the productions playing at
a given venue, the artwork on these program
covers was far from generic artistically
speaking. Often done in the prevailing
graphic style of the day, these colorful
programs added a nice bit of whimsy to the
theatergoer's evening.

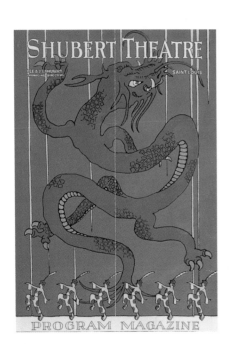

National Theatre, Washington, D.C., (left to right) Bernard B. Jacobs, Alma Viator (press representative for La Cage aux Folles at the National), and Gerald Schoenfeld, 1985. First established in 1835, the National had already been through several incarnations (and U.S. presidents) when the theater fell on hard times in the 1970s. Although it is one of the most respected playhouses in the country, the changing landscape of inner-city Washington and the growing popularity of the new "uptown" Kennedy Center for the Performing Arts had made the National undesirable. The playhouse was threatened with financial ruin and demolition. Then a nonprofit organization called the New National Theatre Corporation was formed to take over the affairs of the playhouse and guide it back to health. In 1979, the National entered into a long-term management agreement with the Shubert Organization, which continues to book and manage the theater today. In 1985, with the Shuberts' help, the playhouse's interior and stage machinery were completely renovated, so that now this "Theatre of the Presidents" stands ready to play host to another century of our nation's leaders.

Jones Beach Stadium, Jones Beach, New York, 1930s. Projecting out over Zach's Bay on Long Island, this outdoor performing-arts facility began life in the early 1920s as the Jones Beach Marine Stadium, a temporary wooden structure built as a work-relief project. For several summers during the mid- to late 1930s, the Shuberts, along with Fortune Gallo and his San Carlo Opera Company, leased the venue for the presentation of "Opera under the Stars." Mounting large-scale productions of many of the operettas and musicals in their repertoire, including The Student Prince, Blossom Time, and Countess Maritza, the Shuberts managed to attract nightly audiences numbering around 10,000. Although the playing area was at some distance from the audience, there was evidently a magical quality about these al fresco performances. Robert Francis, critic for the Brooklyn Eagle, noted: "The Jones Beach Stadium is about ideal as a setting for light opera. A huge stage and its orchestra pit rise out of the placid waters of a lagoon facing the vast, semicircular amphitheater. At night, with powerful floodlights playing upon colorful costumes and scenery and with the voices coming across the water, the spectacle takes on a brilliance which is as filling to the eye as the ear. There is a fairyland quality about it all that can't quite be found anywhere else."

Lee and J. J. named many of their new playhouses after Sam.

As a result of declining business on the road during and after the Great Depression, along with the federal government's antitrust suit against the Shuberts during the 1950s, many of these venues passed out of Shubert hands. Some went on to become movie houses, others places of worship, still others were demolished. Today, after years of neglect, some such as the Folly Theater (formerly the Shubert Missouri) in Kansas City, Missouri, are even getting a second chance as performing arts centers.

Forrest Theatre, Philadelphia, Pennsylvania, interior, 1980s. By the 1920s the Shuberts had an interest in at least six venues in the City of Brotherly Love: the Adelphi, the Lyric, the Shubert, the Forrest, the Chestnut Street Opera House, and the Walnut Street Theatre. In 1927, they began construction on the New Forrest Theatre, which would replace the aging Forrest. The new playhouse, which opened in 1928, was designed by Herbert Krapp and was considered to be state-of-the-art, or as Lee and J. J. stated in the program for opening night, "the last word in practical construction," where "the minutest details were given the utmost careful consideration." The theater, named after the great actor Edwin Forrest, boasted a large stage that could accommodate the biggest Broadway shows, an auditorium sumptuously decorated with gilt Adam detailing and silk brocade, and a spectacular crystal chandelier hanging from a domed ceiling. Perhaps the most unusual feature of the house is its dressing rooms. These are housed in a separate four-story building across the theater's alley and connected by an underground tunnel to the Forrest's stage. Today the Forrest is the Shubert Organization's sole Philadelphia venue.

RIGHT:

Shubert Theatre, Los Angeles, California, interior, 1988. The Shubert Theatre in Los Angeles was formally opened to the public on July 21, 1972, with the West Coast premiere of Stephen Sondheim's Follies. *Located in Century City, the 1,829-seat playhouse was designed by architect Henry George Green. It is not only Shubert's first Los Angeles venue, but is the first theater constructed by the company since 1928, and the first new theater to be christened "Shubert" since 1918. In 1988, only sixteen years after its opening, the Shubert was completely remodeled in time to present the Los Angeles premiere of* Les Misérables. *A permanent exhibition drawn from the resources of the Shubert Archive and documenting the history of the Shuberts was also installed at that time.*

The phenomenon of Broadway has long seized the public's imagination, and it will continue to do so as long as the wonder of live performance exists. The United States has no other theatrical venue that enjoys the stature of Broadway, an address whose stamp of critical, professional, and public approval is potent. This prominence continues to be a distinguishing feature in the landscape of American theater.

For a century, Shubert houses have both defined and chronicled Broadway. These historic halls are as familiar as old friends, echoing with memories of past performance. The breathtakingly inconsistent style of their well-behaved decoration defies art-historical categorization, but their exuberance and compactness draw audiences into their intimate, welcoming spaces. There are now seventeen Shubert houses. Built over the course of a hundred years, no two are the same. Even though the Broadhurst and the Plymouth were constructed at the same time (with identical plans from designs by Herbert Krapp), each has its own character.

The history of these buildings astounds in its proof of their adaptability to new forms of presentation. They were built to contain two clearly defined worlds kept apart by a house curtain: one the stage, the other the auditorium. Each theater was decorated differently, lit differently, and furnished differently. All have also been used differently by many kinds of people on both sides of the curtain. In some contemporary productions, the curtain as separating device disappears, and theatrical lighting and rigging (as well as the actors themselves) invade the auditorium, joining its world with that of the stage. Sometimes scenery is completely absent, and the audience views a bare stage. These theatrical techniques accentuate the dis-

Lyceum Theatre interior, 2000. In this shot taken from backstage of the Shuberts' oldest theater, the apron of the stage, the ghost light, and the orchestra, mezzanine, and balcony seats are all visible.

311

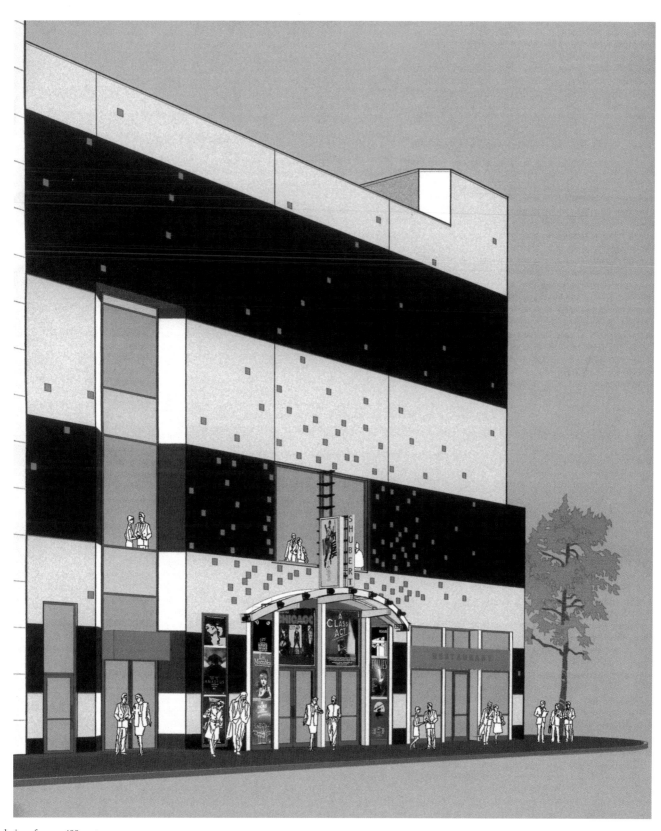

Rendering of a new 499-seat theater (as yet unnamed) on 42nd Street. The space was designed by Hardy Holzman Pfeiffer Associates and is located on the southeast corner of 42nd Street and Dyer Avenue. Its opening is projected for the spring of 2002.

similarity of the theater's two architectural realms, augmenting the performers' authority.

Even when these traditional buildings are used in unconventional ways, their ability to gather the audience in a focused embrace remains constant; there are no finer spaces for bringing people together to see a proscenium production. At their seating capacity, they envelop their audiences with an intimacy that cannot be achieved by contemporary construction.

Current building codes and technical stage requirements do not permit the tight dimensions and simple layouts of Broadway theaters built before 1962.

But what of their future? Can these remarkable buildings continue to nourish life on the stage, or have they, like the operettas and boulevard comedies they were built to house, become obsolete? Some critics say the viability of these theaters has been superseded by the vast cultural centers that have risen across America. These performance places have immense stages, twice the traditional Broadway seating capacity, and support areas whose permanent technical equipment (such as hydraulic lifts, motorized lighting, adjustable acoustics, and sound systems) offer astonishingly elaborate stagecraft.

Yet the very strictures of the Broadway houses are what inspire ingenuity in their staging. Each theater is an empty shell that must be brought to life again with each new production. The lack of permanent technical equipment (other than house lights and counterweight rigging) causes every presentation to be made from scratch, conjuring great creativity from designers, directors, and stagehands alike.

Media experts envision all popular entertainment played out on illuminated screens in a digitized format, but the proliferation of surrogates makes the impact of live performance all the more intense. The experience of watching skilled actors is so primal and so intrinsic to our understanding of the world that no electronic edition can completely replace it. In fact, popular culture relies as much on live entertainment for source material as film or television. The advance of computer technology will unquestionably change the form of live performance, our perceptions of it, and the relationships we forge when we witness it in a theater. But storytelling, exploration of the social condition, and good old-fashioned song and dance will abide. And there's no better place for them than a Broadway house.

No matter what electronic simulations await us, the design dexterity these theaters manifest when people gather for live performance is a triumph, one that will keep them in use far into the future. Not only do these houses represent the romance and excitement of Broadway, but they also enjoy an intimacy that cannot be duplicated. These theaters handsomely meet the challenge of making performers important. Their configuration and ornamentation enhance the actors' presence, making them larger than life. We celebrate, cherish, and watch these theaters as new generations discover their cultural and architectural legacy.

—Hugh Hardy, FAIA

Shubert Theaters Past and Present

Over the course of the twentieth century, the Shubert Brothers and the company they founded either purchased, leased, or managed more than two hundred theaters. Sometimes the company's involvement with a given venue was short-lived—perhaps a matter of a year or two—other times it was long-standing. The Shuberts also booked shows into more than a thousand theaters that were actually owned or managed by other interests. The complexity and wide reach of their holdings, along with gaps in the company's historical records, make it impossible to compile a complete roster of Shubert theaters past and present. What follows, then, is a partial list of playhouses, organized by city and totaling two hundred fifteen, that the Shubert Organization has owned, leased, or managed during the twentieth century and into the twenty-first.

As was common during the early part of the century, the Shuberts most often adopted the British spelling of the word *theatre* (as opposed to *theater*) when naming their playhouses. For the sake of brevity, the word is not repeated each time a building name is given but can be assumed unless otherwise indicated.

Theaters marked with an asterisk are still owned, operated, or managed by the Shubert Organization.

Albany, New York
Capitol
Harmanus Bleecker Hall

Atlanta, Georgia
Grand Opera House

Atlantic City, New Jersey
Globe
Nixon's-Apollo

Baltimore, Maryland
Academy of Music
Auditorium
Ford's
New Lyceum

Boston, Massachusetts
Boston Opera House
Colonial
Columbia
Copley
Hollis
Majestic
Plymouth
Selwyn (also known as
    the Park Square)
*Shubert
Tremont
Wilbur

Buffalo, New York
Lyric
Star
Teck

Chattanooga, Tennessee
Shubert

Chicago, Illinois
Apollo
Auditorium
Blackstone
Central
Colonial
4 Cohans
Garrick
Great Northern
Harris
Illinois
La Salle
Olympic
Playhouse
Powers
Princess
Selwyn
Shubert (also known as
    the Majestic)
Studebaker

Cincinnati, Ohio
Cox
Grand
Lyric
Shubert

Cleveland, Ohio
Colonial
Hanna
Ohio

Columbus, Ohio
Colonial
Shubert Opera House

Danville, Illinois
Grand Opera House

Denver, Colorado
Auditorium
Broadway

Detroit, Michigan
Cadillac
Cass
Detroit Opera House
Downtown
Garrick
Michigan
Shubert-Lafayette
Wilson

Easton, Pennsylvania
Colonial
Opera House
Orpheum

Glens Falls, New York
Empire

Hartford, Connecticut
Parsons

Indianapolis, Indiana
English's Opera House
Murat

Jersey City, New Jersey
Majestic

Kansas City, Kansas
Missouri
Shubert

London, England
Adelphi
Apollo
Gaiety
His Majesty's
Shaftsbury
Waldorf
Winter Garden

Los Angeles, California
Shubert

Louisville, Kentucky
Mary Anderson
Masonic (also known as
    the Shubert-Strand)

Milwaukee, Wisconsin
Davidson
Shubert

Minneapolis, Minnesota
Lyric
Metropolitan
Shubert

Montreal, Canada
His Majesty's

New Haven, Connecticut
Shubert

New Orleans, Louisiana
St. Charles
Shubert
Tulane

New York, New York
*Ambassador
Apollo
Astor
*Barrymore
*Belasco
Bijou
*Booth
*Broadhurst
Broadway (41st Street)
*Broadway (53rd Street)
Broadway (Brooklyn)
Bronx Opera House (Bronx)
Casino
Central
Century
Century Roof
Comedy
*Cort
Cosmopolitan
Crescent (Brooklyn)
Daly's
DeKalb (Brooklyn)
44th Street
46th Street
48th Street
49th Street
Forrest (also known as
   the Eugene O'Neill)
Gallo
Garrick
*Golden
Harris
Herald Square
Hippodrome
Hudson
*Imperial
Jolson
Jones Beach Stadium
Lincoln Square
*Longacre
*Lyceum

Lyric
Madison Square
*Majestic
Majestic (Brooklyn)
Mansfield
Maxine Elliott
Metropolis (Bronx)
Morosco
*Music Box
National
Nora Bayes
*Plymouth
Princess
Ritz
*Royale
St. James
Selwyn
*Shubert
Shubert (Brooklyn)
Shubert-Riviera
Spooner
Teller-Shubert (Brooklyn)
39th Street (also known as
   the Nazimova)
Times Square
West End
Windsor
*Winter Garden
Yorkville

Newark, New Jersey
Broad
Rialto
Shubert (also known as Keeney's)

Philadelphia, Pennsylvania
Adelphi
Broad Street
Chestnut Street Opera House
Erlanger
*Forrest

Garrick
Locust Street
Lyric
Shubert
Walnut Street

Pittsburgh, Pennsylvania
Duquesne (Belasco)
Lyceum
Nixon
Pitt
Shubert
Shubert-Alvin
Shubert-Victoria-Aldine

Portland, Maine
Jefferson

Providence, Rhode Island
Providence Opera House
Shubert-Majestic

Rochester, New York
New Baker
Shubert

St. Joseph, Missouri
Shubert's Tootle

St. Louis, Missouri
American
Empress
Garrick
Jefferson
Shubert-Rialto

St. Paul, Minnesota
Metropolitan

San Francisco, California
Curran
Geary

Schenectady, New York
Van Curler Opera House

Springfield, Illinois
Chatterton Opera House

Springfield, Massachusetts
Nelson

Syracuse, New York
Bastable
Grand Opera House
Wieting Opera House

Toledo, Ohio
Auditorium
Capitol
Town Hall Theatre

Toronto, Canada
Princess
Royal Alexandra

Troy, New York
Griswald's Opera House
Rand's Opera House

Utica, New York
Utica Opera House

Washington, D.C.
Belasco
Garrick
*National
Poli's

Wilmington, Delaware
Playhouse

Worcester, Massachusetts
Worcester

Selected Bibliography

Baral, Robert. *Revue: The Great Broadway Period* (New York: Fleet Press Corporation, 1962).

Best Plays. Series with various editors (various publishers, 1921–99).

Blum, Daniel. *A Pictorial History of the American Theatre, 1860–1985* (New York: Crown Publishers, 1986).

Bordman, Gerald. *American Musical Theatre* (New York: Oxford University Press, Inc., 1978).

—————. *The Oxford Companion to American Theatre* (New York: Oxford University Press, Inc., 1992).

Botto, Louis. *At This Theatre* (New York: Dodd, Mead, 1984).

Ewen, David. *New Complete Book of the American Musical Theater* (New York: Holt, Rinehart, and Winston, 1970).

—————. *American Songwriters* (New York: H. W. Wilson Co., 1987).

Goldman, Herbert G. *Jolson* (New York: Oxford University Press, 1988).

Green, Stanley. *Encyclopaedia of the Musical Theatre* (New York: Dodd, Mead & Co., 1976).

Henderson, Mary C. *The City and the Theatre* (Clifton, N.J.: James T. White, 1973).

Jackson, Kenneth T., ed. *The Encyclopedia of New York City* (New Haven: Yale University Press and New York: The New-York Historical Society, 1995).

Landmarks Preservation Commission, New York, N.Y. *Designation Lists* (1974–88).

Liebling, A. J. "The Boys from Syracuse," *The New Yorker* (Nov. 18, 25, Dec. 2, 1939).

McNamara, Brooks. *The Shuberts of Broadway* (New York: Oxford University Press, 1990).

Morrison, William. *Broadway Theatres: History and Architecture* (New York: Dover, 2000).

Norton, Elliot. *Broadway Down East* (Boston: Boston Public Library, 1978).

Owen, Bobbi. *Costume Design on Broadway: Designers and Their Credits, 1915–1985* (New York: Greenwood Publishing Group, 1987).

—————. *Scenic Design on Broadway: Designers and Their Credits, 1915–1990* (New York: Greenwood Publishing Group, 1991).

"The Passing Show: the Newsletter of the Shubert Archive," various editors (New York: the Shubert Archive, 1977–).

Stagg, Jerry. *The Brothers Shubert* (New York: Random House, 1968).

Suskin, Steven. *Opening Night on Broadway: A Critical Quotebook of the Golden Age of the Musical Theatre, "Oklahoma!" (1943) to "Fiddler on the Roof" (1964)* (New York: Schirmer Books, 1990).

Traubner, Richard. *Operetta: A Theatrical History* (Garden City, N.Y.: Doubleday, 1983).

Van Hoogstraten, Nicholas. *Lost Broadway Theatres* (New York: Princeton Architectural Press, 1991).

Wilmeth, Don B., and Tice L. Miller, eds. *The Cambridge Guide to American Theatre* (New York: Cambridge University Press, 1993).

© AP Wide World Photos: 17.

© Clive Barda/PAL: 76.

Courtesy of Broadway Cares/Equity Fights AIDS: 105.

© Susan Cook: 115 bottom.

Whitney Cox: case binding, endpapers 2–4, 9 banner details, 34–35, 37–41, 48, 49 right and banner details, 50–51, 64, 65 bottom left and right and banner details, 66–67, 77, 79 banner details, 81–83, 86–88, 106–7, 109 banner details, 110–12, 118, 119 banner details, 120–21, 134, 135 banner details, 136–37, 146, 147 banner details, 148–50, 170–71, 178–81, 179 banner details, 190, 191 right and banner details, 192–93, 206–7, 208–11, 220–21, 230, 231 banner details, 232–33, 242, 243 top and banner details, 244–45, 256, 257 banner details, 258, 259, 260, 266, 267 banner details, 310.

© Anthony Crickmay: courtesy of the Theatre Museum, National Museum of the Performing Arts, Victoria and Albert Museum, 249 top right

© Culver Pictures: 43 bottom, 52 top and bottom, 65 top.

© Peter Cunningham: 239 bottom.

© Michal Daniel: 217.

© Zoe Dominic: 226 bottom.

Courtesy of Paul Elson: 96.

© John Engstead / MPTV.net: 280.

© T. Charles Erickson: 240.

Permission to reproduce *The Shubert Alley–Intermission* granted by the Estate of Lydia and Don Freeman: 99.

© Steve Friedman: 20 top.

Courtesy of The Ira and Lenore Gershwin Trusts: 138.

Nichols and May image (124 top) © 2001 Milton H. Greene Archives, Inc. www.archivesmhg.com.

Rendering by Marina Berendeeva / Hardy Holzman Pfeiffer Associates: 312.

The Harvard Theater Collection, The Houghton Library: 300 top, Angus McBean: 195.

Courtesy of Doug Johnson: 47.

© Michael Le Poer Trench: 265 top and bottom.

Billy Rose Theatre Collection, The New York Public Library for the Performing Arts, Astor, Lenox & Tilden Foundations: 56, 115 top, 214 bottom, 216, 238, 239 top, 249 top left. Zinn Arthur: 45 top, 176 bottom. Friedman/Abeles: 90, 197, 248 bottom. H. Charles DeKoven: 185 top. Carl S. Peretz: 94 top. White Studio: 44, 172 bottom, 222 bottom left, 301 top. Van Williams: 186.

© Joan Marcus: 46, 57 bottom, 95 bottom, 125 bottom, 189, 201, 226 top, 227 bottom, 241, 250.

Museum of the City of New York: 36 bottom, 71, 93 top, 104, 174, 182 bottom, 231, 235, 248 top. Joseph Abeles: 58 (Gift of Mary Bryant), 142 top (Gift of Harold Friedlander), 262, 282. Gift of Robert Able: 183. Byron Collection: 13, 147 top and bottom, 301 bottom. Anthony

Crickmay: 249 top right (Gift of Seymour Krawitz). Eileen Darby: 225. Zoe Dominic: 283 bottom. T. Charles Erickson: 117 bottom. Eileen Darby for Graphic House: 196 (Gift of Harold Friedlander). Fred Fehl: 281 top and bottom. Gift of Harold Friedlander: 68, 224. Sy Friedman: 177 top. Friedman-Abeles: 94 bottom and 141 bottom (Gift of Harold Friedlander), 143, 198 (Gift of Albert Fenn). Impact Photos, Inc.: 199 (Gift of John L. Toohey). Gift of Mrs. Bert Lahr: 123 bottom. Lucas-Pritchard: 93 top. Gift of the Burns Mantle Estate: 222 top and bottom right. Gift of The New York Public Library: 139. Martha Swope: 152 bottom (Gift of Solters & Roskin). Talbot: 70 top (Gift of Harold Friedlander). Vandamm Studio: 53 top, 55 top, 89 top, 113 bottom, 114 top, 140 (Gift of Harold Friedlander), 141 top (Gift of Harold Friedlander), 152 top (Gift of the Vandamm Studio), 153 top (Gift of Harold Friedlander), 175 bottom (Gift of Mary Martin), 176 top (Gift of the Burns Mantle Estate), 237, 247. The Wurts Collection: 243 bottom, 299.

Collection of The New York Historical Society: 78.

© Michael Norcia: 284 bottom.

Photofest: 72–73.

The Rodgers & Hammerstein Organization: 70 bottom, 142 bottom.

© Carol Rosegg: 98, 189 bottom.

The Shubert Archive: 6 banner details, 8, 11, 14 top and bottom, 15 top and bottom, 16, 18 bottom, 19, 22, 23, 24, 25, 28, 29 bottom, 30 bottom, 31–33, 36 top, 42, 49 top, 53 bottom, 55 bottom, 57 top, 59–62, 63, 79, 89 bottom, 92 bottom, 96, 100, 102–3, 108, 109, 119, 123 top, 126–28, 130, 131, 132, 151, 155–69, 172 top, 173, 177 bottom, 182 top, 184, 188, 191, 194, 204, 205, 213 top, 214 top, 219, 223 bottom, 228–29, 236, 246, 251, 252–53, 257 left and right, 261, 264, 267, 271, 272 middle and bottom, 273, 274 inset, 279 bottom, 285–88, 289 bottom, 290 top and bottom, 293–96, 298, 299 banner details, 300 middle and bottom, 302–5, 306 bottom, 307, 308, 309 bottom and banner details. Apeda Studio: 92 top, 269 top and bottom, 270 bottom. Artkraft Strauss & Co.: 218. Brunning: 254–55. Byron Collection: 43 top. Clovis: 45 bottom. DeMirjian: 133 top and bottom, 212, 215, 292 bottom. Drucker: 26–27. Dufor: 309 top. Courtesy of Mrs. Peggie Elson: 202–3. Alex Freund: 20 bottom. Friedman-Abeles: 114 bottom. Hall: 267 top, 268. Sydney Hub: 62 inset. Courtesy of Mrs. Betty Jacobs: 21. Murray Korman: 30 top right, 63 inset bottom, 291 top & bottom. Lucas-Pritchard: 54 bottom, 93 bottom. Mayo: 219. Mollet: 122. J. C. Olsen: 290 middle. Ben Pinchot: 272 top. Rocky Mt. Photo Co., Denver: 275–78. Rutter: 296–97. Otto Sarony: 18 top. Talbot: 213 bottom. Underwood & Underwood: 12, 30 top left, 127 inset. Vandamm: 91, 223 top, 274. Walery-Paris: 289 top and middle. White Studios: 29 top, 113 top, 126–27, 129, 131 bottom, 175 top, 270 top, 279 top, 289 bottom, 292 top. Verne O. William: 304 bottom. Photographs by Zindman/Fremont, New York: 8, 14 bottom, 16, 19, 29 bottom, 42, 45 bottom, 47, 53 bottom, 57 top, 59, 60 top and bottom, 63 inset top, 89 bottom, 92 bottom, 96, 108, 123, 130–32, 155 inset, 156 top and bottom, 157–61, 163–69, 172–73, 177 bottom, 188, 194, 213, 228–29, 246, 251, 261, 272 bottom, 274 inset, 285–86, 287 left, 302–3, 305.

© Nigel Teare: 284 top.

Theater Historical Society of America, Elmhurst, Illinois: 306 top.

TimePix: Bill Eppridge: 73 inset, 101. Henry Groskinsky: 84–85. George Karger: 1. Martha Swope: 5, 74, 75, 95 top, 96, 97, 116, 117 top, 124 bottom, 125 top, 144 top & bottom, 145 top & bottom, 153 bottom, 154, 185 bottom, 187, 200, 227 top, 249 bottom, 263, 283 top.

Acknowledgments

The Shuberts Present, like just about every other theatrical project, has been a collaborative effort, and the authors would like to acknowledge many people and institutions that helped make this book possible. First and foremost, without the support of The Shubert Organization, this book would never have come to fruition. We are always indebted to Rebecca Robertson who conceived the initial idea for the book. A special acknowledgment is due to Gerald Schoenfeld, Chairman, and Philip J. Smith, President, who guided the project, read early drafts of the manuscript, and sent us in the right direction. We are also extremely grateful to Shubert's Board of Directors—John W. Kluge, Lee J. Seidler, Michael I. Sovern, President, Shubert Foundation, and Irving M. Wall—in addition to Robert E. Wankel, Executive Vice President, whose enthusiasm and commitment were unwavering.

Many individuals within the Shubert Organization helped us with their insight and advice and smoothed the way for some of our more difficult requests. We would like to thank Lynn Seidler, former Executive Director of The Shubert Foundation, and Brooks McNamara, former Director of the Shubert Archive, whose foresight, energy, and acumen helped establish the Shubert Archive—the main source of research material for the book—and who guided the archive through its first twenty-three years. We much appreciate the input and encouragement we received from The Shubert Foundation—Vicki Reiss (Executive Director), Constance Harvey, and Amy Dorfman—and individuals in various departments of The Shubert Organization, especially, Elliot Greene (Vice President, Finance) as well as Mary Assandri, Peggy Delany, Anthony LaMattina, Sacha McClymont, Brian Mahoney, Kim Mercer, Julio Peterson, Lisa Spagnuolo, Dan Spurgeon, and Jennifer Tattenbaum. Special thanks also should go to Mary Knorr and Peter Entin, both of the Theatre Operations Department, who made it possible for Whitney Cox and his crew to have access to all of the Shubert venues. Lastly, we are indebted to the following engineers and electricians who assisted with the photographing of the theaters: Randy Martin, Adam Piskadlo, Steve Altman, Richard Beck, Jimmy Billings, Ronnie Burns, John Caggiano, John Cooper, Paul Dean, Charlie DeVerna, Manny Diaz, Neil Hannan, Lee Iwanski, Vince Jacobi, Leslie Ann Kilian, Herb Messing, George Milne, and Sylvia Yoshioka.

Whitney Cox's contribution to this project was invaluable. His specially commissioned photographs of the Shubert Organization's seventeen New York playhouses made it seem as if we were seeing those cherished buildings for the first time. Also inestimable was the assistance of our visual consultant Kevin Kwan, whose skill at picture editing is unmatched and whose keen artistic eye helped shape the design of the book.

Although the bulk of research materials and images for the book were drawn from the Shubert Archive's own materials, we consulted several other sources and are grateful for the assistance we received from the following institutions and their staffs: Broadway Cares/Equity Fights AIDS; Dodger Theatricals (Michael David and Amy Wigler); The Ira and Lenore Gershwin Trusts (Mark Trent Goldberg and Camille Kuznetz); Hardy, Holzman, Pfeiffer Associates (Hugh Hardy and Susan Packard); King Display (Ken Lubin); The Theatre Collection of the Museum of the City of New York (Marty Jacobs and Marguerite Lavin); the Billy Rose Theatre Collection of the New York Public Library for the Performing Arts (Jeremy Megraw); Photofest (Ron Mandelbaum); The Publicity Office (Michael S. Borowski); The Rodgers and Hammerstein Organization (Bert Fink and Robin Walton); TimePix (Rebecca Karamehmedovic); and Triton Gallery (Roger Puckett).

Thanks also to X. Theodore Barber and William Morrison, whose brief essays on Raphael Kirchner and Herbert J. Krapp, respectively, contributed significantly to this project; to Amy Ward Brimmer, who assisted in the editing of the text; to Alan Zindman and Lucy Fremont, whose skillful copy photography was indispensable; to Terry Davis and Lainey Friedlander at Modernage, who ably assisted us with image reproduction; to Adrian Bryan-Brown and Joan Marcus for their considerable guidance and help with picture sources; to Doug Johnson for his generous permission to reproduce his artwork; to Mary Higgins for her restoration skills; and to William Ndini for his most generous donation of early Shubert memorabilia.